INTERNATIONAL CONGRESS AND SYMPOSIUM SERIES NUMBER 155

Editor-in-Chief: **Lord Walton of Detchant**

Major Chemical Disasters—
Medical Aspects of Management

*Proceedings of a meeting arranged by
the Section of Occupational Medicine of
the Royal Society of Medicine, held in
London 21 and 22 February, 1989*

Edited by

Virginia Murray

GW00503001

ROYAL SOCIETY OF MEDICINE SERVICES
LONDON · NEW YORK
1990

Royal Society of Medicine Services Limited
1 Wimpole Street   London W1M 8AE
7 East 60th Street   New York NY 10022

These proceedings are published by Royal Society of Medicine Services Ltd with financial support from the sponsor. The contributors are responsible for the scientific content and for the views expressed, which are not necessarily those of the sponsor, of the editor of the series or of the volume, of the Royal Society of Medicine or of Royal Society of Medicine Services Ltd. Distribution has been in accordance with the wishes of the sponsor but a copy is available to any Fellow of the Society at a privileged price.

British Library Cataloguing in Publication Data
Major chemical disasters—medical aspects of management:
 Proceedings of a meeting arranged by the Section of Occupational Medicine of the
 Royal Society of Medicine, held in London 21st February, 1989
 (International Congress and Symposium Series : ISSN 0142-2367; 155)
 1. Dangerous industrial chemicals. Medical aspects
 I. Series
 363.1'79

 ISBN 1-85315-104-1

Library of Congress Cataloging in Publication Data
Major chemical disasters.
 (International congress and symposium series; no. 155)
 ''Proceedings of a meeting arranged by the Section of Occupational Medicine
 of the Royal Society of Medicine, held in London 21st February 1989.''
 Includes bibliographies.
 1. Environmental health—Management—Congresses.   2. Toxicological emergencies—
 Management—Congresses.   3. Chemical industry—Accidents—Health aspects—
 Management—Congresses.   4. Chemical industry—Accidents—Environmental aspects—
 Management—Congresses.   5. Disaster medicine—Congresses.   I. Murray, V.
 II. Royal Society of Medicine (Great Britain). Section of Occupational Medicine.   III.
 Series.   [DNLM: 1. Disasters—prevention—congresses.   2. Emergency Medical
 Services—organization & administration—congresses.   3. Hazardous Substances—
 adverse effects—congresses.
 W3 IN207 no. 155 / WB 105 M234 1989]
 RA565.H2M35 1989   363.17'91   89-10283

 ISBN 1-85315-104-1 (pbk.)

Phototypeset by Dobbie Typesetting Limited, Plymouth, Devon
Printed in Great Britain at the Alden Press, Oxford

Contributors

Editor

Virginia Murray
Honorary Consultant Occupational
Toxicologist,
National Poisons Unit,
Guy's Hospital,
St Thomas' Street,
London SE1 9RT, UK

Dr Murray trained in occupational medicine before joining the National Poisons Unit in 1980. She has played a key role in the collaboration by the Unit with projects organised by the International Programme on Chemical Safety (WHO/ILO/UNEP) and the Commission of the European Communities. Currently, she is developing the Unit's ability to respond to clinical problems arising from major chemical disasters.

Contributors

Wilson Adam
Hazardous Chemicals Subgroup,
Medical and Survival Committee,
Royal National Lifeboat
Institution,
Poole, Dorset, UK

Dr Adam, a general practitioner, was Honorary Medical Adviser to the Poole Lifeboat, and is Deputy Chairman of the Medical and Survival Committee and a member of the Management Committee to the Royal National Lifeboat Institution.

Neil Andersson
Centenary Institute of
Occupational Health,
London School of Hygiene &
Tropical Medicine,
Kepple Street, London WC1, UK

Now Professor of Epidemiology and Tropical Medicine, Centre for Tropical Disease Research (CIET), Faculty of Medicine, Universidad Autonoma de Guerrero, Apdo 25A Acapulco, Mexico.

Peter Baxter
Consultant Occupational Physician,
Cambridge University and
Addenbrooke's Hospital,
Department of Community Medicine,
Fenner's, Gresham Road,
Cambridge CB1 2ES, UK

Dr Baxter worked for the Health and Safety Executive—both at headquarters and in the field. He developed an interest in toxic disease outbreaks while working as medical epidemiologist at the Centers for Disease Control, Atlanta, USA.

John Beare
Western Ophthalmic Hospital,
Marylebone Road,
London NW1, UK

Dr Beare trained in ophthalmology in Oxford and at Moorfields Eye Hospital and is currently Senior Registrar at St Mary's Hospital, Paddington, London. His interest in chemical burns of the eye stems from the large number of non-accidental ocular injuries seen at St Mary's.

Brendan P. Bleasdale
*Principal Engineer, Emergency
    Planning,
Nuclear Safety Operations Branch,
The Central Electricity Generating
    Board,
Courtenay House, 18 Warwick Lane,
London EC4P 4EB, UK*

Mr Bleasdale is a health physicist in the CEGB's Nuclear Safety Operations Branch. His work entails coordination of the emergency arrangements for CEGB nuclear sites. He worked at Dungeness Nuclear Station for seven years, and for the last six years has been at the Board headquarters in the Health and Safety Department.

J. W. Bridges
*Director, Robens Institute of
    Industrial and Environmental
    Health and Safety,
University of Surrey,
Guildford, Surrey, UK*

Professor Bridges is a recent President of the Federation of European Societies of Toxicology and a Member of various Government Committees concerned with toxic substances and their effects in man and on the environment. His main research interest is in the mechanisms of toxicity and the use of such information in risk assessment.

Ian C. Canadine
*Company Distribution Adviser,
ICI Group Headquarters,
9 Millbank,
London SW1P 3JF, UK*

Dr Canadine trained as a chemical engineer and has worked for ICI for 26 years in design, research, plant management, techno-commercial work and distribution. He is currently corporate distribution adviser based in London, and is Vice-chairman of the Distribution Advisory Group of the Chemical Industries Association and of the 'Safety in Distribution' Committee of CEFIC—the European Federation of Chemical Industry Associations.

Keith Cassidy
*HM Superintendent Specialist
    Inspector,
Health and Safety Executive,
Magdalen House,
Stanley Precinct,
Bootle,
Merseyside L20 307, UK*

Mr Cassidy worked in the textiles, engineering and chemical industries (commissioning, production and transport experience) before joining HM Factory Inspectorate, and subsequently the UK Health and Safety Executive. He has served in various parts of the UK as an operational inspector and at HQ. In his current job, heading the Process Safety Group in HSE's Technology Division, he is particularly concerned with technical aspects of the control of major chemical hazards and risks.

Vera Dallos
*Consultant in Charge, Accident
    and Emergency Department,
Whipps Cross Hospital,
Whipps Cross Road,
Leytonstone,
London E11, UK*

Dr Dallos is Consultant in charge of a major Accident and Emergency Department in East London, dealing with approximately 76 000 new patients per year. She is an Examiner at the Final Fellowship in A&E Medicine of the Royal College of Physicians and Surgeons of Edinburgh, and immediate Past President of the A&E Section of the Royal Society of Medicine.

Denis Edwards
Director, Intensive Care Unit,
University Hospital,
South Manchester ME20 8LE, UK

Dr Edwards graduated from Edinburgh University in 1971 and was appointed Consultant Physician in 1981 at University Hospital in Manchester, having previously worked in London, Manchester and Rotterdam. He is a co-founder of the South Manchester Accident Rescue Team and has been involved in a number of national disasters including those at Golbourne Mine, Abbeystead, Bolton Chemical, Manchester Airport, Armenia and Locherbie.

John S. C. English
Department of Occupational
Dermatoses,
St John's Hospital for Diseases
of the Skin,
5 Lisle Street, Leicester Square,
London WC2H 7BJ, UK

Dr English has been Senior Registrar in the Department of Occupational Dermatoses for four years, and is now Consultant Dermatologist at the North Staffs Hospital, Stoke on Trent.

John Ferguson-Smith
Occupational Health,
ICI Chemicals & Polymers Ltd,
Billingham,
Cleveland TS23 1LB, UK

Dr Ferguson-Smith has been with ICI at Billingham for four years, and is presently Area Medical Officer for Billingham and North Tees sites and associated businesses. For six years previously he worked as part-time Medical Officer for BP Chemicals at Grangemouth.

Michel Gilbert
International Programme on
Chemical Safety,
WHO/ICO/UNEP,
Geneva, Switzerland

Dr Gilbert, a physical chemist, has worked with the International Programme of Chemical Safety since 1987. Prior to this he worked with the United Nations Environment Programme and the International Register of Potentially Toxic Chemicals.

Monique Govaerts-Lepicard
Centre Anti poisons,
Rue Joseph Stallaert 1,
B-1060 Brussels,
Belgium

Dr Govaerts-Lepicard is trained in toxicology and public health. Founder of the Poison Control programme in Belgium, she is the head of the Poison Centre and is particularly interested in prevention and the public health implications of toxic agents.

Ian Graham-Bryce
Environmental Affairs Division,
Shell Internationale
Petroleum Maatschappij BV,
The Hague,
The Netherlands

Dr Graham-Bryce is Head of the Environmental Affairs Division of Shell International Petroleum based in The Hague. With a degree in physical chemistry, most of his career has been spent in research in industry, universities and research institutes. He was previously Director of East Malling Research Station, Past President of the Society of the Chemical Industry and Past President of the Association of Applied Biologists.

William J. Guild
Hazardous Chemicals Subgroup,
Medical and Survival Committee
Royal National Lifeboat
Institution,
Poole, Dorset, UK

Dr Guild, a physiologist at Edinburgh University, specializes in first aid, including its research and training, and has particular interest in the problems of exposure, hypothermia and casualty handling. He is responsible for the Royal National Lifeboat Institution's First Aid Training Panel and is a member of the Institution's Medical and Survival Committee.

David Jerrom
West Midlands Fire Brigade,
Fire Service Headquarters,
Lancaster Circus,
Queensway, Birmingham
  B4 7DE, UK

Mr Jerrom is Assistant Chief Officer (Operations) of the West Midlands Fire Service which covers half of the City of Birmingham, including the City centre. He has served for 25 years in the Fire Service in Cambridgeshire, Staffordshire, Somerset and Nottinghamshire.

Per Kulling
Swedish Poisons Information Centre,
Karolinska Hospital,
Box 60500 S-104 01,
Stockholm, Sweden

Dr Kulling is a consultant physician in anaesthesiology, intensive care and clinical toxicology at the Swedish Poison Information Centre with which he has been associated since 1978. He has had a special interest in chemical disasters since 1981.

M. Mercier
Manager, International Programme
  on Chemical Safety,
World Health Organization,
Geneva, Switzerland

Dr Mercier, a pharmacological scientist with a toxicology background, has been the Manager of the International Programme of Chemical Safety (WHO/ILO/UNEP) since 1981. He is also the Visiting Professor in Toxicology at the Faculty of Medicine of the University of Louvain, Belgium and in Preventive Medicine at the Shanghai Medical University, Peoples Republic of China.

W. G. Payne
Metropolitan Police Territorial
  Operations 22,
New Scotland Yard,
London SW1H 0BG, UK
New address:-
Bexley London Borough
  Directorate of Administration,
Bexley Civic Offices,
Broadway, Bexley Heath,
Kent DA6 7LB, UK

Superintendent Payne* is in charge of Territorial Operations 22 and 23 Branch at New Scotland Yard, responsible for contingency planning matters including civil disaster planning and civil protection duties. He is Secretary of the London Emergency Services Liaison Panel comprising representatives from the Metropolitan, City of London and British Transport police forces, the London Fire Brigade, the London Ambulance Service and representatives of the London Fire and Civil Defence Authority. He is a member of the British Institute of Management and the Institute of Administrative Management.
*Mr Payne is now Emergency Planning Officer at Bexley Heath. (See new address.)

Robin Philipp
Director, WHO Collaborating
  Centre for Environmental
  Health Promotion and Ecology,
University of Bristol,
Bristol, UK

Dr Philipp is a Consultant Senior Lecturer in Public Health Medicine, and Director of the WHO Collaborating Centre for Environmental Health Promotion and Ecology, both in the Department of Epidemiology and Public Health Medicine, University of Bristol. He is also Deputy South Western Regional Adviser for the Faculty of Occupational Medicine, Royal College of Physicians, and Chairman of the Environmental Health Courses sub-committee of the Royal Institute of Public Health and Hygiene.

Martin Sibson
County Emergency Planning Officer,
Chief Executive and
* Clerk's Department,*
Essex County Council,
County Hall,
Chelmsford CM1 1LX, UK

Following a career in the police service with Cambridgeshire and on secondment at the Police Staff College, Mr Sibson was appointed CEPO Essex in 1981. He is an adviser on major hazards issues to the Association of County Councils and the Society of Local Authority Chief Executives (SOLACE) and a member of the Health and Safety Executive 'Seveso' *ad hoc* Committee. He is President of the CEPO Society.

D. A. D. Slattery (Chairman)
Royal College of Physicians,
St Andrew's Place,
Regent's Park,
London NW1 4LE, UK

Dr Slattery is the Chief Medical Officer for Rolls Royce plc and is currently the Dean of the Faculty of Occupational Medicine.

Sir George Smart
Hazardous Chemicals Subgroup,
Medical and Survival Committee,
Royal National Lifeboat
* Institution,*
Poole, Dorset, UK

Professor Sir George Smart was educated at Durham University and was a Commonwealth Fund fellow from 1948–49; a Lecturer in Medicine at the University of Bristol from 1946–58 and a Reader in Medicine at the University of Durham 1950–56. He was Professor of Medicine at Newcastle-upon-Tyne from 1968–71 and Senior Vice President from 1972–73. He is a Director of the British Postgraduate Medical Federation. Sir George has been a member of the RNLI since 1971, and on the Medical Survival Committee (of which he is a past Chairman) from 1979–84.

Edward Smith (Chairman)
IPCS,
World Health Organization,
1211 Geneva,
Switzerland

Dr Smith is an occupational physician and toxicologist working in the Division of Environmental Health as part of the unit co-ordinating the International Programme on Chemical Safety (WHO/ILO/UNEP). He has extensive experience in government and industry.

John Stealey
Head of Civil Defence Research,
Home Office,
Horseferry House,
Dean Ryle Street,
London SW1P 2AW, UK

Dr Stealey worked in the food industry for four years, during which he graduated MIBiol. He studied at the Lister Institute of Preventive Medicine and obtained his PhD in 1973. He joined the Home Office in the same year and has carried out research and development projects for Civil Defence, Fire Department and Police Divisions. He became Head of Civil Defence Research in 1985. His main areas of interest are radiation effects in nuclear war, chemical warfare, damage and casualty assessments and modelling, policy analysis and training.

A. N. B. Stott (Chairman)
Head of Medical Services,
John Lewis Partnership,
10–12 Old Cavendish Street,
London W1A 1EX, UK

Dr Stott, an occupational physician, is the Head of Medical Services to the John Lewis Partnership and and was President of the Society of Occupational Medicine 1988–1989.

Derek Taylor (Chairman)
President, Section of
  Occupational Medicine,
Royal Society of Medicine,
1 Wimpole Street,
London W1M 8AE, UK

Dr Taylor is currently the Chief Medical Officer of Britain's major national and international retailer, Marks & Spencer, and is President of the Section of Occupational Medicine (1989/90).

James Thompson
Department of Psychiatry,
Middlesex Hospital,
Riding House Street,
London W1N 8AA, UK

Dr Thompson is carrying out research into the effectiveness of psychological therapy for survivors of disasters, and is part of a team providing a clinical service for survivors.

Theodore G. Tong
Arizona Poison and Drug
  Information Center (APDIC),
The University of Arizona,
Tucson, Arizona,
USA

Dr Tong is currently Director, APDIC, Professor of Pharmacy Practice, Pharmacology and Toxicology at the University of Arizona, and Associate Dean for Academic Affairs, College of Pharmacy. He is Secretary of the American Association of Poison Control Centers, and co-founder and program Director from 1979–82 of the San Francisco Bay Area Regional Poison Center, University of California. He is a Fellow of the American Academy of Clinical Toxicology, and Diplomat of the American Board of Applied Toxicology.

Michael I. Willis
Chief Ambulance Officer,
Norfolk Ambulance Service,
Ambulance Headquarters,
Hospital Lane,
Hellesdon,
Norwich NR6 5NA, UK

Mr Willis joined the Ambulance Service in 1967. He has been involved in the training of ambulance staff since 1974. He was previously Assistant Chief Ambulanceman in the West Yorkshire Metropolitan Service. He is a Fellow of the Ambulance Service Institute and Member of the National Health Service Training Authority.

Glyn N. Volans
Director,
National Poisons Unit,
Guy's Hospital,
St Thomas' Street
London SE1 9RT, UK

Dr Volans trained in medicine and clinical pharmacology. He is Consultant Physician and Director of the National Poisons Unit at Guy's Hospital, Member of the Committee on Toxicity of Chemicals in Food and the Environment, and a former Meetings Secretary to the British Toxicology Society.

List of Abbreviations

ACMH   Advisory Committee on Major Hazards

ACPO   Association of Chief Police Officers

ACDS   Advisory Committee on Dangerous Substances

BASIC   British Association for Immediate Care

CEFIC   European Federation of Chemical Industry Associations

CEGB   Central Electricity Generating Board

CEPO   County Emergency Planning Officer

CIA   Chemical Industries Association

CIMAH   Control of Industrial Major Accident Hazard

CSA   Casualty Surgeons Association

DH   Department of Health

DHSS   Department of Health and Social Security

EEC   European Economic Community

EPGLA   Emergency Planning Guidance to Local Authorities

EPCC   Emergency Planning Consultative Committee

HASAWA   Health and Safety at Work Act

HSE   Health and Safety Executive

ILO   International Labour Organisation

IPCS   International Programme on Chemical Safety

NAIR   National Arrangements for Incidents Involving Radioactivity

NCEC   National Chemical Emergency Centre

NIHHS   Notification of Installations Handling Hazardous Substances

NII   Nuclear Installations Inspectorate

NIOSH   National Institute for Occupational Safety and Health (USA)

NRPB   National Radiological Protection Board

LCLC   Local Community Liaison Council

OECD   Organisation for Economic Cooperation and Development

SIESO   Society of Industrial Emergency Service Officers

UKAEA   United Kingdom Atomic Energy Authority

UN   United Nations

UNEP   United Nations Environment Programme

WAEDM   World Association for Emergency and Disaster Medicine

WHO   World Health Organization

Contents

PREFACE

Worldwide, the manufacture and use of chemicals have increased dramatically during the last 25–30 years, and chemical disasters have occurred as a result of releases from industrial sources during manufacture, processing, storage, transport and general use. Contaminated air, water and even food have led to toxic exposure in humans and animals, and the environment. The consequences of these exposures to humans have led to acute and/or chronic clinical effects which may be immediate or delayed in onset.

The UK has responded by planning for chemical emergencies and this has received a new impetus with the CIMAH 1984 Regulations, which placed new obligations upon local authorities and emergency services to prepare for accidents involving certain types of chemical installations.

The International Programme on Chemical Safety is active in supporting national programmes for the prevention and treatment of poisonings involving chemicals. These are related to medical aspects of the more general objective of IPCS 'to promote effective international cooperation with respect to emergencies and accidents involving chemicals'.

Inter alia, areas identified for international collaboration were the establishment of guidelines for poison control and the establishment of a mechanism for exchange of experience in the role of poison centres in responding to major accidents involving chemicals.

Events such as Seveso, Bhopal and Basel have shown how toxic incidents may rapidly escalate beyond the capabilities of local emergency services, and that national and international expertise may be required for successful management of a chemical disaster, particularly as toxicological information about the hazards and risks from chemicals is sparse. Thus the current situation in the UK suggests that practical advice given for the management of chemical disasters could be incomplete, conflicting, confusing, delayed or duplicated.

In this context, the promotion of training of the manpower required in major chemical disasters is paramount. As well as UK and other national initiatives, the IPCS is currently preparing self-contained packages. The topics are related to the prevention of, and preparedness for, emergencies in the chemical and process industries, planning operations and training, on-site emergency response, and off-site emergency response.

Most importantly, medical management, which should be seen as a central issue in the planning and response phases and fundamental to the assessment of the

Major chemical disasters—medical aspects of management, edited by Virginia Murray, 1990: Royal Society of Medicine Services International Congress and Symposium Series No. 155, published by Royal Society of Medicine Services Limited.

impact of the incident on humans, has been given relatively little attention when compared with the tasks of search and rescue and on-site planning, carried out by emergency and other non-medical services.

For these reasons the Section of Occupational Medicine of the Royal Society of Medicine organized this meeting to discuss medical aspects of the management of major chemical disasters. The key aim of the meeting was to bring together experts from medical specialities, emergency services, and industry to identify gaps in current planning for medical intervention after major chemical accidents and to provide possible solutions for remedying this situation.

Dr Derek Taylor
Dr Virgina Murray
Dr Robin Philipp
Dr Michel Gilbert

SESSION I

INTRODUCTION

Chairman: Dr Edward Smith

Introductory remarks

M. Mercier

International Programme on Chemical Safety, World Health Organization, Geneva, Switzerland

Chemicals have become an essential and indispensable part of man's life, sustaining his activities and development, preventing and controlling many diseases, increasing agricultural productivity. However, many chemicals may, especially when they are misused, exert adverse effects on human health and on the integrity of the environment. One of the reasons for our concern is the significant number of poisonings by chemicals and the increasing number of accidents throughout the world involving chemicals, as well as the recognition of the association between the incidence of certain diseases and the exposure to certain chemicals, both natural and synthetic. This concern includes the realization that international trade in chemicals is worldwide and increasingly involves the less industrialized countries, and that accidents and poisonings involving chemicals are problems faced by all countries. The build-up of knowledge and of institutional capacity to respond to these problems has become a pressing need in all parts of the world.

The massive chemical poisoning disaster in Bhopal which claimed over 2500 lives has demonstrated, in tragic fashion, the risks involved in the ever-expanding production and use of chemicals and has illustrated the lack, or inadequacy of international cooperation in chemical safety in a third world country, desperate to develop and prosper through industrialization. That disaster, which may only be the tip of the iceberg, has drawn world attention to the consequences of inadequate information and safety precautions when dealing with highly dangerous chemicals. It has also stirred the world's conscience and has led to legal action with global implications.

But however horrific, Bhopal is only a dramatic example of a larger, more pervasive problem that touches practically everyone, especially in developing countries: how to live with chemicals in our daily lives. Over the past few years, there have been almost daily reports of chemical spills, leakages, plant breakdowns, and tens of thousands of chemical 'time bombs' waiting to go off in hazardous waste dumps. Alarmed by this 'série noire' of chemical accidents which have occurred in industrialized, as well as newly industrializing countries, the public is increasingly sensitive to the potential dangers of chemicals manufacture and handling, both for human health and the environment.

Although we know that there are hazards attached to every industrial activity and that it is impossible to remove the risk of a major accident completely, steps

Major chemical disasters—medical aspects of management, edited by Virginia Murray, 1990: Royal Society of Medicine Services International Congress and Symposium Series No. 155, published by Royal Society of Medicine Services Limited.

can nevertheless be taken to try to avert such accidents, and to limit their impact on human health and the environment, should they occur.

With incidents of major accidents in many different sectors of the chemical industry seeming to have reached epidemic proportions, and with increasing international impact and repercussions, a major international effort to focus attention on these critical issues is long overdue.

The management/organizational failures which are of concern are common to all cultures and sectors, as well as to large and small, public and private organizations worldwide. Since these failures are cross-cultural and cross-sectoral, a major effort which includes all these dimensions is most likely to produce the desired results.

Chemical safety is an international problem and national management should benefit from international collaboration in the planning and implementation of feasible control measures, in the strengthening of health education programmes to promote chemical safety and public awareness, exchange of validated information, and prevention and response to chemical accidents.

Meaningful international cooperation is the only key, and this catch-phrase has been translated into action by the three organizations of the United Nations family, UNEP, ILO and WHO who decided, in 1980, to set up jointly the IPCS, as a coordinated, intersectorial and international response to the challenge to human health and the environment made by the widespread utilization of an ever-increasing quantity of chemicals throughout the world.

One of the major roles of the IPCS is to collaborate with Member States in improving their national capabilities to ensure chemical safety, including preparedness and response to chemical emergencies and poisonings. The activities which we have developed during the last few years in this context include the provision of guidance material on prevention and response to chemical accidents, information systems on diagnosis and treatment of poisonings by chemicals, validation and availability of appropriate treatment, training of the necessary personnel, development and/or strengthening of poison control facilities and related toxicological services, etc.

I congratulate the organizers for having chosen this extremely important subject for this meeting, and for convening it at a very timely period. As a scientist working within an international organization dedicated to the health of all peoples, I am grateful for the guidance from the experts here on possible future directions which will enable us to better assist Member States in their endeavours to tackle the difficult and complex task of prevention of and response to chemical disasters.

Review of major chemical incidents and their medical management

P. J. Baxter

University of Cambridge Clinical School, Department of Community Medicine, Cambridge, UK

INTRODUCTION

Medical management in disasters is usually about the rescue and immediate treatment of casualties (e.g. maintenance of the airway, arresting haemorrhage, resuscitation, etc.), triage if there are numerous casualties, emergency hospital treatment and subsequent rehabilitation, and the welfare of temporary evacuees or refugees. In factory accidents or spillages of chemicals during their transportation, for example, decontamination of patients is added to the list (1). However, in most, if not all, major chemical incidents the medical management requires a broader approach than these traditional measures allow for the following reasons at least.

Chemical releases into the community from industrial sources can be through the three main routes of air, food, and water, with the result that many thousands of individuals can be exposed through ingestion, inhalation, or skin contact, depending upon the type of incident. There may be few acute effects from such exposures and instead most concern may focus on possible long-term health effects due to chemical injury, examples of which are given in Table 1. These effects may be characteristic of the chemical involved, but more often they will be indistinguishable from those having natural causes and can only be linked with chemical exposure through epidemiological studies. In addition, such mass exposures may be due to a single chemical or a mixture of chemicals whose toxicological properties, both short and long term, may be virtually unknown. A complete health hazard assessment is available for only 7% of chemicals used in pesticides, cosmetics, drugs and food additives, and there is no toxicity information available on 44% of these widely used substances; but for other chemicals the situation is much worse as there are virtually none on which a complete health hazard assessment has been made, and in 80% there is no toxicity information available at all (2).

Thus, in a major chemical incident a population can be exposed to a potentially wide range of health hazards which at the time of the event may be only dimly foreseen, and against which medical treatment may have little effect. In the

Major chemical disasters—medical aspects of management, edited by Virginia Murray, 1990: Royal Society of Medicine Services International Congress and Symposium Series No. 155, published by Royal Society of Medicine Services Limited.

Table 1 *Some long-term medical effects reported, or suspected, in major chemical incidents*

Category	Example	Incident
Carcinogenic	Primary liver cancer (suspected)	Polychlorinated biphenyls (Japan) (45)
Teratogenic	Cerebral palsy syndrome	Organic mercury (Japan) (35)
Immunological	Abnormal lymphocyte function	Polybrominated biphenyls (Michigan) (68)
Neurological	Distal motor neuropathy	Tri-o-cresyl phosphate (e.g. USA, 1930) (19)
Pulmonary	Parenchymal damage	Methyl isocyanate (India) (55)
Hepatic	Porphyria cutanea tarda	Hexachlorobenzene (Turkey) (40)
Dermatological	Sicca syndrome	Toxic oil syndrome (Spain) (48)

emergency phase, treatment of acute symptoms with specific antidotes is applicable to only a handful of chemicals, and preventive measures to eliminate further exposure (primary prevention) or mitigate its effects (secondary prevention) are of paramount importance.

The purpose of this paper is to use examples of previous major incidents to illustrate these points and their implications for chemical disaster planning.

ACUTE CHEMICAL INCIDENTS INVOLVING WATER, FOOD AND DRINK

The designation of certain chemical incidents as acute is inevitably arbitrary but may be applied to those incidents in which the latent period (the time between first exposure and the manifestation of the illness) is either short, i.e. within hours or a few days, or longer but the outbreak of the illness is explosive, resembling an acute infectious disease with which it can be readily confused. The epidemiological methods for the investigation of acute toxic and infectious disease outbreaks are similar, but the unravelling of the causal chemical, its impact on the community and the appropriate preventive health measures to arrest its spread, may pose special problems.

Two main types of acute incident can occur. First, an accident may arise in the manufacture or the supply of the product resulting in a normally safe chemical additive being added in excess with unexpected health consequences for the consumers. Occasionally a brand new additive used in a recommended amount may lead to an outbreak of disease. Secondly, contamination with a dangerous chemical may occur during the transport of the food, drink or water to the user, and in the case of food and drink there may be deliberate adulteration or the illicit use of industrial chemicals.

Water: additives and contaminants

Acute incidents involving additives to water supplies have been relatively minor in their health impact because the suppliers or the consumers are soon alerted to a change in water quality, though a spill of hydrofluorosilicic acid into the Annapolis public water supply on 13 November 1979 was linked to the death of one patient undergoing renal dialysis (3). Other incidents involving fluoridation have been recorded in the United States. Sodium hydroxide (4) and aluminium sulphate (5) are examples of chemicals normally added to make water potable which, when they have inadvertently been added in excess, have caused incidents of acute illness with gastrointestinal upset and skin irritation as the main features. Contamination of drinking water by chemicals may be accidental through faults in public water lines or through deliberate sabotage; in the USA, both types of incident have occurred with the pesticide chlordane (6). In the UK an accidental spillage of phenol into the River Dee in 1984 led to its appearance in the tap water of two million consumers (7); phenol spillages can contaminate drinking water from wells for years (8).

Food and drink: additives

In the USA bread (9) and cornmeal flour (10) have been associated with two outbreaks of transient illness characterized by facial flushing and an erythemato-macular rash on the face or upper arms coming on within 15–30 minutes of eating food containing high levels of the additive niacin; previous outbreaks have been linked with excessive levels of niacin in meat and meat products. An outbreak in South Africa in 1968 involved the flour improver potassium bromate, with hundreds of people developing an acute severe gastrointestinal illness (11). In Quebec in 1965–66 a cobalt additive in beer led to the hospitalization over several months of 48 patients with cardiomyopathy (12).

Of special interest is the outbreak of Margarine Disease in the Netherlands in 1960 (13). Two years previously a similar outbreak had occurred in West Germany when the disease was initially believed to be viral (i.e. erythema infectiosum, or fifth disease). In the Netherlands outbreak 600 000 people consumed Planta margarine containing a new additive with anti-splatter properties. The illness affected about 50 000 people and was characterized by a rash, fever, leucocytosis and eosinophilia starting within 1–23 days of consuming the margarine and lasting several days. The erythemato-macular rash had a sudden onset and became generalized in 2–24 hours; it was accompanied by severe itching and burning. The number of deaths was small. In Holland the emulgator was soon withdrawn from the margarine and the epidemic lasted only a few weeks, but in West Germany its use had continued for at least six months. Thus toxic causes should always be considered in the epidemiological investigation of acute disease outbreaks even before an infectious aetiology has been ruled out, otherwise delays in identifying a chemical culprit may result in many thousands of people becoming needlessly exposed.

Food and drink: contaminants/adulterants

Lead has been a serious contaminant of food and drink for centuries, either as a deliberate adulterant (14) or through accidental or unwitting contamination during food and drink manufacture. For example, illicit whisky stills made from lead pipes and automobile radiators containing lead solder caused severe lead poisoning in drinkers of 'moonshine' in rural areas of Georgia in the past (15). A recent outbreak of lead poisoning on the West Bank occurred through the use of lead to stabilize the metal parts of stone mills (16). Lead drinking bowls and water distributed through lead pipes was commonplace in Roman times, but pottery with lead glaze is still common in certain parts of the world (17,18).

Another important cause of severe neurological disability in many countries has been the contamination of food and drink with triorthocresylphosphate (TOCP) (19,20). This weak organophosphate compound is used as an industrial lubricant and hydraulic fluid, but as a clear oily liquid it has been an adulterant of edible oil (e.g. Morocco 1959 (21)). Edible oil has also been contaminated through its storage in drums which formerly contained TOCP (22). In the Jamaica Ginger Paralysis in the United States in 1930 thousands of Americans were poisoned by 'jake', an illicit extract of Jamaica ginger containing TOCP that was used as an alcoholic beverage during Prohibition (19). The clinical manifestations are a delayed neurotoxic syndrome with the development of acute, mainly motor, peripheral neuropathy and distal weakness (wrist and foot drop). The latent period is from 3–28 days and consequently it is relatively easy to link an outbreak with a specific exposure. The clinical picture of an acute paralysis of distal limb muscles is so characteristic that this chemical should always be suspected in an outbreak of polyneuropathy.

The transportation of flour has been associated with numerous recorded incidents, including one involving TOCP (23). Fatal outbreaks of parathion poisoning have occurred, for example, in Jamaica (24) and Sierra Leone (25), and outbreaks of endrin poisoning have occurred in several countries (26–28). In these incidents sacks of flour were conveyed in ships' holds or trucks used previously to transport pesticides. Diggory *et al.* (24) state that between 1956–76 there were 14 recorded outbreaks of disease with 249 deaths reported as caused by the contamination of foods with pesticides during storage or shipment. The now widespread use of containers in shipping, together with other measures, should reduce the risk. Contamination of food crops with misapplied pesticides can also lead to acute intoxication in consumers and in the United States such outbreaks have recently involved melons (29,30), and hydroponic cucumbers (31), and the carbamate pesticide Aldicarb. Pesticide poisoning always needs to be considered in outbreaks of gastrointestinal illness, and signs of anticholinesterase intoxication, including convulsions, should always be sought.

Jaundice is an uncommon presentation of chemical food poisoning, but the Epping Jaundice incident in England in 1965 is instructive (32). During the month of February 84 cases appeared, the illness affecting professionals who fell ill at about the same time. In many sufferers upper abdominal pain ensued a few hours following the consumption of a particular type of wholemeal bread, and jaundice appeared several days later. In some patients the jaundice persisted for months, but the cause was soon tracked down to a contaminated sack of flour transported to the bakery on 21 January: a plastic jar containing a chemical liquid had spilled its contents on to the hessian flour sack in the van. The chemical, the plastic hardener methylene dianiline, caused a characteristic hepatitis (33), and is a suspect carcinogen. Nowadays in the UK flour is packaged in 3-ply paper bags and the risk of such incidents going unnoticed is in consequence less.

CHRONIC INCIDENTS INVOLVING FOOD

If the latent period is months, or the exposure is long term and insidious, then the emergence of cases of toxic illness may also be drawn out over time. With chemical carcinogens the latency may be many years. An important consequence of a long latent period is that large numbers of people may become exposed before the the first appearance of the disease draws attention to the contamination problem. Moreover, it may be a complex and difficult task to determine the environmental cause of such an outbreak, particularly when more time may elapse before the seriousness, or the chemical nature, of the outbreak becomes recognized. It is therefore not surprising that some of the most serious chemical incidents have been of this type. Another type of contamination episode is one which is discovered after the event but which does not give rise to acute illness, e.g. the contamination of the food chain with polybrominated biphenyl in Michigan, 1973 (34). The major chronic incidents to date have all involved food and some examples now follow.

Methyl mercury, Minamata, Japan (1956 to present)

The first patients with an unusual neurological disease which was initially thought to be of infectious origin and later known as Minamata Disease (35), presented in Minamata in 1956. Not until three years later did suspicion fall upon mercury as the causal agent when the disease was seen to resemble industrial organic mercury poisoning and mercury was identified in effluent entering Minamata Bay from the city's chemical factory. In 1960 organic mercury was identified in sea food and in 1963 the government announced that methyl mercury was likely to be the chemical culprit. Controversy continued over the source of the methyl mercury until 1968, when it was accepted that it came from the factory's acetaldehyde process. The first victims were poor fishermen and their families who were unable to afford any other items than fish in their diet and who had moved into the area after the Second World War, but exposure also involved over 50 000 others. To date over 2000 cases of Minamata Disease have been certified, including 28 recognized congenital cases (a syndrome resembling cerebral palsy) and an unknown number of spontaneous abortions which were identified early in the outbreak. Epidemiological studies were slow to start and incomplete, and not until 1968 was a fishing ban imposed in the Bay area, though this was voluntary. The severity of this classical outbreak was probably linked to the long duration of exposure before the chemical cause was fully accepted and action taken to eliminate exposure: a massive 10-year operation of dredging the contaminated Bay was not completed until 1987.

Methyl mercury, Iraq, 1971/2 and
hexachlorobenzene, Turkey, 1955–61

The latent period in Minamata was probably over 10 years, but in another outbreak of methyl mercury poisoning in Iraq (December 1971–March 1972) the average latency period was only 32 days with a maximum of about three months (36,37). The exposure was through the consumption of bread made from seed grain which had been treated with methyl mercury as a fungicide, and it resulted in 459 deaths and 6530 hospital admissions, many including children. Cases of congenital organic mercury poisoning were also recorded (38). The cause of this outbreak was soon identified and the exposure time was only two weeks to two months, with the result that the disease had a better outcome than at Minamata (39). The use of methyl mercury as a seed dressing has been widespread, resulting in several other outbreaks in Iraq and around the world. Another major incident involving flour from treated seed grain, this time with hexachlorobenzene, was in Turkey in 1955–61. The latent period was about six months (40), with the appearance of 3000–4000 cases of porphyria cutanea tarda, a liver condition in which the skin, becoming unusually sensitive to light and trauma, heals poorly and is readily infected. The outbreak appeared slowly at first and a genetic origin was considered. The true cause was not identified until 1958, but consumption of the wheat continued after that time as the treated seed grain bore no distinguishing mark and there were food shortages (42–43). The consequences were severe and many survivors are to be found in Turkey today suffering from neurological, dermatological and orthopaedic abnormalities.

One of the most important lessons of these outbreaks is the need for urgency in the investigation of suspected toxic disease, so that the causal agent can be identified and the exposure of the population eliminated as soon as possible, as medical treatment has little to offer in comparison with halting the organ damage caused by the exposure. Another observation is the vulnerability of the poor who may have little choice but to continue to consume food they fear is contaminated.

Yusho epidemic, Japan, 1968 and the Toxic Oil Syndrome, Spain, 1981

In the Yusho ('oil disease') episode in southern Japan in 1968 about 10 000 people ingested rice oil which was later found to have been contaminated with polychlorinated biphenyls during its manufacture: 64% of the consumers were affected by an illness whose hallmark was the skin condition, chloracne (44,45). Some children born to exposed mothers also showed evidence of contamination (e.g. stained skin and low birth weight) and following an almost identical outbreak in Taiwan in 1979 it was confirmed that PCBs caused developmental abnormalities (46). Rice oil was not a commonly used edible oil and some victims were aware that they had developed symptoms as a result of consuming the oil, but despite this dermatologists were slow to appreciate that there was an epidemic. It was not until early October 1968, several months after the first cases appeared, that the rice oil was submitted to analysis. Initially it was thought that arsenic was present and following the press report of this erroneous finding the government banned the oil on 15 October. A scientific working group formed four days later initiated studies which rapidly led to the identification of an unusual chemical substance in fat biopsies from the patients which was identical to the contaminant in the oil and subsequently identified as Kaneclor-400. The investigation was greatly aided by the fact that half the oil was sold in cans which bore the date when they left the factory, as the disease was eventually linked to rice oil shipped on 5 and 6 February. The average latency was 71 days (47). The lack of appropriate response on the part of medical workers when this disease first appeared points to the potential value of a national surveillance or reporting system for environmental diseases.

Delay in recognizing a toxic outbreak was one of the factors which contributed to confusion in the Toxic Oil Syndrome in Spain in 1981. An explosive outbreak of pneumonia in Madrid and the provinces north-west of Madrid beginning on 1 May was at first regarded as infectious and the possibility of a toxic cause, though considered, was not as actively pursued (48,49). There were eventually about 11 000 acute hospital admissions and, at the height of the outbreak, at the rate of 600 per day. Over 20 000 cases and 330 deaths were recorded. Soon after the outbreak began an epidemiological survey was undertaken using a questionnaire which enquired into numerous possible aetiological factors, but without success. In the meantime hospital clinicians decided that a common factor in the patients' diets had been a cheap adulterated edible oil sold by itinerant salesmen. On 10 June the government announced the possible link with this oil and on 11 June the epidemiological study was repeated, this time with a questionnaire which included the consumption of edible oil. A strong association was found and on 30 June the government offered to replace rape-seed oil samples with genuine olive oil. This was now two months after the epidemic began and, to make matters worse, inadequate care was taken to record which oil samples came from affected households, and many people brought cheap oil to exchange for the more expensive olive oil. About 30% of the patients who had recovered from pneumonia soon developed chronic complications, the main features being neuropathy, myopathy, sicca syndrome and a scleroderma-like skin disease.

The oil was illicitly refined, denatured rape-seed oil originally intended for industrial purposes. Apart from the presence of the industrial marker aniline, a chemical contaminant in the oil responsible for the outbreak has not been found. Comparisons between the Yusho and Toxic Oil syndromes reveal some important differences as to why the chemical culprit was found in the former, and not the latter, epidemic. In the Yusho outbreak some patients themselves were able to link the oil with their disease because the rice oil was not widely consumed in the everyday diet as was the rape-seed oil in Spain. Part of the rice oil production was sold in cans marked with the date of manufacture and not only in unmarked bottles as in Spain. The preventive measure of recalling contaminated oil was much more effective in the Japanese population which soon stopped using the rice oil.

In the initial phases of the Toxic Oil Syndrome speculation over possible environmental causal factors actually impeded the investigation. Such confusion would have been minimized if the lessons of previous outbreaks had been followed. In many major chemical incidents involving food and drink five vehicles stand out as obvious candidates for urgent consideration. These are edible oil, flour, dairy products (milk, meat, eggs), alcoholic beverages, and water (fish, if this is the staple food). Epidemiological surveys should routinely include these in their questionnaires when investigating outbreaks if a toxic cause is suspected. The Toxic Oil Syndrome showed the necessity of collecting and storing samples of these vehicles from affected households at the earliest opportunity. Delays may result in the suspect food being lost through being eaten or destroyed so that laboratory identification of a chemical contaminant becomes impossible.

AIRBORNE RELEASES

In these releases the chemical is emitted over a short time into a localized geographic area, e.g. around an industrial plant. The potential for exposure exists in the period it takes for the chemical cloud to disperse, or for a material deposited in the environment to break down or be removed. Health effects may be immediate or delayed as in incidents involving food and water. The chemicals may be raw materials, processed products, the intermediate products of chemical reactions, combustion products, or a mixture of any of these. Air sampling to collect chemical emissions in an emergency is seldom feasible in practice even in fires lasting for several hours. Thus, in determining the substances released reliance has to be placed upon after-the-event studies of the process inside the plant and its chemicals together with any materials deposited in the environment. The plant inside the factory has to be carefully examined to piece together the events leading up to the release. In most accidental releases there is no warning and so there is usually little possibility of the population being evacuated before some degree of exposure has occurred.

Seveso, Italy, 1976

The release of 2,3,7,8-tetrachlorodibenzodioxin (TCDD) at Seveso in 1976 (50) is another example of how delay in recognizing the severity of an incident can lead to the continuing exposure of local populations. The Icmesa factory manufactured 245-trichlorophenol by an exothermic reaction which went out of control on 10 July with the result that 1.3 kg of TCDD (51) were released into the air to contaminate the surrounding area. Three days later birds, animals and vegetables died in what later became designated as Zone A (the most polluted zone) downwind from the plant, but it was only on 17 July that the presence of TCDD was suspected. Further delays occurred until its presence was confirmed on 23 July and then not until 26 July was the evacuation of the 735 residents in Zone A begun, a measure which should have been considered from the outset. Subsequent studies show that the soil in this zone had become heavily contaminated with TCDD, the most toxic synthetic chemical known and one highly resistant to environmental degradation. Widespread fears arose over its carcinogenicity and teratogenicity (52), as well as other health effects. Bruzzi (53) mentions two factors that characterize the history of epidemiological studies in Seveso: the lack of proper studies in the early phase, and problems in defining exposure. Reasons for these deficiencies included poor cooperation from the exposed population, the inadequacy of proper protocols and the absence of control groups in the initial studies. It was erroneously considered at first that refined studies would be unnecessary as the health effects would be self-evident, and it was not until 1979 that epidemiological studies were begun. So far the only well substantiated disorder attributed to TCDD exposure has been chloracne in 187 children. As in some other incidents (e.g. Yusho) laboratory techniques for measuring the chemical agent in human serum were slow to be developed, but in 1988 samples of serum collected in residents after the incident were submitted for analysis by a new technique (54) developed at the Centers for Disease Control: the highest levels ever reported in humans were found in persons in from Zone A, confirming the human exposure which had occurred in 1976 (51).

Bhopal, India, 1984

The world's worst industrial disaster to date occurred at Bhopal when about 200 000 people were exposed to a cloud of 40 tonnes of methyl isocyanate released from the Union Carbide plant during an estimated 90-minute period in the early hours of 3 December 1984 (55). Most of the deaths occurred in the hours or days after the release, and the hospitals were swamped with casualties suffering from severe eye and lung irritation. About 2500 people died, mostly from pulmonary oedema or its sequelae. There was a delay in chemical engineers gaining entry to the plant to study the process and the cause of the leak remains disputed. The epidemiological follow-up and medical records of survivors have been incomplete. The lack of appropriate clinical investigations, including the storage of blood samples during the immediate emergency phase, led to controversy over whether cyanide was present in the gas (56,57), a subject which clouded both the acute and longer term treatment of the victims. Proper coordination of toxicological advice and investigations in the early key stages of the disaster was especially needed as information on the human effects of methyl isocyanate was virtually non-existent before this catastrophe.

B & R Hauliers, Salford, 1982

Late on the night of 25 September 1982 a warehouse containing some 2000 tonnes of chemicals, including over 20 tonnes of sodium chlorate, and located in the midst of a built up area in Salford, England, was deliberately set alight (58). An explosion destroyed the warehouse building whereupon several hundred people were urgently evacuated from their homes until it was deemed safe, on wholly inadequate grounds, for them to return the next morning after the fire had come under control. Sixty people suffering from smoke and fume related complaints were treated at the local hospital, but no attempt was made either to identify, or to do a health survey on, the exposed population. A layer of chemical powder up to half-an-inch thick had fallen as far as 14 miles away downwind on to houses and gardens. The residents were advised to sweep up the powder even though no-one knew what it contained. Two days after the fire a laboratory confirmed that the dust was relatively harmless and contained titanium dioxide and para- and ortho-dichlorobenzene. However, reassurances on safety were given before the dust had been analysed and it was not known whether other materials had been released from the warehouse; a further four weeks elapsed before an inventory could be compiled since the company's records had been consumed in the fire. Fortunately this incident did not seem to have any serious health impact but it did highlight the lack of preparedness of local emergency services in the UK for dealing with major toxic incidents, a deficiency which has since been partially addressed for certain activities which fall under the CIMAH Regulations 1984 (59).

Mount St Helens eruption, USA, 1980 and the Lake Nyos gas burst, Cameroon, 1986

Merchant (60) has described the response to the eruption of Mount St Helens on 18 May 1980 as an exemplary model of how to cope with disaster through the proper use of technology, public education, a coordinated emergency response, and a thorough evaluation of the health effects arising from exposure. A volcanic eruption has many parallels with an industrial release as volcanoes can emit toxic gases or ash over a wide area. In this eruption the main concerns were the toxic and respiratory effects of the ash which had fallen in a thick layer over the central part of Washington State. An emergency response involving many different agencies and coordinated by the Federal Emergency Management Agency resulted in the rapid setting up of short- and long-term epidemiological and laboratory studies. The outcome was a virtually complete evaluation of the health hazard (61).

In complete contrast, a gas burst from Lake Nyos, Cameroon, on the night of 21 August 1986 left about 1700 people dead and illustrates how the absence of immediate medical investigations, including autopsies, can make a re-creation of events in a disaster almost impossible. The finding of skin lesions on pressure points, together with neurological palsies (wrist and foot drop) in some survivors, and which resolved in about two weeks, supported accounts that numerous victims of the gassing had been unconscious for hours following the gas release. However, language and cultural factors made retrospective epidemiological studies impossible and the only revealing finding was a high concentration of dissolved carbon dioxide in the lake water. The exact nature of this event and its health impact remains poorly understood as investigators took too long before arriving in this remote area. The clinical signs, together with the evidence of CO_2 in the water, indicated that carbon dioxide from a volcanic source was the major if not the only lethal gas released and that a CO_2-in-air mixture had been responsible for the effects observed. This explanation, inadequate though it may be, is the only one that can be reasonably drawn from the limited data available (62).

Environmental assessment and animal sentinels

Some of the above mentioned incidents have shown the need for careful environmental studies as an adjunct to investigations in human subjects. Chemical analysis of environmental samples for evidence of contamination is not routinely performed, but in some instances, e.g. fires, the testing for such prime hazards as lead, asbestos, and sometimes polychlorinated biphenyls and TCDD should be considered. On the other hand damage to vegetation may give important clues to the potential toxicity to humans, or record the path of a gas plume, e.g. at Bhopal (63) and Seveso (50). The absence of damage to the vegetation at Lake Nyos was most important in excluding hot or acidic gases as the cause of the skin lesions, and made the hypothesis that a volcanic eruption had been the source of the gas less likely. In Seveso the deaths of rabbits, chickens and birds in the first few days after the disaster should have alerted health officials to the presence of a serious health hazard in the contaminated Zone A and the need for immediate evacuation (50). The deaths of birds, cats, dogs and 43 horses led to the uncovering of a serious toxic waste problem in Missouri, USA, where in 1971 waste contaminated with TCDD from a plant manufacturing trichlorophenol had been sprayed on to horse arenas to suppress dust. By 1986 in residential, commercial and recreational areas of eastern Missouri, near St Louis, 40 sites had been identified as having received contaminated waste from the plant, and human exposure to TCDD has been demonstrated (64,65). Warning of serious chemical contamination of fish was given at Minamata a few years before the human cases appeared when cats who ate the fish developed fatal neurological problems (cat dancing disease) (35). In the Yusho epidemic the deaths in March 1986 of broiler chickens whose feed contained oil from the culprit plant could well have alerted officials to a breach in the manufacturing process in advance of the outbreak of human disease shortly afterwards (45). In Michigan in 1973 dairy produce and meat became contaminated with polybrominated biphenyls (PBB) as a result of the accidental substitution of the fire-retardant 'Firemaster' (PBB) for 'Nutrimaster' (a magnesium oxide feed additive for dairy cattle). The first indication of the accident was sickness in cattle that had consumed the contaminated feed (66). Subsequently, 8 million of Michigan's 9.1 million residents were shown to have detectable body burdens of PBB (67) and immunological abnormalities have been described (68). Similar incidents involving animal feedstuffs with potential for contamination of the human food chain have been reported (69,70). Thus in an emergency situation careful environmental and animal studies may be crucial in determining whether a human health hazard exists or not.

CONCLUSION

The presentation of a major chemical incident depends on whether the exposure route is air, food or water, but the same general principles of medical management apply. When a large number of people become exposed the emergency response is of a different order from that seen in the common accidents involving the transport or distribution of chemicals which are usually routinely handled by the emergency services. The medical management of the incidents described above can be easily faulted in retrospect. The key deficiency can be seen to be the delay, for a variety of reasons, in properly identifying the health hazard with the result that the medical management could not proceed on an adequately informed basis. The health-risk assessment must begin as soon as possible after the incident

Table 2 *An overview of the medical management of major chemical incidents*

1. *Urgent evaluation of the health risk* using multidisciplinary expertise:

   Clinical
   Laboratory
   Epidemiological
   Toxicological
   Environmental

2. *Provision of authoritative advice* based on this evaluation for:

   Management of exposed
   Treatment of casualties
   Primary and secondary prevention
   Reassurance

3. *Coordination* of all the above, plus:

   Media
   Clinical/epidemiological follow up
   Collaboration with national/international agencies

occurs, or a health hazard is suspected, and has to be continually updated as the situation unfolds. An outline summary of the multi-disciplinary approach needed is shown in Table 2; the importance of the adequate scientific investigation of major toxic incidents has been elaborated upon elsewhere (71–74). As the resources required for effective medical management are likely to be beyond local emergency services, planning for such events should therefore include national and international agencies.

ACKNOWLEDGMENT

I acknowledge the support of a NATO Fellowship in the preparation of this paper.

REFERENCES

(1) Baskett P, Weller R, eds. *Medicine for disasters*. London: Wright, 1988.
(2) Magos L. Thoughts on life with untested and adequately tested chemicals. *Br J Ind Med* 1988; **45**: 721–6.
(3) Centers for Disease Control. Fluoride intoxication in a dialysis unit—Maryland. *MMWR* 1980; **29**: 134–6.
(4) Centers for Disease Control. Community water supply contaminated with caustic soda—Georgia. *MMWR* 1981; **30**: 67–73.
(5) *New Scientist*. A nasty taste. 21 January 1989, p. 23.
(6) Centers for Disease Control. Chlordane contamination of a public water supply—Pittsburgh, Pennsylvania. *MMWR* 1981; **30**: 571–8.
(7) Jarvis SN, Straube RC, Williams ALJ, Bartlett CLR. Illness associated with contamination of drinking water supplies with phenol. *Br Med J* 1985; **290**: 1800–2.
(8) Baker EL, Landrigan PJ, Bertozzi PE, Field PH, Basteyns BJ, Skinner HG. Phenol poisoning due to contaminated drinking water. *Arch Environ Health* 1978; **33**: 89–94.
(9) Centers for Disease Control. Niacin intoxication from pumpernickel bagels—New York. *MMWR* 1983; **32**: 305.
(10) Centers for Disease Control. Illness associated with high levels of niacin in cornmeal—Illinois. *MMWR* 1981; **30**: 11–12.

(11) Stewart TH, Sherman Y, Politzer WM. An outbreak of food-poisoning due to a flour improver, potassium bromate. *S Afr Med J* 1969; **43**: 200–2.

(12) Morin YL, Foley AR, Martineau G, Roussel J. Quebec beer-drinkers' cardiomyopathy: forty-eight cases. *Can Med Assoc J* 1967; **97**: 881–3.

(13) Doeglas HMG, Hermans EH, Huisman J. The Margarine Disease. *Arch Dermatol* 1961; **83**: 837–43.

(14) Burnett J. *Plenty and want: a social history of diet in England from 1815 to the present day.* London: Scolar Press, 1979.

(15) Crutcher JC. Clinical manifestations and therapy of acute lead intoxication due to the ingestion of illicitly distilled alcohol. *Ann Intern Med* 1963; **59**: 707–15.

(16) Hershko C, Abrahamov A, Moreb J, *et al.* Lead poisoning in a West Bank Arab village. *Arch Intern Med* 1984; **144**: 1969–73.

(17) Klein M, Namer R, Harpur E, Corbin R. Earthenware containers as a source of fatal lead poisoning. *New Engl J Med* 1970; **283**: 669–72.

(18) Acra A, Raffoul Z, Dajani R, Karahagopian Y. Lead-glazed pottery: a potential health hazard in the Middle East. *Lancet* 1981; **i**: 433–4.

(19) Morgan JP. The Jamaica Ginger Paralysis. *JAMA* 1982; **248**: 1864–7.

(20) Morgan JP, Penovich P. Jamaica Ginger Paralysis. Forty-seven-year follow-up. *Arch Neurol* 1978; **35**: 530–2.

(21) Smith HV, Spalding JMK. Outbreak of paralysis in Morocco due to *ortho*-cresyl phosphate poisoning. *Lancet* 1959; **ii**: 1019–21.

(22) Senanayake N, Jeyaratnam J. Toxic polyneuropathy due to gingli oil contaminated with tri-cresyl phosphate affecting adolescent girls in Sri Lanka. *Lancet* 1981; **i**: 88–9.

(23) Sorokin M. Orthocresyl phosphate neuropathy: report of an outbreak in Fiji. *Med J Aust* 1969; **1**: 506–8.

(24) Diggory HJP, Landrigan PJ, Latimer KP, *et al.* Fatal parathion poisoning caused by contamination of flour in international commerce. *Am J Epidemiol* 1977; **106**: 145–53.

(25) Etzel RA, Forthal DN, Hill, Jr, RH, Demby A. Fatal parathion poisoning in Sierra Leone. *Bull WHO* 1987; **65**: 645–9.

(26) Davies GM, Lewis I. Outbreak of food-poisoning from bread made of chemically contaminated flour. *Br Med J* 1956; **2**: 393–8.

(27) Centers for Disease Control. Acute Convulsions Associated with endrin poisoning—Pakistan. *MMWR* 1984; **33**: 687–93.

(28) Weeks DE. Endrin food-poisoning. *Bull WHO* 1967; **37**: 499–512.

(29) Green MA, Heumann MA, Wehr HM, *et al.* An outbreak of watermelon-borne pesticide toxicity. *Am J Public Health* 1987; **77**: 1431–4.

(30) Centers for Disease Control. Aldicarb food poisoning from contaminated melons—California. *MMWR* 1986; **35**: 254–8.

(31) Goes EA, Savage EP, Gibbons G, Aaronson M, Ford SA, Wheeler HW. Suspected foodborne carbamate pesticide intoxications associated with ingestion of hydroponic cucumbers. *Am J Epidemiol* 1980; **111**: 254–60.

(32) Kopelman H, Robertson MH, Sanders PG. The Epping Jaundice. *Br Med J* 1966; **1**: 514–16.

(33) Kopelman H, Scheuer PJ, Williams R. The liver lesion of the Epping Jaundice. *Q J Med* 1966; **35**: 553–64.

(34) Wolfe MS, Anderson HA, Selikoff IJ. Human tissue burdens of halogenated aromatic chemicals in Michigan. *JAMA* 1982; **247**: 2112–16.

(35) Tsubaki T, Irukayama K (eds). *Minamata disease.* Amsterdam: Elsevier Scientific Publishing Co, 1977.

(36) Al-Tikriti K, Al-Mufti AW. An outbreak of organomercury poisoning among Iraqi farmers. *Bull WHO* 1976; **53**(suppl): 15–21.

(37) Al-Mufti AW, Copplestone JF, Kazantzis G, Mahmoud RM, Majid MA. Epidemiology of organomercury poisoning in Iraq. 1. Incidence in a defined area and relationship to the eating of contaminated bread. *Bull WHO* 1976; **53**(suppl): 23–36.

(38) Amin-Zaki L, Elhassani S, Majeed MA, Clarkson TW, Doherty RA, Greenwood M. Intra-uterine methyl mercury poisoning in Iraq. *Pediatrics* 1974; **54**: 587–95.

(39) Amin-Zaki L, Majeed MA, Clarkson TW, Greenwood MR. Methyl mercury poisoning in Iraqi children: clinical observations over two years. *Br Med J* 1978; **1**: 613–16.

(40) Cripps DJ, Peters HA, Gocmen A, Dogramici I. Porphyria turcica due to hexa-chlorobenzene: a 20–30 year follow-up study on 204 patients. *Br J Dermatol* 1984; **111**: 413–22.

(41) Cam C, Nigogosyan G. Acquired porphyria cutanea tarda due to hexachlorobenzene. *JAMA* 1963; **183**: 88–91.

(42) Dean G. The Turkish epidemic of porphyria. *S Afr Med J* 1961; **35**: 509–11.

(43) Schmid R. Cutaneous porphyria in Turkey. *JAMA* 1960; **263**: 397–8.

(44) Kuratsune M, Yoshimura T, Matsuzaka J, Yamaguchi A. Yusho, a poisoning caused by rice oil contaminated with polychlorinated biphenyls. *HSMHA Health Rep*, 1971; **86**: 1083–91.

(45) Kuratsune M, Yoshimura T, Matsuzaka J, Yamaguchi A. Epidemiological Study on Yusho, a poisoning caused by ingestion of rice oil contaminated with a commercial brand of polychlorinated biphenyls. *Environ Health Perspect*, 1972; No 1: 119–28.

(46) Rogan WJ, Gladen BC, Hung K-L, *et al.* Congenital poisoning by polychlorinated biphenyls and their contaminants in Taiwan. *Science* 1988; **241**: 334–6.

(47) Hayabuchi H, Yoshimura T, Kuratsune M. Consumption of toxic rice oil by 'Yusho' patients and its relation to the clinical response and latent period. *Food Cosmetics Toxicol* 1979; **17**: 455–61.

(48) World Health Organisation. *Toxic Oil Syndrome*. Copenhagen: WHO, 1984.

(49) Centers for Disease Control. Follow up on toxic pneumonia—Spain. *MMWR* 1981; **30**: 436–8.

(50) Hay A. *The chemical scythe*. New York: Plenum Press, 1982.

(51) Centers for Disease Control. Preliminary Report: 2,3,7,8-tetrachlorodibenzo-p-dioxin. Exposure to humans—Seveso, Italy. *MMWR* 1988; **37**: 733–6.

(52) Mastroiacovo P, Spagnolo A, Marvi E, Meazza L, Bertollini R, Segni G. Birth defects in the Seveso area after TCDD contamination. *JAMA* 1988; **259**: 1668–72.

(53) Bruzzi P. Health impact of the accidental release of TCDD at Seveso. In: Coulston F, Pocchiari F (eds), *Accidental exposure to dioxins: Human health aspects*. New York: Academic Press 1983: 215–28.

(54) Patterson DG, Hampton L, Lapeza, Jr, CR, *et al.* High resolution gas chromatographic/high resolution mass spectrometric analysis of human serum on a whole weight and lipid basis for 2,3,7,8-tetrachlorodibenzo-p-dioxin. *Analyt Chem* 1987; **59**: 2000–5.

(55) Hazarika S. *Bhopal: The lessons of a tragedy*. New Delhi: Penguin Books India, 1987.

(56) Salmon AG. Bright red blood of Bhopal victims: cyanide or MIC? *Br J Ind Med* 1986; **43**: 502–4.

(57) Nemery B. Bright red blood of Bhopal victims? *Br J Ind Med* 1987; **44**: 287–8.

(58) Health & Safety Executive. *The fire and explosions at B & R Hauliers, Salford, 25 September 1982*. London: HMSO, 1983.

(59) Baxter PJ. From Flixborough to Bhopal: is legislation enough? *Br J Ind Med* 1986; **43**: 1–5.

(60) Merchant JA. Preparing for disaster. *Am J Pub Health* 1986; **76**: 233–5.

(61) Buist AS, Bernstein RS, eds. Health effects of volcanoes: an approach to evaluating the health effects of an environmental hazard. *Am J Pub Health* 1986; **76**(suppl): 1–90.

(62) Baxter PJ, Kapila M, Mfonfu D. Lake Nyos disaster, Cameroon, 1986: the medical effects of large scale emission of carbon dioxide? *Br Med J* 1989; **298**: 1437–41.

(63) Singh MP, Ghosh S. Bhopal gas tragedy: model simulation of the dispersion scenario. *J Hazard Mat* 1987; **17**: 1–22.

(64) Hoffman RE, Stehr-Green PA, Webb KB, *et al.* Health effects of long-term exposure to 2,3,7,8-tetrachlorodibenzo-p-dioxin. *JAMA* 1986; **225**: 2031–8.

(65) Patterson DG, Hoffman RE, Needham LL, *et al.* 2,3,7,8-tetrachlorodibenzo-p-dioxin levels in adipose tissue of exposed and control persons in Missouri. *JAMA* 1986; **256**: 2683–6.

(66) Halbert FL, Jackson TF. A toxic syndrome associated with the feeding of polybrominated biphenyl-contaminated protein concentrate to dairy cattle. *J Am Vet Med Assoc* 1974; **165**: 437–9.

(67) Brilliant LB, Van Amburg G, Isbister J, *et al.* Breast milk monitoring to measure Michigan's contamination with polybrominated biphenyls. *Lancet* 1978; **ii**: 643–6.

(68) Bekesi JG, Holland JF, Anderson HA, *et al.* Lymphocyte function of Michigan dairy farmers exposed to polybrominated biphenyls. *Science* 1978; **199**: 1207–9.

(69) Firestone D. Etiology of Chick Edema Disease. *Environ Health Perspect* 1973; **5**: 59–66.

(70) Drotman DP, Baxter PJ, Liddle JA, Brokopp CD, Skinner MD. Contamination of the food chain by polychlorinated biphenyls from a broken transformer. *Am J Public Health* 1983; **73**: 290–2.

(71) Aldridge WN. Toxic disasters with food contaminants. In: Chambers PL, ed. *Toxicology in the European Economic Community.* London: Wiley, 1987: 57–71.

(72) Aldridge WN, Connors TA. Chemical accidents and toxicology. *Human Toxicol* 1985; **4**: 477–9.

(73) Lawther PJ. Epidemics of non-infectious disease. *Proc R Soc Lond* 1979; **205**: 63–75.

(74) Environmental Health Criteria 72. *Principles of studies on diseases of suspected chemical etiology and their prevention.* Geneva: WHO 1987.

SESSION II

LIKELY CAUSES OF FUTURE MAJOR INCIDENTS INVOLVING CHEMICALS

National and international legislation on major chemical hazards

K. Cassidy

Technology Division, Health and Safety Executive, Magdalen House, Stanley Precinct, Bootle, Merseyside, UK

INTRODUCTION

There is nothing new about major hazards; it is only their character which has changed over the years. Initially, of course, large scale threats to man and his environment had a natural origin, mainly storm, flood and fire, although the archeological record amply demonstrates the potential for disaster which arose from early man's attempt to harness the potential of fire. In the Middle Ages, the manufacture, storage and accidental ignition of black powder may well provide the first examples of large-scale damage from manufactured substances and artefacts; and in the last couple of centuries, large scale water dam failure and boiler explosions heralded the onset of the Industrial Revolution.

The entrance of chemistry and particularly chemical engineering on this stage has been relatively recent; and it is even more recently that the threats posed by large-scale chemical engineering and energy processes have attracted the attention, first of risk analysts, and then of legislators, as a response to growing public concern. The justification for such concern has been highlighted at regular intervals, by a succession of incidents causing widespread death and damage. Many lists of such incidents could be produced; most would include catastrophes such as Oppau; Texas City; Flixborough; Seveso and Manfredonia; Bantry Bay; San Carlos; San Juan Ihautepec; and Bhopal, all of which have been seminal in terms of public and regulatory response. Nor is the catalogue confined to damage to humans. Many major hazard risks have an element (which may indeed, predominate) of environmental damage where effects may persist long-term. The incident at Morley, Leeds earlier this decade, and the major Rhine pollution following the fire at the Sandoz site at Sweitzerhalle, Basle in 1986, point up this environmental dimension (a dimension shared, incidentally, by Seveso, Manfredonia, et al.).

For all that they are burned into our corporate consciousness, such disasters are, in real terms, relatively rare; they make only a small contribution to total deaths from accident, in an industrial or any other context. Why, then, are they special? There are, of course, economic implications, on both a micro and macro scale; there are humanitarian considerations; but above all it is the 'aversion factor'

Major chemical disasters—medical aspects of management, edited by Virginia Murray, 1990: Royal Society of Medicine Services International Congress and Symposium Series No. 155, published by Royal Society of Medicine Services Limited.

in public response (and its logic or otherwise is irrelevant), with the concomitant political implications, which results in action in a democratic society, leading to tighter control.

THE UK APPROACH

The UK has been a leading architect in the framing of legislative control for major industrial hazards. We have a system, based mainly on the advice of the Advisory Committee on Major Hazards (1) and confirming the European requirements, (2) which is centred on the following concepts (3):

1. Identification—via the Notification of Installations Handling Hazardous Substances (NIHHS) regulations (4)
2. Assessment and control—via the Control of Industrial Major Accident Hazards (CIMAH) regulations (5) and, of course, Health and Safety at Work Act (HASAWA) (6)
3. Mitigation—via the CIMAH regulations (involving emergency planning and information to the public), and land-use planning control (7,8)

This approach is very much an interdependent package of controls and responses, appropriately tailored to the relevant risks.

IDENTIFICATION

There are some 1750 installations under NIHHS, and several hundred more now notified under CIMAH, many of the latter in particular presenting environmental, as well as human-damage risks. The very requirement for statutory notification has a number of effects: it prioritizes HSE attention; it permits identification of such sites to land-use and emergency planners, and to emergency services; and hopefully, it stimulates a greater on-site awareness of the hazards and risks.

ASSESSMENT AND CONTROL

The general requirements of the CIMAH Regulations apply to sites which store or use hazardous substances which satisfy criteria related to toxicity, flammability, reactivity or explosibility. Several thousand such substances have been identified as being in regular use in industry. In such cases, the operator of the site must:

1. Notify the Health and Safety Executive (HSE) of any major accident which has occurred on his site, with details of steps taken to prevent its recurrence (note—a major accident need only have the potential to harm)
2. Be prepared to demonstrate to an Inspector, on request (and produce documentary evidence as appropriate), that he has considered the potential for major accidents from his operations, and has taken all appropriate steps both to prevent their occurrence and to mitigate the consequences of any which may occur

Further, more specific duties under the Regulations apply to sites on which are stored or used named substances in excess of specified thresholds. These sites are known as large inventory top tier sites (LITTS) which store large quantities of flammable toxic or explosive materials or small inventory top tier sites, which store or use substances which are considered particularly toxic, and for which much lower thresholds (1 tonne or less) are prescribed. In the UK there are currently over 250 LITTS, and more than a hundred small inventory top tier sites (SITTS) notified to HSE. (These numbers will increase substantially, when the second amendment to the 'Seveso' Directive is carried into UK law.) The additional duties which fall to the occupiers of such sites are:

1. The preparation of on- and off-site emergency plans
2. The provision of appropriate information to the public
3. The submission to HSE of a 'safety case'

THE SAFETY CASE

Emergency planning and information to the public are measures primarily designed to mitigate the consequences of any major incident, should it occur (the probability of a major accident should, however, be remote) or, in the case of some aspects of emergency planning, to intervene in the escalation process. This latter approach apart, however, such questions should be concerned with the residual risk after all appropriate, reasonably practicable precautions have been taken. In other words they are concerned with the mitigation aspect of control. The 'safety case' however is, in concept at least, central to assessment and control; the 'written report' format merely formalizes the approach.

The Safety case should (9)

1. Identify the nature and scale of use of dangerous substances
2. Place the installation in its geographical and social context
3. Identify the type, consequences, and relative likelihood of potential major accidents
4. Identify the control regimes and systems on the site, and in so doing demonstrate that the operator of the site has considered and (presumably) is satisfied with the adequacy of his controls, and that any residual risks are at an acceptable level.

Essentially, the case consists of facts about the site, and reasoned arguments and conclusions about the risks from the site. It is a mixture of fact and prediction, leading to informed judgements (both technical and social) about the acceptability of the site in its physical location. But is is not licensing; nor is it, despite the role of HSE as a 'competent authority', within Europe, one of approval. It is, however a quintessential management approach (10), applying relevant management techniques to major hazard control. It identifies the critical areas, which can then be addressed on a concentrated and continuing basis; and the hazard analysis carried out an early stage of the assessment process highlights, *inter alia*, the relevant areas for potential mitigation.

MITIGATION

The main elements of mitigation are emergency planning, information to the public, and location.

Emergency planning

CIMAH requires effective arrangements for on and off-site emergency plans, involving close cooperation between the site operator, the local authority, the county authority and the emergency services. General advice on emergency planning has been published in the UK by both the HSE (11) and industry (12,13). The SIESO 'all hazards' approach is a significant addition to this corpus of advice (14). Similar guidance is being produced in other countries, e.g. the USA (15). Many organizations are now developing expert systems to assist in emergency planning and responses.

Information to the public

Any emergency planning depends for its success on an appropriate response from those covered by the plan, and this necessitates adequate briefing of those liable to be affected. On-site personnel should receive this briefing (and training, as appropriate) as part of the preparation and realization of the site emergency plan. Off-site, however, such detailed briefing and preparation will rarely be possible. For this reason the CIMAH Regulations impose an additional duty to inform persons who are within an area which it is for the HSE to define (often the land-use planning consultation distance). The minimum information to be given, currently, is:

1. That the hazardous installation is notifiable, and has been notified to HSE
2. A description of the operations on site, and of the hazards and risks which might affect the recipient of the information; and
3. Of any emergency measures (including appropriate personal behaviour) to be taken in the event of an incident.

Methods of information-giving will, of course, vary, as will frequency. Advance and regular information can be given to those resident or working in the area; those in control of public amenities can be similarly informed. Transients may well, however, only receive the information in an emergency situation.

Adequate and relevant information is, therefore, a prerequisite for control and response in an emergency situation.

This requirement for limited openness in the provision of information about risks to those who might be affected, is, of course, part of a much wider initiative in respect of freedom of information. HSE has already published a discussion document relating to the industrial context (16). Discussion documents on 'tolerable' risk are in the course of preparation. Freedom of information is a cornerstone of the approach in some other countries (e.g. Canada (17) and the USA (18)).

The second amendment to the 'Seveso' Directive has included changes in information provision requirements, which will need to be carried forward into UK law. The amendment closely followed current UK advice in HS(R)21, which suggested that an appropriate package of advice might include:

- Name and address of site
- Name and position of informant
- Confirmation that the site is notifiable and has been so notified
- A simple explanation of the site activities
- The common names (where possible) of the 'major accident' substances on site, with an indication of their principal harmful characteristics
- Details of how the population will be informed in the event of an accident

- General advice on the actions and behaviour appropriate to warning situations
- An assurance that adequate arrangements (including liaison with the emergency services) exist to deal with forseeable accidents and to minimize their effects
- A reference to the off-site emergency plan, including advice on cooperation with emergency services
- Details of sources of further information

Location

Adequate mitigation of major hazard risks is best achieved by planning control of incompatible land uses. In the UK, land use and development is controlled by planning law (19). ACMH confirmed that such controls remained appropriate for the location of hazardous installations and for developments in their vicinity. Despite the setting up administratively of liaison and advice arrangements in 1972, planning law as it then stood was not capable of dealing with all aspects of the risks from such installations, and there have been more recent developments, both in the law (6,7) and in liaison (20), which have closed some of the loopholes. Further developments are imminent—The Housing and Planning Act (21), introduced to Parliament early in 1986, contains proposals for 'consent' procedures for hazardous installations control, operated by planning authorities advised by HSE. Regulations will soon introduce this enabling Act, on the basis of application to NIHHS and (perhaps some) CIMAH sites. Such 'consent' will relate to description of the land, and of the substance(s), the maximum quantity permitted of each substance, and may include conditions as to how and where any hazardous substance is to be kept or used. The imposition of such conditions will involve statutory consultation with the HSE.

These are planning controls, and proposals for control, for the present and future. What of the present legacy of past mistakes? It is clear that in the UK not all hazardous installations are ideally located; indeed some locations are far from ideal. The costs to society of preventing incompatible developments in advance of their taking place are generally relatively small; whereas the cost of intervention to relocate from existing incompatibility may be enormous. Where the risk warrants it such action may be justified; but in most cases the expense involved would not justify the costs. This explains the apparent paradox in some HSE advice, against further development at a range greater than developments currently existing. Consent will assist in mitigating any problems where this paradox is real, rather than apparent.

ENVIRONMENTAL RISKS

The overall strategy outlined above was developed on the basis of incidents which, in general, had direct effects on humans, and where any environmental effects were secondary. Indeed, where environmental risks from major chemical hazards (i.e., the uncovenanted rather than the covenanted release) were perceived, they tended to be approached as the vector for indirect human risk rather than damage to other flora and fauna. The 'Seveso' Directive and the CIMAH Regulations have, however, always had an environmental dimension; indeed the risk nature of some SITT substances may be dominantly ecotoxic. The transfrontier consequences of fire water run-off pollution at Basle in 1986 has concentrated international attention on such risks (some implications of this are discussed later in this paper), and supplements more local effort. In the UK, the HSE has carried out substantial investigative work on CIMAH environmental risks, through its research agreement with the Safety and Reliability Directorate of UKAEA, and has done other work in collaboration with other government departments, and water authorities (22). Arrangements are in place in the UK to ensure appropriate liaison and cooperation between relevant government departments and other enforcing authorities in respect of CIMAH environmental risks.

THE EUROPEAN RESPONSE TO THE 'SEVESO' DIRECTIVE

Earlier parts of this paper have outlined the UK input to a European strategy, and the application of the European strategy to the domestic scene. Although member states of the EC are required to conform to Directive standards, there is, currently, some variation in approach and response. Not all member states had in place the legislative and enforcement framework to put the requirements of the Directive into effect; and where such frameworks are in place, implementation dates vary. Enforcement and compliance approaches also vary, as does the scale of any problems.

A particular example of variety of approach is that of the use of quantification in hazard and risk assessments (either *per se* or as part of 'reasonable practicability' or cost benefit considerations). The UK occupies something of the middle ground on this issue between the highly quantified approach of the Netherlands (23,24) and the standard-meeting approach of West Germany, with the implicit assumptions that conformity to detailed engineering and other technical, performance related standards is sufficient to reduce the probability/frequency of major accident hazards to an 'acceptable' level.

Short term reviews

There have already been two short term reviews of Directive 82/501. The first of these has already been carried into UK law (25). The changes introduced by this amendment:

1. Tidy up the situation re ammonium nitrate
2. Reduce the threshold quantities for certain substances (e.g. chlorine, phosgene and methyl isocyanate)
3. Increase the threshold quantities for certain substances (e.g. cobalt and nickel metal, oxides, carbonates, sulphides, as powders) and
4. Add certain substances (e.g. liquid oxygen, sulphur trioxide)

Probably the most important changes are to clarify that the definition of industrial undertaking in Article 1 of the Directive (Schedule 4 of CIMAH) is inclusive, not exclusive and to add 'treatment' to the production and processing of energy gases.

The Basle incident amply demonstrated that the previously voiced doubts about the validity of the distinction 'isolated storage' and process were well founded, particularly in emergency situations and in the 'warehousing' context, especially when environmental hazards and risks had to be considered. The second amendment to the Directive has therefore centred on:

1. The extension of the list of named substances held in 'isolated' storage or process
2. The reduction in thresholds of certain named substances in 'isolated storage' or process

3. The application of generic categories of substances and preparation, both isolated storage and process (the categorisation based on the so called 'Sixth Amendment' Directive) (26)
4. The aggregation of partial fractions of generic categories of dangerous substances

and will bring within the terms of the 'top tier' legislation several hundred more sites, many of them in the warehousing sector. The 'generic' categories and thresholds are as follows:

	General (tonnes)	Top tier
'Very toxic'	5	20
'Toxic'[a] 'oxidizing' 'explosive'	10	200
'Highly flammable' gases[b]	50	200
'Highly/extremely flammable'	5000	50 000

[a] Except where the substances, etc., are not in a state which gives them properties capable of causing a major accident hazard.
[b] At normal temperature and pressure.

Long term review

The EC has already commissioned numerous investigations into various aspects of the 'Seveso Directive' both on the content of the Directive, and its implementation and effects, generally and locally, in terms of emergency planning, information to the public, and safety reports. A number of concepts are being debated, including hazard equivalence (e.g. 27), research into major technological risks, information to the public (28), detail (29), pipeline risks, transportation, and non-acute risks, including carcinogenicity and teratogenicity, from major accident hazard incidents. Problems associated with criteria are also being investigated. It is perhaps too early to anticipate the effects these and other reviews will have on the future content and form of any fundamentally revised Directive.

INTERNATIONAL DEVELOPMENTS

The principles of the European control strategy have been accepted internationally, and are being increasingly adopted, particularly in the so called 'developed' world. A particular initiative has come via the World Bank (30) and similar work has stemmed from the Warren Centre and others, in respect of Australasian and Pacific Basin, major industrial hazards (31,32). In terms of the industrialized world, variations in acceptance and adoption are, in general, of degree and timing rather than type. This is not, however, the case with the developing countries, and it is significant that a number of incidents have recently occurred in such countries.

The problems of developing countries

The predominance of economic factors, the lack of necessary expertise and appropriate training, and the lack of adequate enforcement machinery are all in the forefront of international deliberations on the problems of the transfer of technology to the developing world. There is substantial UN (33) CEFIC (34) and ILO (35) input. All these initiatives may have an effect, subsequently, on control legislation in the industrialized world. The ILO has been particularly active with respect to major hazards in the developing world (36,37) and has produced guidelines on the establishment and organization of major hazard controls there (38) which take into account the particular problems of the 'Third World'. These controls are based on the European approach, but modified to take account of relevant social and economic features.

Initiative by the OECD

The Organisation for Economic Co-operation and Development (and in particular the Environmental Directorate) has recently become significantly more involved in industrial major accident hazard issues, and it may well be that OECD initiatives could be combined with current internal European considerations in any fundamental review or changes in the EC Major Hazards Directive.

Topics currently under consideration include (39)

1. Harmonization of regulatory controls and procedures for approval of new installations
2. Common principles of accident response
3. Siting policies
4. Arrangements for handling transfrontier emergencies, and for mutual assistance
5. Exchange of technical information
6. Harmonized methods of assessment in terms of standards for the safe operation of installations
7. Exchange of data on past accidents
8. Setting up of a major accident database
9. Information to the public
10. Chemicals safety testing
11. Comprehensive risk management
12. Enforcement harmonization
13. Public participation in risk decisions
14. Licensing and/or approval regimes

TRANSPORTATION RISKS

There is already a substantial corpus of international regulation of the transportation of harmful substances (generally converted into national legislation) by sea, air, road and rail. Most are based on UN standards (40) modified with mode relevance (40–45). All such regulation is based on the principles of

1. Classification of hazard   (i.e. identification)
2. Identification of dangerous substances   (i.e. labelling)
3. Containment   (i.e. avoidance/prevention)
4. Emergency response   (i.e. mitigation)

Many major hazard incidents involving hazardous substances have occurred in the transport mode and one of the valedictory recommendations of the Advisory Committee on Major Hazards involved the assessment of the hazards and risks associated with the transportation (including interchange and marshalling) of major hazard quantities of dangerous substances. This task has been taken up, in the UK, by a sub-committee of the Advisory Committee on Dangerous Substances, which in turn has formed Technical Working Groups whose task is to appraise, and if necessary derive relevant assessment methodology and criteria for, both individual and societal risk, for each major transportation mode. When this task is completed, the ACDS sub-committee will be able to reach informed judgements on the levels of risk(s) and to make appropriate recommendations for further controls (if needed) to government. Members of the sub-committee and working groups are aware of the major internationally based effort which is continuing on this subject, and are in contact with many of the workers in the field. It would not be appropriate to anticipate the conclusions of either group, but clearly any necessary controls will relate to quantities, transport mode direction, routing, and mode prohibition, as well as conventional controls, including siting of interchange and concentration points, and developments in their vicinity.

OTHER ISSUES

In the longer term, other issues currently being debated, investigated, or even identified, may need resolution. It is not within the scope of this paper to consider these issues. It is clear, however, that issues such as risk criteria, quantification of risk, and risk equivalence, perceived and real, will need to be addressed in due course. Inevitably this will introduce consideration of processes or operations (e.g. handling of pathogens, genetic engineering, etc.) which are perceived to present similar hazards.

CONCLUSIONS

A fairly comprehensive framework of control for 'static' major accident hazards exists at the UK and European level, which is being extended to other parts of the industrialized world, and, with appropriate modifications, to developing countries. Substantial effort is being deployed in the revision and updating of these controls. Risks from transportation, currently being assessed, may warrant similar controls. The extension of such controls to other hazards and risks remains a matter for future debate.

NOTE

The views expressed in this paper are the author's, and except where the context indicates otherwise, not necessarily definitive statements of HSE policy.

REFERENCES

(1) Advisory Committee on Major Hazards. *Three Reports* 1976, 1979, 1984. HMSO.
(2) Directive No 82/501/EEC. OJEC.
(3) Cassidy K. The national and international framework of legislation for major industrial accident hazards. *I Chem E Symposium Series* No 110, 1988.
(4) *Notification of Installations Handling Hazardous Substances Regulations.* HMSO, 1982.
(5) *Control of Industrial Major Accident Hazard Regulations.* HMSO, 1984.

(6) *Health and Safety at Work, etc, Act 1974.*
(7) *Town and Country Planning (General Development) (Amendment) Order, 1984.*
(8) *Town and Country Planning (Use classes) (Amendment) Order 1984.*
(9) *A Guide to the CIMAH Regulations,* HS(R)21, HMSO, 1984.
(10) Cassidy K. CIMAH safety cases—the HSE approach. *Chem Eng Loss Prevention Suppl* August 1987.
(11) *CIMAH Regulations 1984: Further guidance on emergency plans,* HS(G)25. HMSO, 1984.
(12) *Recommended procedures for handing major emergencies.* CIA, 1977 (and supplement 1985).
(13) *General guidance on emergency planning within the CIMAH Regulations for chlorine installations* CLA, 1986.
(14) *Guide to Emergency Planning.* SIESO 1986.
(15) *Hazardous materials emergency planning guide.* National Response Team Report NRT 1 March 1987.
(16) *Disclosure of information to the public.* HSE Discussion Document, 1985.
(17) *An Act to amend the occupational Health and Safety Act 1980.* Ontario 1987.
(18) *Emergency Planning and Community Right to Know Act,* Washington 1986.
(19) *Town and Country Planning Act 1947.*
(20) *Department of Environment Circular 9/84.* HMSO.
(21) *Housing and Planning Act 1986.* HMSO.
(22) Cassidy K. *Some implications of releases of toxic substances into water supplies.* EC Inspectors Workshop London. December 1987.
(23) *Operational safety report—guidelines for the compilation.* Netherlands Labour Inspectorate.
(24) *Environmental programme of the Netherlands 1986–90.*
(25) *The Control of Industrial Major Accident Hazards (Amendment) Regulations 1988.* HMSO.
(26) Directive 67/548/EEC as amended by 69/91/EEC, 70/189/EEC, 71/144/EEC, 73/409/EEC, 79/831/EEC with adaptions to technical progress 79/907, 79/370, 81/957, 82/232, 83/467, 84/449.
(27) Marshall VC. *EX XI/706/85 Final Review Report.*
(28) Walker GP. *The Seveso Directive: Public information in the UK.* Lancaster University, 1987.
(29) B Harve-Bazin *Review of Annex IV of 82/501/EC.* 1987.
(30) *Manual of industrial hazard assessment techniques.* World Bank, 1985.
(31) *Major industrial hazards project report.* Warren Centre, University of Sydney, 1986.
(32) *Statement by Environmental Protection Agency on evaluation of industrial risks and hazards in Western Australia,* 1986.
(33) *International code of conduct on the transfer of technology.* UN (in draft).
(34) *Guidelines for the transfer of technology.* CEFIC (in draft).
(35) *Operational safety, health and working conditions and the transfer of technology.* Geneva: ILO, 1985.
(36) *Working paper on control of major hazards in industry and prevention of major accidents.* MHC 1985/1. Geneva: ILO.
(37) *Report on tripartite ad-hoc meeting of consultants on methods of prevention of major hazards in industry.* MHC 1985/6/(Rev). Geneva: ILO.
(38) Ellis AF. *The establishment and organisation of major hazard control in developing countries.* Rome, 1987.
(39) *OECD chemicals programme (and associated documentation).* OECD, 1987.
(40) *The transport of dangerous goods: UN code of practice.* New York: UN, 1977.
(41) *International maritime dangerous goods code.* IMCO, 1977.
(42) *Regulations on the safe transport of radioactive materials.* IAEA, 1973.
(43) *Restricted articles regulations,* IATA.
(44) *Reglement international concernant le transport des matierea dangereuses* RID Annex EEC.
(45) *Accord european relatif an transport international des matieres dangereuses per route.* ADR EEC.

The possibility of major incidents in chemical distribution

Ian C. Canadine

ICI Group Headquarters, London, UK

BACKGROUND

It is perhaps worth making the point that not all chemicals are dangerous goods and not all dangerous goods are chemicals. 'Dangerous goods' in distribution terms are those goods which are classified as dangerous using the criteria developed by the United Nations Committee of Experts on the Transport of Dangerous Goods and published in the so called 'Orange Book'. These criteria cover nine possible classes of hazard, for example, Flammable, Toxic and Corrosive which fall into United Nations hazard classes 3, 6 and 8, respectively. Dangerous goods in each class are required to carry the appropriate United Nations hazard warning label with explanatory symbol and distinctive colour. These labels, of course, have the familiar diamond shape which was the theme of the 'diamonds are for danger' television information campaign of some years ago.

It is also worth noting that 'chemicals' as defined by the Chemical Industries Association and in Government statistics are separate and different from 'petroleum products'. There are obviously many similarities and overlaps between the two industries but in the main the petroleum industry concerns itself with flammable liquids and gases which are used as fuel in many different ways. The chemical industry's products find a rather wider range of end uses affecting all aspects of our society.

THE INDUSTRY

The size and importance of the petroleum industry seems to be self-evident and fairly well understood by society in general. In the United Kingdom it distributes by pipeline, water, rail and road more than 200 million tons of products every year. Everyone who remembers the effect of fuel shortages on transport, heating, and many other essentials in our modern life is well aware of the vital importance of petroleum products and the price to be paid when they are not available.

This awareness was illustrated in a MORI poll carried out for the Chemical Industries Association in the UK in autumn 1987 when 34% of those interviewed felt that they knew a fair amount about the oil and petrol industries compared

Major chemical disasters—medical aspects of management, edited by Virginia Murray, 1990: Royal Society of Medicine Services International Congress and Symposium Series No. 155, published by Royal Society of Medicine Services Limited.

with only 15% who felt the same about the chemical industry. The same poll showed that 55% felt largely favourable towards the oil and petrol industries compared with only 32% who felt favourable towards the chemical industry. Since there are no obvious safety-related reasons for such a disparity of opinion it seems likely that the chemical industry suffers from a general lack of understanding of its role and importance.

The chemical industry in the UK contributes about 10% of the wealth created by manufacturing industry and is the sector's biggest single export earner with a net surplus of well over £2 billion. Total sales in 1987 were approximately £23 billion of which about a half were exported. The industry provides employment for about 340 000 people of whom roughly 34 000 (10%) are involved in distribution, i.e., transport and warehousing.

The complete dependence of modern society on the chemical industry is frequently underestimated. It is very difficult to find anything in our lives which is not either entirely made from the products of the chemical industry or at least heavily dependent upon them. Even so-called natural products such as wood, cotton and wool can only be produced, processed and used under modern high volume conditions with the aid of literally hundreds of different chemicals.

Chemicals, even dangerous ones, are not an optional alternative in the society in which we live; they are an integral part of it.

DISTRIBUTION IN THE UK

The petroleum industry transports over 200 million tons of crude oil and final products in the UK each year. However, almost half of this moves by pipeline and only a third in total by road. Water transport is smaller but still significant whilst rail now amounts to only 4% of the total. Although road transport only accounts for about one third of the total movements of petroleum products it does, of course, constitute by far the biggest proportion of movements of petroleum spirit to filling stations. A very high proportion of the petroleum industry's products are moved in bulk tankers rather than in small packages—a situation which is quite different from that in the chemical industry.

The chemical industry transports about 80 million tons of chemical a year by road in the UK—about 25 million tons of which are fertilizers. Of the total about half is moved in bulk road tankers and container tanks and the other half in packages such as drums, cylinders and bottles. Powders, crystals and pellets which are not classified as hazardous are usually carried in sacks. A high proportion of the packaged chemicals transported are not classified as dangerous, and neither are more than half of the chemicals moved in tankers. About 4000 road tankers are involved in the transportation of chemicals compared with about 12 000 which are used to carry petroleum spirit.

Chemicals are also transported in the UK by water, rail, and pipeline but the proportions are much smaller than for the petroleum industry. Rail movements are only about 5% of the amount moved by road.

MAJOR INCIDENTS IN UK CHEMICAL TRANSPORT

The definition of a major incident is of course open to many variations. The UK Advisory Committee on Dangerous Substances has set up a 'Sub-Committee On The Major Hazard Aspects Of The Transport of Dangerous Substances'. Its terms of reference are 'to give further consideration to aspects of the transport of large quantities of dangerous substances (excluding radio-active substances) by road, rail or water which have the potential to present major accident hazards of fire, explosion or toxic release to employees or to the public, to identify appropriate voluntary and mandatory control measures and to advise on any additional action which might be necessary'. The Sub-Committee decided as a working rule of thumb to consider major accident hazards as dangerous substances and situations which might have the potential to cause more than ten fatalities. They decided that this seemed likely to include substances in the following categories:

- Explosives
- Flammable gases
- Toxic gases
- Highly flammable liquids, flash point less than 21°C
- Flammable liquids, flash point between 21°C and 55°C
- Flammable solids (including substances viable to spontaneous combustion)
- Oxidising substances including liquid oxygen
- Toxic liquids

Historical data available from various sources would seem to confirm initial conclusions of the UK Major Hazards Sub-Committee on the classes of substances requiring further investigation. The 'chemical cocktail' much beloved by the media has been notably absent as a cause of significant incidents in transport. This is perhaps hardly surprising as mixed loads normally consist of packages of chemicals each of which is much smaller than a bulk load and inherently has less potential for causing injury. This is in no way to minimize the difficulties of the firemen and other emergency services personnel in tackling incidents involving such loads and in the immediate area of the load they can be difficult to deal with and hazardous. However, almost by definition a major incident requires sufficient quantity of the dangerous substance to affect people at a significant distance from the load.

The chemical industry in the UK believes that the last member of the public to die as the result of a release of chemicals in a transport incident was in 1972 when a crash on the M6 motorway resulted in the release of significant quantities of oleum. Two later incidents in 1973 and 1976 resulted in death of the chemical driver, but in both cases the actual collision was severe and may have played a significant part in the fatalities.

During the same period there have been eight deaths attributable to petroleum products, but not more than two in any one incident. Most of these deaths have involved the driver of the vehicle involved, but the contribution of the load to death was not always clear in accident situations which resulted in fire. It has to be remembered in comparing figures that considerably more petroleum products than chemicals are carried in bulk by road. More significant, however, is that the total road deaths due to hazardous goods average less than one per year, compared with road traffic deaths of about 5000 per year.

In the period 1977-88 British Rail suffered four incidents involving dangerous goods—all of them petroleum products. There were no fatalities because of the dangerous goods although the collision alongside the motorway at Eccles in 1984 resulted in three deaths and 68 injuries from the collision and not from the resulting serious fire.

The derailment in the Summit tunnel in 1984 resulted in a large petroleum spirit fire which burned out of control for several days and captured media headline attention. Fortunately no-one was injured but again it was a potentially serious incident.

Even the large scale transport of chlorine in the UK has so far been achieved without fatalities. The safety record of ICI's chlorine road tankers is impressive. In more than 60 years of operation, only two cases of leakage are known. These were due to incompletely closed valves and were quickly rectified by tightening the valves and end caps. In neither case were injuries caused.

The safety record of rail tankers is similarly good in that there has never been a major release of chlorine or the puncture of a rail tanker. This is despite the fact that rail movements in bulk started during the First World War under the control of the Ministry of Munitions and continued under Brunner Mond, one of ICI's original constituent companies. The total number of rail tanks operated by ICI reached 100 in 1938 and almost 300 in the early 1950s. These unbraked 14 tonne capacity wagons were taken out of service in the 1960s and 70s and replaced by a smaller number of modern braked wagons with a 28 tonne load. For various logistical reasons, however, the carriage of chlorine by rail continues to decline and ICI now operates only about 40 rail tanks.

Since there have so far been no 'major incidents' (according to the ACDS Sub-Committee definition) in the UK, it seems sensible to look at the possible lessons to be learned from abroad.

MAJOR INCIDENTS IN WORLD CHEMICAL TRANSPORT

There is no reliable information on transport accidents involving hazardous goods on a worldwide basis. Industrialized countries in the West tend to publish details of incidents, but there are many countries which do not. For example there were reports of an incident in Fushun, China in 1985 in which a rail tanker leaked chlorine into a crowded area. The only details reported were that 2000 people were forced to seek medical help.

The number of people injured is not necessarily directly related to the amount of toxic materials released, or to the size of any fire or explosion. The famous Mississauga incident in Canada in 1979 was in an urban area, and the accident involved 22 rail tank cars of chemicals. There was an explosion, a large fire and a tank containing 90 tonnes of chlorine was ruptured. Because of the magnitude of the incident about 250 000 people were evacuated, but in fact there were no fatalities. Proximity to the public, weather conditions and emergency response all have considerably potential impact on the situation.

Despite the occasional freak occurrence, the situations which have usually caused significant fatalities abroad are bulk quantities of the substances identified by the ACDS Sub-Committee. There have been one or two incidents involving toxic gases (chlorine and ammonia) and one or two involving toxic combustion products from fires. In the main though, the casualties seem to have been from fires and explosions, the worst in terms of number being the rupture of an overfilled road tanker of propylene near a camp site in San Carlos, Spain in 1978. The propylene ignited, causing a fire ball which swept over the camp site causing 215 deaths.

Road incidents seem to occur more frequently than rail incidents but probably no more (or even less) than would be expected from the relative volumes of dangerous goods moved. Movements by water (inland and coastal) and by pipeline also contribute to the total incidents, but in the latter case most significant incidents seem to have been in the USA and have largely involved natural gas.

PRECAUTIONS TAKEN IN THE UK

The United Kingdom has been fortunate in avoiding major incidents in transport so far. Whilst adequate regulations and luck are some of the factors responsible, there are others. For example the UK chemical industry has a long history of self-regulation. Driver training for hazardous goods, the Hazchem code, safety auditing of hauliers were all developed and introduced voluntarily by the industry although the first two are now incorporated in the law. The industry (represented by the CIA) is still developing and introducing safety measures quite independently of legislation.

The apparently poor performance of the USA in pipeline safety is due, at least in part, to the fact that they were amongst the first to build such pipelines and hence many are now old. The UK was able to gain by experience and build to higher standards as well as insisting upon regulated inspection and maintenance under the supervision of the Health and Safety Executive. One recent development is the use of the so-called 'intelligent pig' which is pumped through the line, and is able to measure and record wall thickness and faults at the same time as it removes solid deposits. As several pipeline failures have been caused by corrosion, this is a particularly important development.

The performance of bulk road and rail tankers for liquified gases is particularly important in avoiding major incidents and the UK has an excellent record in this area. To take chlorine as an example again ICI specifies the use of low carbon highly ductile steel for the manufacture of liquid chlorine tanker vessels—and indeed for most other similar duties on liquified gases including both drums and cylinders. If an abnormal incident, such as a collision, occurs there is a great deal of energy to be absorbed and experience in various parts of the world has shown that the high yield steels used there have a tendency to fracture with a relatively small amount of elongation or deformation. Their ability to absorb energy is significantly less than that of ductile steels which can deform to a significant extent without rupturing.

Experience with rail tankers and with cylinders has proved the ability of low carbon steel to absorb energy in a safe manner. An instance is known of a full cylinder of chlorine falling down the shaft of a well in Libya and being virtually flattened without any release of the contents.

In 1976 ICI introduced the concept of additional side and rear protection on its chlorine road tankers to resist penetration, absorb energy and spread the load in case of collision. The protection takes the form of twin-lengths of motorway crash barriers mounted onto the support ribs of the tanker using relatively weak brackets which deform preferentially in case of a crash. This arrangement (which has since been used on various tankers for other products) has proved to be a most efficient means of protection.

The most serious UK road accident involving chlorine occurred in 1985 when an ICI chlorine tanker was travelling uphill outside Baslow in Derbyshire. It was hit by a 38 tonne articulated lorry which was travelling at an estimated 60 miles per hour down the hill. This vehicle veered diagonally across the road and hit the chlorine tank on its front off-side stopping it instantaneously and driving it sideways off the road. The side protection on the chlorine tank absorbed the majority of the collision energy and spread the load as it was designed to do. Apart from deformation of a bracket, the tank was not damaged in any way and was able to resume service, after full inspection, with no repairs other than straightening the bracket. The severity of the impact which it withstood can be judged by the damage to both the side protection and to the other vehicle involved.

Similarly ICI pioneered in the UK the use of rail tanker 'buffer-override' protection. This is a reinforced hollow steel section mounted above the buffers across the width of the tank. It has been found to be most effective in cases of collision or heavy shunting in preventing damage to the pressure vessel by buffers or couplings and in preventing 'jack-knifing' and consequent increased damage. 'Buffer-override' protection is now required by British Rail for certain types of rail tanker.

Since the introduction of the larger rail tanker about 20 years ago accidents have been confined to minor derailments and collisions in marshalling yards. The older type of rail tanker, however, was involved in some major collisions including one in which a loaded chlorine tanker hit a signal box at 60 miles per hour and demolished it. Another (during the Second World War) was struck on its valve chest by a locomotive and dragged along for some distance. A military recovery team subsequently allowed it to fall down the railway embankment! However, neither of these incidents resulted in leakage.

Just as important as careful construction of course are all the other requirements for safety such as inspection and maintenance, correct operation, driver selection and training, labelling and emergency procedure.

QUANTIFICATION AND RISK

Because major chemical hazards in distribution occur so infrequently, it is not possible to estimate the risk they pose with any accuracy from purely historical data. Techniques have been developed to construct mathematical models of transport situations and hence to estimate probabilities of accidental events and consequences—so called Quantified Risk Analysis.

The UK Major Hazards Sub-Committee decided to carry out some initial studies on flammable and toxic gases and flammable liquids. It has now carried out quantitative risk analyses for the rail mode and partially for road transport, in both cases using governmental technical resources with monitoring by industry. It has also commissioned a risk analysis of marine transport which will also be monitored by industrial experts and the Sub-Committee.

The more difficult job of interpreting the figures produced and suggesting acceptable levels of risk has yet to be carried out and can only really be completed when the figures are available for all alternative modes of transport.

Quantitative risk analysis (QRA) is, relatively, still in its infancy and it is absolutely essential to understand the approximations in the assumptions which have to be made and the weaknesses and limitations in the model used to calculate the final results. The Sub-Committee feels that the enormous amount of work put into this British study has produced a model which is at least as reliable and robust as any currently in existence. It is anxious therefore to produce results before other, and in some cases less reliable, results gain international credibility.

The accuracy of QRA calculations, the assumptions made, the models used and the sensitivity of the final result to all these things remain a matter of concern and debate. However, if all the problems were resolved and the calculations themselves were undisputably accurate, it is doubtful if it would make the final decisions much easier. Having decided in quantitative terms how dangerous any particular activity is, one still has to decide whether it is acceptable to the public. The 'logical' approach is to follow the example of the early work justifying nuclear power stations and to compare the risk with many other risks in everyday life such as air travel, travel by road or rail or working in an office. However, as the nuclear debate has clearly shown, an activity which is a thousand times safer than another which appears to be accepted by society is not necessarily itself acceptable.

SUMMARY

Historical information shows that the risk of a major chemical transport accident in the UK is very low. Quantitative studies are in hand which hopefully will confirm this, but in any case should expose any operations or parts of operations which need improvement. However low the probability, accidents can still happen, and history overseas shows that they can be very severe. Experience shows that a major transport incident (harming more than a few people) is likely to involve large quantities of material, i.e. bulk road or rail tanks or ships or pipelines rather than packages.'

The largest number of serious incidents have arisen with flammable gas or liquids (partially because of the volume moved) with some incidents from toxic gases and toxic fumes (including products of combustion).

Environmental impact

Ian Graham-Bryce

Environmental Affairs Division, Shell Internationale Petroleum Maatschappij BV, The Hague, The Netherlands

INTRODUCTION

The nature of the environmental impact from a major chemical incident should obviously determine in principle how we manage the disaster. In that sense my subject is central to the issues discussed in this symposium. My brief is to provide a broad overview of some of the key considerations which determine environmental impact as a background to the other papers, the majority of which will deal with the practical and policy aspects of disaster management.

DEFINING ENVIRONMENT

Environmental impact is a vast and complex subject with many areas of remaining scientific uncertainty, and I can only skim the surface in this brief presentation. We need first to establish a definition of the environment, because the term means different things to different people. In the medical context obviously the emphasis is anthropocentric and the first attention is to the direct effects on man. However if we are to take full account of environmental impact we should also include not only the indirect effects on man, some of which can be long delayed, but also the whole range of possible other effects on that myriad of components of the environment. For example, at Seveso the observable effects were predominantly on domestic animals and wildlife, and following the Basle incident, effects on fish and eels were prominently reported.

In defining environmental impact, therefore, we must consider the combined effects, direct and indirect, of physical and chemical factors on the non-living and living components of the receiving environment. Indirect effects may be via bio-accumulation, by oxygen depletion, by effects on food sources, etc. Furthermore, while we concentrate on the individual in the case of man, with other organisms in the environment, we are often concerned with effects on populations, and consequent effects on eco-system structure and function. Indeed, certain issues must be considered on a global basis. That is obviously true for airborne contaminants, as was demonstrated for radioactive materials in the case of Chernobyl, but any comprehensive view also has to consider the long range effects of substances such as polychlorinated biphenyls (PCBs), organochlorines, dioxins and ultimately the currently prominent topics of ozone depletion and the greenhouse effect.

Major chemical disasters—medical aspects of management, edited by Virginia Murray, 1990: Royal Society of Medicine Services International Congress and Symposium Series No. 155, published by Royal Society of Medicine Services Limited.

ECOTOXICOLOGY

Clearly all of the above topics cannot be covered in this brief paper which will concentrate primarily on direct toxic effects, and begin by recalling a few guiding principles. The first cardinal precept of ecotoxicology is that the potential effect of any toxic agent is a function of both the toxicity and of the exposure to which a receiving organism is subjected. Toxicity is, of course, an intrinsic property depending on the molecular structure; exposure, on the other hand, depends not only on the molecular properties, but also to a large extent on the circumstances of the incident and the nature of the environment. In mathematical terms the exposure is a function of both the concentration and the time. To be rigorous, it can be equated with the integral of concentration with respect to time which has been called 'availance'. A further important point is that the concentration we are concerned with is the bio-available concentration, which can differ markedly from the bulk concentration as a result of various sorption and partition processes. Let us briefly consider the components of these relationships.

Toxicity

Toxicity values can vary greatly, not only in absolute terms but in relative terms between species. Table 1 gives examples taken from an exercise to compare the most potent toxicants from different classes while Table 2 illustrates selectivity.

The most active on a weight for weight basis are the mammalian toxins, with materials of natural origin being the most toxic of all. Insecticides are deliberately toxic to one set of organisms, but nevertheless have to have favourable selectivity, particularly with respect to mammals, especially man. Within this group there is an enormous range of different selectivity values, with some modern compounds such as the synthetic pyrethroid bioresmethrin having a particularly favourable toxicity. It is, in fact, safer than many substances commonly consumed.

There is an increasing understanding of the mechanistic basis for these properties. One other aspect of toxicity which must be addressed briefly is the matter of indirect toxicity, particularly as manifested in the phenomena of bio-accumulation and bio-magnification. There is a potential for confusion here and it is important to be clear about the basic pharmacokinetic principles. The level of any toxicant within an organism is determined by the rate of intake, less the rate of metabolism and excretion. For compounds which are unreactive and resistant to degradation and which are also lipophilic, so they have a strong affinity for fatty tissues, the removal processes are not very active and a large proportion of the intake is retained. Intake will be favoured if the supplying medium itself does not have a strong affinity for the compound, so that, for example, fish exposed to water containing PCBs or organochlorine pesticides, or earthworms in contaminated soil, will accumulate the contaminant to much higher concentrations than the surrounding water or soil. This process is bio-concentration, which can be regarded as a partition between phases, and expressed in a mathematical form. For example, the bio-concentration factor (BCF) can be related to the octanol/water partition coefficient P according to the relationship: $\log BCF = 0.87 \log P - 0.62$ (derived by G. G. Briggs). The octanol/water partition coefficient can itself be calculated from the molecular structure.

The extent of the accumulation can obviously be very substantial: for compounds like dichlorodiphenyltrichloroethane (DDT) and PCBs it can be several hundred—or even thousand-fold. The first organism to acquire a contaminant may form

Table 1 *Intrinsic activity of different toxicants*

Toxicant	Species	Approximate, LD_{50} mg/kg
Botulinum toxin	Human	0.00002
Tetrachlorodibenzo-p-dioxin	Guinea pig	0.0006
Synergised deltamethrin	Housefly	0.002
Paraoxon	Asparagus beetle	0.03
Cycloheximide	Yeast	0.38
Carbendazim	Bread mould (neurospora)	1–2
Parathion	Housefly	2
DDT and analogues	Housefly	7–14

LD_{50} = lethal dose causing death in 50% of exposed group

Table 2 *Relative toxicity of insecticides to insects and mammals*

Insecticide	LD_{50} to rats $\mu g/g$ (acute oral)	LD_{50} to M. Domestica $\mu g/g$ (topical)	Ratio rats/houseflies
Parathion	3–6	0.9	5
DDT	118–250	10	18
Dieldrin	40	0.5	80
Dimethoate	200–300	0.7	357
Malathion	1400–1900	18	917
Bioresmethrin	8600	0.2	43000

the food source for other organisms, for example predatory birds, and this contamination can continue along the food chain, to man. Again, the amounts which are retained depend on the basic pharmacokinetics. A further concentration of toxicant would not be expected, unless the predator has a higher relative fat content than its diet, because the processes of excretion and metabolism following the initial ingestion would tend to reduce the concentration. However, levels may be achieved sufficient to cause damage, especially if the predator is susceptible during vulnerable life stages, such as reproduction, or when body fat levels are reduced as a result of decreased food availability.

Exposure

Fascinating though toxicity is, it is the behaviour of the chemical in the environment, as manifested in the exposure, which largely determines the significance of the inherent toxicity. Exposure is a function of bio-available concentration and the time over which that exerts its effects. Those factors are determined by the various transport and degradation processes which affect the chemical once it has been released, and which in turn depend on the nature of the chemical and the characteristics of the particular environment.

Degradation

The environment is an integrated system of different phases. However, for the purposes of discussion and study it is convenient to distinguish various compartments and examine the processes in each separately. Degradation

Table 3 *Representative half-lives for degradation in different environmental compartments*

Substance	Process	Half-life
Trichloromethylbenzene	Hydrolysis in water	19 seconds
Methyl acetate	Hydrolysis in water	2 years
Formaldehyde	Phototransformation in air	6 hours
Bromomethane	Phototransformation in air	400 years
Phenol	Degradation in marine sediment	2 days
Cypermethrin	Degradation in soil	8 weeks
DDT	Degradation in soil	4 years

eliminates the parent compound and in that sense differs from the transport processes which dilute the substance and move it to other parts of the environment, but do not actually remove it. The degradation processes to consider fall under the following headings—biodegradation processes involving metabolism by various organisms, photochemical processes which can be either direct or indirect, and finally chemical reactions.

The environment is largely aerobic and contains water, so oxidation and hydrolysis are common reactions, but anaerobic areas do exist so reduction and other reactions may also occur.

Pathways and rates of degradation depend on the chemical structure of the compound and the features of the environment, but despite the complexities of the systems involved it is possible to characterize persistence in terms of the half life—the time taken for the concentration to fall to half of that originally present.

The range of possible half lives can be enormous, from hours to centuries, in air, earth and water (Table 3).

Transport processes

Transport processes redistribute the chemical and partition it between the different compartments in the environment. First are the advective processes, i.e. processes in which the chemical is carried along with the movement of the medium in which it is contained (rather as a river carries along dissolved material), often called bulk flow. Then there are the various dispersive and diffusion processes which spread the chemical essentially in three dimensions from the initial distribution. Finally, there are partition processes, typified by evaporation into the air, and sorption onto the solid phases. The range of dispersion and diffusion values is substantial, with at one end, the molecular diffusion processes, and at the other the hydrodynamic and aerodynamic spreading processes.

The slowest of these processes is molecular diffusion in soil which gives average displacements of only a few centimetres in a week, even for fumigant chemicals like ethylene dibromide. By contrast, aerodynamic dispersion can cover as much as 100 kilometres a week. Movement by dispersion processes is usually less than advection processes: wind velocities can reach 100 miles an hour or more at ground level, and it is these faster processes which result in the global redistribution of persistent compounds that are so familiar, the PCBs, the organochlorine pesticides, dioxins, etc.

Advection values can be expressed by means of another concept, that of the residence time in different environmental compartments. In air the mixing layer for the lower atmosphere may remove compounds within a day, whereas the stratospheric residence time for complete exchange is approximately seven years. Persistent compounds which get into the stratosphere therefore stay there for

Table 4   *Typical half-lives for evaporation*

From water	
Benzene	: 10 hours
1,5,4′ Trichlorobiphenyl	: 8 days
From soil	
1,3-Dichloropropene	: 1 week
Dieldrin	: 4 years

Table 5   *Environmental distribution at equilibrium (%)*

	Air	Water	Soil/sediment
Heptane	92	4	4
Benzene	52	47	1
Sulfolane	0	100	0
Ionol	4	8	88

a long time, where they may contribute to ozone depletion and the greenhouse effect.

Turning to the aqueous environment, typical residence time in the River Thames is seven days; North Sea ocean currents can retain substances for a year. In soil there is a wide range, but a typical value for a strongly sorbed compound might be 100 years, assuming no degradation. However, a small proportion may leak into ground water much more rapidly.

Finally, one must consider the exchange between compartments. Typical values for evaporation from soil and water to air are shown in Table 4.

The relative importance of the different transport and degradation processes will obviously depend on the proportion of the compound that is in each environmental compartment or medium. This is determined first by the circumstances of its initial introduction into the environment, but thereafter by the way it partitions between the different phases via these intercompartmental transport processes. For any given situation partition depends first on the physical and chemical properties of the substance. The partition between water and air, for example, is determined by the ratio of solubility to vapour pressure as indicated by Henry's Law constant. Partition between soil solids or sediments and the aqueous phase is determined by the extent of adsorption which can be measured conveniently in the laboratory.

Such calculations can be of great value in identifying the compartments to which greatest attention should be given when considering potential exposure following release. For example, Table 5 shows calculations of the equilibrium partition between environmental compartments for representative compounds.

PREDICTION OF HAZARD DEVELOPMENT FOLLOWING ACCIDENT

It will be clear from the foregoing account that we now have a highly developed knowledge of the properties and the relationships which determine environmental behaviour, and that these can be expressed in mathematical terms. Starting with molecular structure, basic physicochemical properties can be estimated, including polarity and from that adsorption, partition, bio-accumulation, diffusion and other transport processes. Computerized modelling of environmental behaviour can then be extended to predict distribution in air or in water from any particular

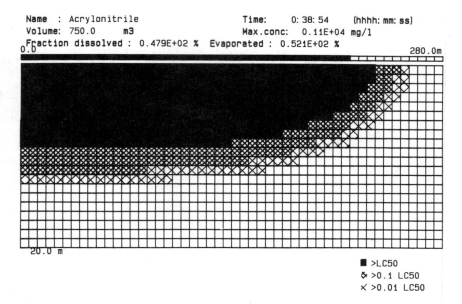

Name : Acrylonitrile   Time: 0: 38: 54   (hhhh: mm: ss)
Volume: 750.0   m3   Max.conc: 0.11E+04 mg/1
Fraction dissolved : 0.479E+02 % Evaporated : 0.521E+02 %

■ >LC50
✧ >0.1 LC50
✕ >0.01 LC50

Figure 1 *Example of simulation using CHEMSPILL model, showing distribution of acetonitrile following a spill at sea initiating at upper left of the chart. Shaded areas denote the zones on the surface and in the water column exceeding toxicity categories indicated.*

release pattern, such as a major accident. For example, a model developed by the Environmental Affairs Division of Shell International is called 'Chemspill' and is used to predict the hazards in the aquatic environment which would be associated with a major accident at sea. Beginning with the basic properties of the compound and knowledge of all the various processes, the spreading, evaporation, dissolution and so on, the model allows prediction of the extent of contamination with time, and then in turn, the zones in which different toxic effects could be expected. This type of model is increasingly used in the process of environmental impact assessment, which is the structured approach to assessing in advance the potential impact of any new major project. It is increasingly required by authorities and is relevant to major incident preparedness. Figure 1 illustrates the results which can be obtained using this model.

The complementary activity to modelling is, of course, measurement, i.e. observation of behaviour in the environment either to provide basic information or to validate models. The assessment of behaviour is most advanced in the case of agrochemicals where there is an extensive battery of tests required to provide the data needed for registration. These activities account for about 50% of the $40 million now required to develop a new agrochemical product. Over a period of years these tests have done much to establish the essential principles determining behaviour in the environment. They range from tests in small experimental plots, to monitoring of behaviour in full scale practical field application.

A valuable intermediate tool is the use of 'mesocosms'—outdoor experimental systems that are small enough to allow detailed study and replication but large enough to represent accurately the behaviour in large scale practical situations. For instance, in artificial ponds at Shell Sittingbourne Research Station in Kent, the natural ecosystems with sediment and plant and animal life are established so that chemicals can be applied under controlled conditions. The advantage is that one can study simultaneously the fate and behaviour of the chemical, and its toxicological effects on the various components of the environment.

Such studies reveal very clearly how the intrinsic toxicology, which is measured in the laboratory, can be dramatically altered by exposure considerations, such as the processes of degradation, partition and transport, which modify the original pattern of concentration. Indeed, compounds which are acutely toxic when applied directly, say to fish in laboratory tests, may have relatively little impact in real situations even when applied directly to the water.

In conclusion, therefore, the central guiding principle is that hazard is a function of both toxicity and exposure, and both must be considered carefully in developing management strategies or contingency plans.

SESSION III

MANAGEMENT OF A MAJOR CHEMICAL DISASTER: IMMEDIATE AND PLANNED RESPONSES

Chairman: Dr A. N. B. Stott

Immediate response:
The Fire Brigade—the first response

David A. Jerrom

West Midlands Fire Service, Headquarters, Birmingham, UK

INTRODUCTION

Since the beginning of recorded time, and more particularly over the past two centuries, man has been creating, storing and refining materials which have proved to have unexpected and unwelcome characteristics.

From the earliest production of gunpowder and the first attempts to work with pressurized steam, every effort by mankind to progress has been bought at the expense of the lives of the innovators and sometimes of their fellow citizens. As his knowledge and ability in the fields of physics and chemistry have advanced, so man has ensured a continuing chain of disasters, which worldwide, have cost hundreds of thousands of lives.

The pattern has been repeated time and time again as new developments, usually of great social and commerical benefit in themselves, are discovered to possess a destructive potential undreamed of by their originators.

In the United Kingdom, attempts have been made in the past to enact effective legislation in order to prevent the circumstances which lead to disaster occurring. It must be admitted, however, that such legislative safeguards usually lag behind the problem as they are rarely initiated until after a tragic and costly disaster has taken place.

EXAMPLES OF MAJOR INCIDENTS

First let us consider a few fairly recent disasters which have occurred in Britain, resulting in a firmer and more realistic attitude among planners and legislators alike.

Braehead Container Depot, Renfrew, January 1977

A fire started by children resulted in an explosion in stored chemicals (sodium chlorate in drums) equivalent in destructive power to between five and ten tonnes of TNT. The power of the explosion was such that girders were found on the roof of a nearby power station and some debris reached the banks of the River Clyde.

Major chemical disasters—medical aspects of management, edited by Virginia Murray, 1990: Royal Society of Medicine Services International Congress and Symposium Series No. 155, published by Royal Society of Medicine Services Limited.

B & R Hauliers, Salford, September 1982

Again, a fire started by vandals in a warehouse storing chemicals for transit, resulted in a series of shattering explosions. The extent of damage, as well as distance covered by fragments and missiles, caused serious concern.

Nypro (UK) Limited, Flixborough Works, June 1974

The most significant incident, however, in the United Kingdom for a very long time, was undoubtedly the Flixborough disaster. In this explosion and fire, 28 people lost their lives, millions of pounds in value of product and plant was lost and damage to buildings resulted over several square miles.

ADVISORY COMMITTEE MAJOR HAZARDS

The reason that Flixborough is seen as a particularly significant event is that, as a result of the very thorough enquiry which followed, the Health and Safety Commission appointed an Advisory Committee on Major Hazards (ACMH) to consider the problems and make recommendations.

The ACMH was clear on one point in particular. The responsibility for control and minimizing of hazards at work should be accepted by those who created the risks. The ultimate result of the Health and Safety Commission's interpretation of the ACMH's reports was the enactment of the Notification of Installations Handling Hazardous Substances Regulations 1982.

These Regulations *require* the user of certain, listed dangerous materials to notify the Health and Safety Executive. Notification is required if quantities of dangerous substances exceed those laid down in the Schedule of the Regulations.

While the implications of Flixborough were being considered, however, a series of serious chemical accidents occurred in Europe, culminating in the Seveso incident in 1976.

So horrifying were both the direct consequences of this incident and its implications for the future, that the control of dangerous substances became a concern of the European Community as a whole. In 1977 the Commission for the European Community set about preparing a directive on Major Accident Hazards. The document when completed became known as 'The Seveso Edict' and regulations have been enacted in UK which ensure compliance with the requirements of the edict.

The regulations referred to are known as the Control of Industrial Major Accident Hazard Regulations 1984 and the operation of these CIMAH Regulations, in conjunction with the NIHHS Regulations, of 1982, provides a substantial part of the on-site planning at major incidents in Britain today.

NIHHS AND CIMAH REGULATIONS

These Regulations are basically a short schedule of dangerous substances, all of which have a potential for disaster if misused and which are quite common in the current industrial scene. They require any use or storage of listed substances, in quantities above certain limits, to be the subject of notification by the user to the Health and Safety Executive, but those organizations intending to get involved in use or storage of listed products are required to give advance notification *prior to commencing operations*.

How does this 'Notification' help?

First, it allows the HSE to build up a map of the nature and density of hazards in each area. Secondly, it will to some extent permit control, as the HSE will have the opportunity to object if they receive advance notification that a hazardous process is to be set up in an area considered unsuitable either due to density of population or the proximity of incompatible industry. Third, it will enable the HSE to advise on the safest methods of handling the materials and to insist on correct storage. Finally, where the quantities in question are considerably above those listed in NIHHS, it provides an automatic link to the next level of control—which are the CIMAH Regulations, 1984.

As mentioned earlier, these Regulations were formulated as a response to the Seveso Incident in Italy in 1976. They are primarily intended:

> 'to prevent major accidents arising from industrial activities, to limit the effects of such accidents both on men and on the environment, and the harmonisation of control measures to prevent and limit major accidents in the European Community'.

It is also clear that they are intended to complement the NIHHS Regulations and operate in conjunction with them.

The industrial activities covered by the CIMAH Regulations are defined in terms of processes and storage involving specified dangerous substances. This has the effect of embracing most of the chemical and petro-chemical industries using substances which have dangerous, flammable, explosive or toxic properties.

An important feature of the Regulations is that the *storage* of a dangerous substance, not associated with a process, is treated differently from *process use* and a different list of substances is applied.

The requirements of the Regulations can be considered as being at two levels:

- The low level requirements apply widely and require that the person in control of an industrial activity takes the necessary precautions to prevent major accidents, to report those that do arise and to take steps to limit their consequences. These regulations apply only to potentially more hazardous activities using dangerous substances.
- The upper level requirements are stringent and require the person in control of a relevant activity to carry out a safety assessment of the site and to submit a report to HSE. They also require the preparation of on-site and off-site emergency plans and the provision of information to members of the public who may be affected by a major accident.

Plans, on- and off-site

1. The on-site plans that the manufacturer is required to prepare will provide a starting point for the off-site plan which the local authority is required to draw up
2. This on-site plan must be kept available and up to date at all times
3. It must include the name of the site safety officer and the names of those who are authorized to take action as directed by the plan in the case of an emergency (key personnel)
4. Material changes in industrial activity must be taken into account
5. Every person on the site who is affected by the plan must be informed of its relevant provisions

The off-site plan should be a written document, kept up to date as necessary to reflect changes in risks, procedures and personnel. The authors of the plan must address themselves to any relevant aspect including the following:

1. The types of accident to be taken into account
2. Organizations involved including key personnel and responsibilities and liaison arrangements between them
3. Communication links including telephones, radios and standby methods
4. Special equipment including firefighting materials, damage control, and repair items
5. Technical information such as chemical and physical characteristics and dangers of the substances and plant
6. Information about the site including likely locations of dangerous substances, personnel and emergency control rooms
7. Evacuation arrangements
8. Contacts for further advice, e.g. meteorological information, transport, temporary food and accommodation, first aid and hospital services, water and agricultural authorities
9. Arrangements for dealing with the press and other media interests
10. Longer term clean up

Information to the public

People in the vicinity of an industrial activity may be at risk if a major accident occurs. Therefore, this Regulation requires that such members of the public be told about the activity, its associated hazards and what to do in an emergency. In addition to the foregoing, legislation is currently being prepared which will ensure that sites containing even moderate quantities of dangerous substances are clearly marked. The marking of which will be in accordance with the diamond-shaped Hazardous Substances Symbols (Fig. 1). Standard hazard symbols, will warn Emergency Services on arrival of the type of hazard they can expect to encounter on site.

A MAJOR INCIDENT

Although I have not directly mentioned the fact, Fire Service involvement takes place throughout the considering and formulating of plans. In addition, operational personnel regularly visit CIMAH sites and exercises are organized to ensure familiarity, should the need arise. Occasionally, in spite of all the legislation, meticulously interpreted and applied, in spite of safety officers, safety procedures and fail-safe operations, the need *will* arise from time to time!

Response to a major incident—or threat

Let us now look at the resources in terms of planning, procedures, equipment, personnel and specialist advice which we can deploy to deal with the results of a major disaster, should one threaten or take place.

Implementation of major hazard plans

Off-site plans for use in a major disaster are held by:

1. The manufacturer
2. The Police

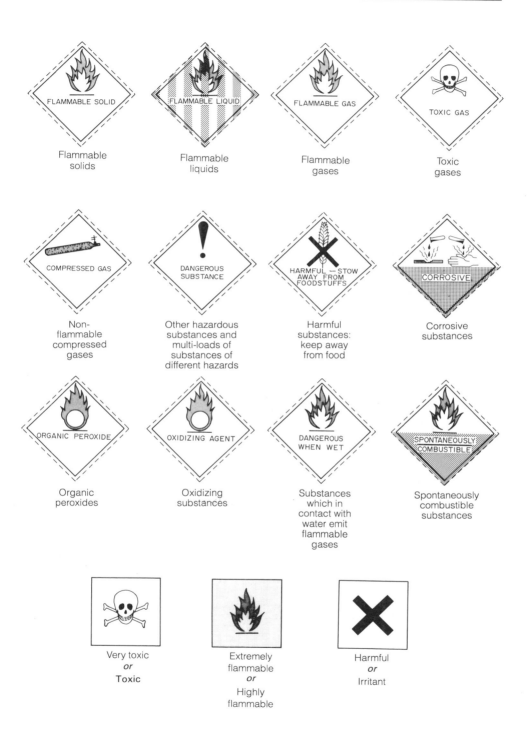

Figure 1 *Hazard warning signs.*

3. The Fire Service
4. The Ambulance Service
5. The District Councils
6. The Emergency Planning Office
7. The Health Authority
8. The Voluntary Services

Attention of the plan will give personnel to each of the above groups the following information for immediate application:

1. Description of the site
2. Activity carried out
3. Main characteristics of substances used
4. Detailed appraisal of the hazard
5. Maps of the site and surrounding area
6. Action by manufacturer to initiate emergency procedure
7. Role of each of the emergency services, quoted separately, in order to avoid overlapping responsibilities
8. Meteorological advice
9. Other relevant information

Thus such responsibilities should be considered to include:

- Should evacuation of any part of the local population be undertaken?
- Who should carry out evacuation, if decided upon?
- Who will provide the necessary transport?
- Where should evacuees be housed?
- How and by whom should they be fed?
- What agency has responsibility for over-all coordination of activities?
- Which hospital is most suited and able to receive casualties in large numbers?

These responsibilities are all apportioned in the plan and therefore, no time should be wasted in discussions or decision-making on the subject of 'who does what?'

While there is no doubt that a disaster is a disaster, by any interpretation of the term, it is equally true that efficient and immediate application of a well coordinated plan can cause the worst effects of any major accident to be considerably reduced. But the activity cannot stop at a well-drilled initial response. The effects of a major accident, even if softened by prompt action and efficient planning, are likely to continue well beyond the short-term business of firefighting and first aid.

On-going considerations

Areas in which a more long-term function must be given to the planning include:

1. If serious damage to housing has taken place, re-housing of evacuees may be necessary
2. In case the casualty list rises to extreme numbers, back-up hospital facilities must be available
3. In cases where toxic escapes are involved, decontamination of buildings, plant, equipment and personnel may have to be undertaken

4. In certain cases decontamination of injured persons may be necessary before treatment of injuries can commence
5. Meteorological advice on expected weather patterns in the area, for days or weeks ahead, may need to be taken into consideration, and many other factors depending upon circumstances

FIRE SERVICE PREPARATIONS

To enable us to be as effective as possible against the threat of chemical disaster, the UK Fire Services have evolved certain plans, procedures, and equipment which have already proved their value in the course of the many, relatively minor incidents which occur regularly in our progressive industrial society. I refer to spillages, pipeline fractures, valve failures, road and rail traffic accidents, etc., in which smaller quantities of dangerous substances are involved.

One of the most important developments to take place, has been the adoption of the de-mountable unit approach to major incident hazards. For a variety of reasons, all of which combined to improve the effectiveness of the service—the West Midlands Fire Service switched to the use of de-mountables some years ago.

Briefly, the system utilizes a small number of tractor units to transport a large variety of specialized equipment and facility containers, which are usually referred to as 'pods'. In this way, one tractor unit on standby can respond to an incident with any one of a selection of pods, deposit the pod at the incident and return to standby in case of a further call.

In the context of a major accident hazard, each of the following pods might well play an important part:

1. Hazardous Substances Unit (HSU)
2. Major Rescue Unit
3. Command Unit
4. Foam Distribution Unit
5. Incident Support Unit
6. Damage Control Unit

Of particular value at a chemical incident of course, is the HSU. Not only for its complement of protective clothing for firemen and absorbent material, etc., but also for the decontamination role it can fulfill. The procedure laid down in the West Midlands Fire Service provides for three types of decontamination:

1. Wet—containment: water spray, residual water with contaminating substance is retained for supervised disposal, later
2. Wet—non-containment: water spray, contaminating substance diluted and washed down drains
3. Dry: for powders mainly, using special vacuum cleaners or Fullers earth

Generally, wet, non-containment decontamination is satisfactory for most types of chemicals followed by full body showers. Disposal of contaminated equipment and clothing is taken into consideration and documentation of all personnel exposed and decontaminated is carried out on the spot for retention on file.

TRANSPORT OF DANGEROUS GOODS

Road transport is on the increase in the United Kingdom as the most cost-effective method of transit. Although the quantities of dangerous substances thus moved do not in general qualify as potential major hazards, considerable damage and alarm can be caused by a 32 tonne tanker, if full of some extremely toxic or flammable substance, and involved in a traffic accident.

In order to deal quickly and safely with such incidents on British roads, the Haz Chem System (Fig. 2) has been devised. This consists of a set of coded symbols which are displayed on vehicles carrying dangerous substances (Fig. 2). Fire Service personnel can de-code the symbols, by using a card designed for the purpose, and thus obtain emergency action advice for dealing with the substance concerned.

In cases where the Haz Chem action code is not sufficiently explicit, or unavailable for some reason, brigades have recourse to the assistance of a system known as Chemdata.

Chemdata computer information

This is an information service produced by the National Chemical Emergency Centre at Harwell. The database uses software suitable for running on a wide variety of computers and contains emergency action details of thousands of chemicals. Subscription covers regular updates of information. The chemical name system caters for the chemical name, United Nations Substance Identification Number or company name. Any one of these three references, if passed to the system, will result in a screening and/or printout of the following details:

1. Product hazard identification
2. Types of protective clothing and equipment required
3. Action to take after spillage or fire
4. Company emergency telephone number
5. Decontamination procedure
6. First aid

When it is borne in mind that this information can be obtained within seconds and relayed by radio directly back to the fire officer in charge of the incident, the advantages are easily appreciated. A mobile data printer on the mobile control unit provides a hard copy of the information.

Transport emergency card

A further safeguard is provided by the transport emergency card, or Trem Card as it is known within the service (Fig. 3). This card, standard A4 size and laid out in a simple, easily recognized format, is familiar to all British fire service personnel. It is carried in the cab of the vehicle and, of course, must be changed for another card when the load of the vehicle is changed.

A Trem Card gives emergency service personnel broadly similar details to those which may be obtained through Chemdata. Carrying of Trem Cards however is not yet mandatory although most reputable transport concerns subscribe to the scheme.

There are a number of other specialized schemes which have been developed through bodies such as the Chemical Industries Association as well as the continental 'ADR' System or marking as used in Europe generally.

Inherent in all the systems so far described is the ability to call on specialist advice at any time. A number of chemicals manufacturers and universities working within the spheres of industrial chemistry or academic research, who have

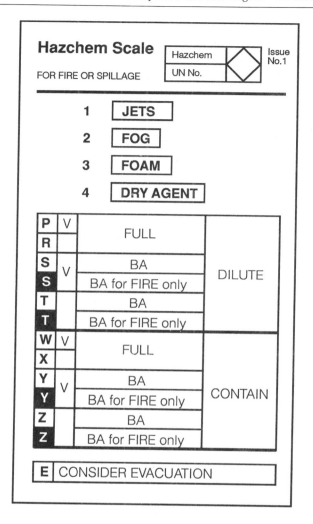

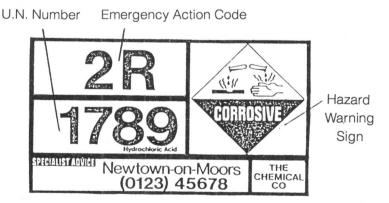

Figure 2   *(a) Hazchem scale; (b) Hazardous load Hazchem plate.*

TRANSPORT EMERGENCY CARD (Road) | **CEFIC TEC(R)–105A 11/1971**

CARGO
SODIUM CYANIDE | **Class 6.1 ADR Item 41a**

*Coloured solid with perceptible odour

NATURE OF HAZARD

*Severe poisoning perhaps fatal when swallowed
*Contact with acids (e.g. from battery) causes toxic fumes

PROTECTIVE DEVICES

*Suitable respiratory protective device
*Goggles giving complete protection to eyes
*Plastic or rubber gloves and boots
*Special first aid equipment
*Eyewash bottle with clean water

EMERGENCY ACTION–Notify police and fire brigade immediately

*Stop the engine
*Mark roads and warn other road users
*Keep public away from danger area
*Keep upwind

SPILLAGE

*Do not repack
*Cover spilled substance and consult an expert
*Keep remaining cargo dry
*If substance has entered a water course or sewer or contaminated soil or vegetation, advise police

FIRE

FIRST AID

*Special treatment by a doctor is required as soon as possible in cases of exposure to the substance or its vapours
*If substance has got into the eyes, immediately wash out with plenty of water. Continue treatment until medical assistance is provided
*Remove contaminated clothing immediately and wash affected skin with plenty of water
*Seek medical treatment when anyone has symptoms apparently due to swallowing, inhalation or contact with skin or eyes
*Even if there are no symptoms resulting from such exposure send to a doctor and show him this card

Additional information **TELEPHONE:**

HI No.: ....

UN No.:........

COPYRIGHT BY CEFIC Prepared by CEFIC, from the best knowledge available; no responsibility is accepted that the information is sufficient or correct in all cases

APPLIES ONLY DURING ROAD TRANSPORT **ENGLISH**

Figure 3 *Transport Emergency Card (Road).*

expressed a willingness for their contact numbers to be available to the Emergency Services on a round-the-clock basis. In cases of extreme need, such people will turn out to attend incidents and advise Fire Service personnel on the spot. This reponse forms part of a scheme known as 'Chemsafe'.

FIRE INFORMATION NATIONAL DATA SERVICE (FINDS)

The Fire Service is currently introducing the Fire Information National Data Service. A system which will provide a private viewdata system for all Fire Brigades, and an electronic mail service which can be used to transfer messages quickly and easily to other brigades. The system includes a special equipment index to assist brigades dealing with difficult or major incidents.

CONCLUSION

I have stressed the importance of good, accurate information. There seems to be a large measure of uncertainty within the industry as to exactly what information the fire service should be privy to. The problem the British fire service has, and Basle proves the case, is that the fire situation is very much a science of the unexpected. There are so many parameters which can change the outcome that we must have access to all available information on a 24 hour basis. We must expect a cocktail of chemicals and we must know what the effects of that cocktail are likely to be. I would emphasize that the responsibility in case of fire rests firmly with the fire officer and to deprive him, whether by accident or design, of the means of making professional judgements is, in my view, unacceptable.

BIBLIOGRAPHY

Notification of Installations Handling Hazardous Substances Regulations, 1982.
Control of Industrial Major Accident Hazard Regulations, 1984.
Petroleum (Consolidation) Act, 1928.
Regulations under the Factories Act.
Fire Services Act, 1947.
Offices, Shops and Railway Premises Act, 1963
Fire Precautions Act, 1971.
Highly Flammable Liquids and LPG Regulations, 1972.
Health and Safety at Work Act, 1974.
Classification, Packaging and Labelling of Dangerous Substances Regulations, 1984.
Dangerous Substances (Notification and Marking of Sites) Regulations, (Consultative Document), 1985
Road Traffic (Carriage of Dangerous Substances in Packages) Regulations, 1986.

Immediate response:
Major incidents—the police response

W. G. Payne

Metropolitan Police, Territorial Operations 22, New Scotland Yard, London, UK
(New address: Bexley London Borough Directorate of Administration, Broadway, Bexley Heath, Kent, UK)

INTRODUCTION

The role of the Police Service at any disaster in the United Kingdom is to control and coordinate the total operation. The basis for the primacy of the police role is historical, and based on the common law police responsibility for the protection of life and property. The powers of the police ultimately derive from their function as representatives of the Coroner, who has overriding authority in relation to investigating the cause of death.

It is essential that from the outset, police primacy is established and maintained.

The following viewpoints reflect the recommendations made on 14 January 1989 by the Police General Purposes Committee (working party on emergency procedures) to the ACPO. The recommendations were accepted by ACPO and circulated to all Chief Officers but it is important to stress that individual Chief Constables are not bound by them. However, should a major incident occur today within the Metropolitan Police District the priorities highlighted would be implemented.

A major incident is any emergency that requires the implementation of special arrangements by one or all of the emergency services for:

1. The rescue and/or transport of large numbers of casualties
2. The involvement directly or indirectly of a large number of people
3. The handling of large numbers of enquiries from both the public and/or the media to the police
4. The requirement to combine the resources of the three emergency services
5. The mobilization and organization of the three emergency services in addition to essential support services, for example, the local authority to meet the demands of the homeless

The primary areas of police responsibility may be summarized as follows:

1. The saving of life in conjunction with the other emergency services
2. Coordination of the Emergency Service's response

Major chemical disasters—medical aspects of management, edited by Virginia Murray, 1990: Royal Society of Medicine Services International Congress and Symposium Series No. 155, published by Royal Society of Medicine Services Limited.

3. The protection and preservation of the scene
4. The investigation of the incident in conjunction with other investigative bodies
5. Identification of victims on behalf of the Coroner
6. The restoration of normality at the earliest opportunity

POLICE CONTROL AND THE COORDINATION OF THE EMERGENCY SERVICE'S RESPONSE

Dependent on the size and location of the incident three levels of police command and control will be developed.

Forward control point

This first control to be established at the scene of the disaster will be responsible for immediate deployment and security. Under the command of the *Incident Officer* the functions of the Forward Control Point may vary considerably dependent on the siting of the *Incident Control Post* (see below). Once established the Incident Control Post may supplant the need for a static Forward Control Point, but a communications link must be maintained.

Incident control post

Will control and coordinate the management and investigation of the incident, providing a central point of contact for all emergency and specialist services. The Incident Control Post will be the responsibility of a *Coordinator* and also under the command of the *Incident Officer*.

Major incident room

The need for such a control is very much dependent on the scope of the incident. In some cases, even though there are a number of casualties all aspects of the operation can be coordinated through the Incident Control Post. However with protracted incidents, where there are ongoing manpower and logistical requirements, a Major Incident Room should be established to coordinate the overall response and provide facilities for senior command functions. This allows the Incident Control Post to fulfil its primary functions of coordinating and managing the operation within the 'controlled area', requesting resources through the Major Incident Room. The Major Incident Room will be under the command of the *Overall Incident Commander*. Its routine also being the responsibility of a *Coordinator*.

Command functions

Whilst the officers nominated may vary dependent on individual force establishments the following command functions should be adopted:

1. Overall Incident Commander
2. Incident Officer
3. Investigating Officer
4. Major Incident Room Coordinator
5. Incident Control Post Coordinator

As these control and command functions are established the multitude of tasks associated with each can be progressively implemented to ensure that the responsibilities of all concerned in the operation are effectively carried out.

Inevitably, however, responsibility will fall to the first officer to arrive at the scene who will act as Incident Officer until replaced by a senior officer and to the Divisional and Force Operations Rooms to undertake the rapid mobilization of resources.

Initial action by the first officer at the scene

The first officer to arrive at the scene of an incident will almost invariably be a constable and his initial action in assessing the situation is all important.

His immediate responsibility is to assume interim command and ensure that other emergency services are informed, if they are not already in attendance. He must *not* get personally involved in rescue work. Despite the enormity of the incident his priorities are to *assess* and *inform*.

The following information must be passed to his radio control without delay:

1. *Exact location*: if not easily identifiable as in isolated areas, landmarks, road junctions, etc., should be used to pinpoint the site
2. *Type of incident*: brief details of types and numbers of vehicles, buildings, aircraft, etc., involved
3. *Hazards present and potential*: should include fuel spillage, debris, weather conditions and terrain as well as the presence of gases, chemicals fire or the danger of explosion
4. *Access*: best routes for emergency vehicles, parking turning points, routes blocked
5. *Casualties*: approximate numbers of fatalities, injured and uninjured
6. *Emergency services*: present and required

Having passed all available information the officer must maintain radio contact with his control to coordinate the response of the emergency services to the scene and act as Incident Officer until relieved by an officer of more senior rank.

Divisional/sub-divisional control

Control Room staff at the Divisional or Sub-Divisional police station on receipt of information that a potentially major incident has occurred must:

1. Inform the Force Operations Room without delay
2. Direct the nearest officer to the scene to assess the situation
3. Inform the senior officer on duty, who will attend and assume the role of Incident Officer
4. Inform the divisional commander or his deputy
5. Deploy divisional personnel as directed by the Incident Officer
6. Commence log and coordinate the divisional response
7. Maintain liaison with Force Operations Room

Force Operations/Control Room

On receipt of information that an incident has occurred that may subsequently be classed as a Major Incident the Duty Officer in the Force Operations Room is responsible for instigating the mobilization of the emergency services, and police manpower, and for establishing communications with the scene.

In addition to the mobilization of police resources, other essential actions to be taken by the Duty Officer will be to alert:

1. Other emergency services (i.e. Fire Service, Ambulance Service, specialist rescue services, designated receiving hospitals)
2. Traffic control
3. Hospital documentation team
4. Photographers
5. Local authority
6. Essential services (i.e. gas, water and electricity)
7. British Transport Police or other interested authorities
8. Voluntary Services

The Force Operations Room will act as the resourcing and communications centre until the Incident Control Post and the Major Incident Room are operational.

SCENE MANAGEMENT

It must be appreciated that the immediate and overriding responsibility of all emergency services at the scene of a major disaster is the saving of life. To this end the Fire and Ambulance Services, together with other specialist rescue services, must be afforded the opportunity to utilize their training and experience. The response of the other services is to provide the necessary support for these skills to be used to their full effect.

During the rescue phase the police coordinating role is vital and, whilst a number of officers may be engaged in rescue work as directed by the Fire Officer in charge of the rescue operation, the Incident Officer must, after a preliminary reconnaissance, ensure that action has been taken to establish:

1. The Incident Control Post
2. Security of the scene
3. Traffic control
4. Casualty clearance
5. Property team
6. Hospital documentation teams
7. Mortuary facilities

When it becomes apparent that no further life can be saved other considerations take precedence:

8. Preservation of the scene
9. Recovery of deceased
10. Investigation
11. Protection of property
12. Identification of deceased

At this time the responsibilities of the Fire and Ambulance Services will be scaled down whilst those of the Police, investigative bodies and the welfare agencies will increase.

Bringing order to chaos as soon as possible will always feature as the primary objective at the scene of any major incident and this can only be achieved by all the emergency services working together in a coordinated way with an understanding of each other's role. It must never be forgotten that none of the emergency services acts in isolation, each relies very heavily upon the other.

Immediate response:
Ambulance Service—The response to chemical incidents

Michael I. Willis

Norfolk Ambulance Service, Ambulance Headquarters, Norwich, UK

INTRODUCTION

This paper presents a view of the general response by Ambulance Services in England and Wales to a major incident, with a particular emphasis on those incidents involving chemicals, but in the space allowed for this presentation it will only be possible to cover the most basic aspects.

Statistical information with regard to the ambulance service has been omitted, as it is not particularly relevant other than to demonstrate that ambulance and medical involvement on a large scale with regard to chemicals is infrequent. However, the potential in all counties, especially Norfolk, for such incidents is significant, due primarily to the large numbers of chemicals in transit.

In all cases, an ambulance service initial response would be the same as for any other major incident.

Experience has shown that the most likely cause of a chemical incident is not the chemical works itself, but the end user or the intermediate carrier. The greatest element of risk lies with the casual transit operator. It is recognized that should either the manufacturer or road haulier be involved then the incident is likely to be substantial, such as the renowned Flixborough disaster. However, in the cases of manufacturing premises, one has the advantage of the Control of Industrial Major Accident Hazard (CIMAH) regulations and the resultant integrated pre-planning required of the three emergency services.

Whilst the title of the symposium is 'Major Chemical Disasters' I feel it is important to consider the implications of incidents that can be regarded as minor, particularly as they have a knock-on effect, not only on the ambulance service, but also the Accident and Emergency Departments.

PREPARATION FOR MAJOR INCIDENTS

Ambulance services in the UK prepare for major incidents on the basis of a circular known as HC (77)1. Whilst it is a little old, its basic concept holds true, providing that updated terminology is used.

Ambulance calls for such incidents are received, for the most part, via the normal British Telecom network, and direct lines from other emergency services provide for any shortfall in the advisory system.

Major chemical disasters—medical aspects of management, edited by Virginia Murray, 1990: Royal Society of Medicine Services International Congress and Symposium Series No. 155, published by Royal Society of Medicine Services Limited.

Response to a major incident

Each call is dealt with on its merits and whilst each may engender a slightly different response, the basic concept will remain constant. The ambulance service has nationally laid down standards. These require that:

1. 50% of all calls be attended within 8 minutes
2. 95% of all calls be attended within 20 minutes

In metropolitan areas these figures reduce to 7 and 14 minutes, respectively.

The number of vehicles responding to the initial call often depends on the source and level of information provided. If a major incident is advised, then an Officer will also be despatched to establish the extent of the incident, and the initial ambulance control point.

Procedures on site

Should the first crew/officer arriving on the scene confirm that the incident is of a size to warrant initiating the Majax Plan, then the following will ensue:

1. Mobilize ambulance control units
2. Inform other Emergency Services
3. Advise first level receiving hospitals
4. Ambulance service to standby
5. Advise surrounding services and centres

From then on, normal major incident procedures are followed. For example, should it be necessary, a hospital team would be conveyed to the site and a triage area established, along with forward control points. If necessary an Incident Medical Officer would attend, together with the medical team, to provide overall medical coordination.

Whilst in most incidents this is a natural process, where chemicals are involved, the freedom to move and to handle casualties has inherent difficulties.

Chemicals cause illness/injury by either ingestion, inhalation, injection or cutaneous absorption, all of which need to be avoided by the rescuer. It is therefore essential that both clean and dirty areas for patients are not only established, but clearly marked. It is also necessary to bear in mind the wind direction, which can be of significant importance, depending on the substance involved.

Although this may seem straightforward, in reality it takes considerable self-discipline not to follow one's instinct and immediately begin the rescue attempt of patients. Ideally, patients should pass through the decontamination process prior to receiving other than life-saving treatment.

The prime warning at this stage to all concerned is *Caution*. While one can appreciate that the training of all medical staff is devoted to saving life, to walk into the scene of a chemical incident without clearance from the Fire Officer, Ambulance Officer or crew on the scene is, to say the least, irresponsible. Recent incidents have demonstrated that reckless action by some team members at the scene of such incidents has inevitably led to risk being incurred by others. In many rural counties pre-hospital care is supported by an immediate care scheme, and it is these doctors who may be first on the scene, or who arrive shortly after the first vehicle.

So far as ambulance service crews are concerned, the guidelines are relatively simple, and can be applied to any attendance at such incidents. These are as follows:

1. Keep in mind that personal safety is paramount—do not make any rescue attempts until access to the incident site is declared safe by the officer in charge
2. Depending on when you arrive, obtain or give a situation report to Ambulance Control of what you can see from a safe distance. This should include:
   The nature of the incident
   Whether the Police or Fire Service are in attendance
   The number of casualties and whether or not they are trapped
   All information displayed—i.e. Hazchem or Kemler identification numbers, UN numbers, product name and any other relevant details
   Whether further assistance is required
3. Be careful not to step into any spilled liquid, touch or smell any substance or vapour which may be harmful
4. Position the ambulance vehicle correctly in relation to the hazard, i.e. approach up-wind, remain uphill if liquids are involved, park at a safe distance (at least 100 metres)
5. Maintain close liaison with Fire, Police and specialist services. The Police are responsible for coordination. The Fire Service is responsible for containing and making safe the hazard, and in the majority of cases for decontaminating casualties and emergency personnel. However, there is a need to consider the degree to which this process can be effected for the majority. The decontamination units are designed for Fire personnel, not patients with varying degrees of injury. Although this facility is becoming more sophisticated, its prime function should be borne in mind
6. After patients have been rescued by the Fire Service, the Control will, from the information provided, obtain instructions on any special first aid measures necessary. However, it is essential that when treating a contaminated patient some form of impervious protective clothing (such as PVC-coated gloves and aprons) are worn
7. **REMEMBER**: one should gain information about the substance involved without putting yourself at risk. You will be of little use to casualties if you succumb to the effects of the chemicals. If the Fire Service needs protective clothing and breathing apparatus to be safe—so do you

Whilst these guidelines may seem basic, they can be the difference between giving medical aid and needing it. One of the most significant incidents highlighting the damage caused by chemicals occurred on the M6 when a tank wagon loaded with oleum was involved in an accident, resulting in extensive spillage. One of the would-be rescuers, a woman, stepped into the product, and only a few of her minor remains were recovered by the Fire Brigade. This may be an extreme example, but one which makes the point.

For the majority of the medical fraternity, work outside the hospital can be regarded as operating in a hostile environment. Therefore the ambulance service will endeavour to provide safe working facilities and conditions. However, very little thought is given to protective clothing for medical teams, and although weather protection may be available, chemical protection is often not. Such protection may also need to be extended to the Accident and Emergency Department itself.

SUMMARY

In summary, experience has shown that basic aspects in such incidents are often overlooked, such as:

1. Patients who have been exposed to chemical fumes can suffer further effects purely due to the confined space and the clothes they are wearing
2. All contaminated clothing should either be left on the scene or bagged and sealed
3. Hospitals need to adopt a specific set of procedures with regard to chemical incidents and not the present 'deal with it at the time' approach
4. Construction of new hospitals should provide appropriate patient and staff decontamination areas
5. Adequate protective clothing should be provided for staff working in an Accident and Emergency Unit faced with contaminated patients, particularly for those who are sent to the scene

All of these issues only scrape the surface of the subject, which cannot be adequately covered in this short paper.

In conclusion I would suggest that the primary aim of ambulance service policy should be:

> Personal safety
> Patient safety
> Give medical aid—do nothing to require it

Immediate response:
Accident and Emergency Departments

Vera Dallos

Accident and Emergency Department, Whipps Cross Hospital, Leytonstone, London, UK

INTRODUCTION

My remit is to give an account of the Accident and Emergency Department's immediate response to a chemical incident. In order to do this I would like to review the existing guidelines and to analyse how far those guidelines were implemented in ten major departments. Chemical incidents are the Cinderella of disasters inasmuch as there is no Department of Health circular to recommend action by health authorities and hospitals in case of such an event.

There are Department of Health and Social Security (DHSS) circulars for action for health authorities and hospitals entitled Health Service Arrangements for dealing with Major Accidents (1), one for action by health authorities and hospitals for Health Service arrangements for dealing with major incidents involving radioactivity (2), and also one for action by health authorities and for information for other interested parties entitled Civil Defence Planning in the NHS (3).

Though there is no such information on the management of chemical incidents, DHSS Health Building Notes 22 for Accident and Emergency Departments in 1969 and 1986, respectively, gave advice on decontamination facilities for victims of toxic materials. The 1969 Building Notes recommend that a room should be set aside for patients whose clothing has been contaminated by injurious chemicals. This room provided shower facilities for one to two patients well enough to stand. It was also suggested that the same facility might be used for decontamination of other substances, including radioactive materials.

The recommendations of the 1986 Building Notes (4) are much more specific. A room should be provided for decontamination of victims of injurious chemicals. This room should be near the entrance of the Accident and Emergency Department and should permit the decontamination of stretcher patients. Adjacent to it should be a decontamination equipment store. The room should have a special drainage system installed. Advice is given to consult the Health and Safety Executive in case of major chemical incident.

In the companion document, Design Briefing System Notebook DBS22 Accident & Emergency Department 1986 (5) the Health Building Note's advice is reinforced.

Major chemical disasters—medical aspects of management, edited by Virginia Murray, 1990: Royal Society of Medicine Services International Congress and Symposium Series No. 155, published by Royal Society of Medicine Services Limited.

Whilst the building notes specifically advise on decontamination facilities, the Casualty Surgeons Association (CSA) Clinical Services Committee drew up Guidelines on Decontamination Procedure for Victims of Accidents involving Toxic Waste (6), using the organizational models for major and radioactive incidents. In 1984 this paper was submitted to the British Medical Association and also the DHSS in the hope that further discussion would follow and DHSS guidelines would be produced. At the same time the Ambulance Service and the British Association for Immediate Care (BASIC) also submitted their respective guidelines for the DHSS consideration.

In 1989 the Academic Committee of the Casualty Surgeons Association produced guidelines on the Early Management of Contamination by Toxic Chemicals (7) reinforcing the earlier documents.

WHAT ARE THE GUIDELINES?

Anticipation of hazards

1. Information should be obtained about local chemical industries and CIMAH sites
2. Telephone numbers of major information sources should be available, e.g. Fire Services, Poison Units, Harwell Chemical Emergency Centre
3. Key reference books for medical staff should be available
4. Arrangements should be made with hospital pharmacists for stocking of common antidotes, especially those relevant to local industries and for obtaining increased supply in case of a major incident

On hearing of the accident

1. Obtain information about the toxic chemical involved
2. Ascertain approximate number of casualties, i.e. a few only, enough to invoke special arrangements by a hospital according to a protocol, or is it a mass disaster?

Action to be taken

At site

When called to attend the site full protective clothing should be worn, i.e. PVC suit, hood, boots, gauntlets, goggles, mask and breathing apparatus.

If doctors and nurses are not going to enter the heavily contaminated zone they will still need ordinary surgical protective clothing, goggles and mask.

In hospital

Decontamination: facilities will be needed for patients who walk in and for stretcher cases who need resuscitation before decontamination:

- Decontamination room
- Isolation facilities
- Hospital protocol for organization

IMPLEMENTATION OF THE GUIDELINES

In order to check how far the CSA's recommendations were observed, I have contacted ten major departments (more than 50 000 new patients per year—range 50 000 to 100 000). The selection was partly subjective in that I had high regard for the quality of medical practice and partly objective as I selected only consultant led units, some in highly industrialized areas, some in seaports and some in inner cities. No consultant had been in post for less than five years and the following questions were put to them.

How common are major chemical incidents in your experience?

The concensus was that major incidents requiring special arrangements were rare. No department had a chemical incident record file. All answers were anecdotal.
   One consultant was involved in three episodes in 15 years:

1. 30 patients inhaled chlorine gas, none were admitted;
2. 45 patients were victims of formaldehyde spillage, none were admitted; and
3. 75 patients were exposed to CS gas. The department was closed for two hours and the patients were managed jointly with the ophthalmologists—four patients were admitted.

Another consultant dealt with two incidents in eight years:

1. A mass casualty scare of chlorine gas escape from an industrial site and evacuation procedure was instituted. The site was managed by ICI and only two patients were sent to hospital.
2. 100 cases were directed to hospital by ICI but only two were admitted.

One department dealt with 40 patients who suffered skin contamination from toxic paint. The department had no shower facilities and the patients were sent home by taxi to have a bath and to change. They returned for examination but none were admitted.
   Seven departments dealt with only isolated cases.

Are you aware of local industry, and, if so, do you have close liaison with their industrial medical officer/nurse or manager?

Two hospitals worked in close cooperation with ICI. They were also aware of local chemical industry and visited smaller units. Site attendance was provided by ICI and they received only patients selected for hospital by ICI.
   Three departments were aware of CIMAH sites and products and they have formed close contact with the Fire Service and attended joint exercises.
   In one region the Emergency Planning Officer called a meeting for organization of mass disaster involving chlorine gas from a local industry.
   Five hospitals tried to find out about local industry but had difficulties. They were not approached by the Managers/Occupational Health Staff of those industries.

What is your source of information about toxic substances?

All departments would approach the Fire Brigade and their local Poison Unit. One department was aware of the Harwell Register; two departments depended primarily on the ICI Information Register.

The departments had a variable collection of literature but did not find this important as they felt that in a crisis more adequate information could be obtained from the above sources.

Have you discussed the antidote list with your pharmacy?

Five departments have done so but left it to the pharmacy to make arrangements for increased supply in case of a major incident. In one hospital the pharmacists added the telephone number of the suppliers on the antidote information card. Five departments did not discuss matters with their pharmacy.

Do you have decontamination facilities?

This was the most contentious item. No hospital had decontamination rooms as recommended by Hospital Building Note 22 1986. Eight hospitals had shower rooms for the use of one or two well patients; one hospital had no shower room; one hospital used to have one but it was allocated for a different purpose.

Decontamination of severely injured patients depended on improvization. The best organized departments were the four National Arrangements for Incidents Involving Radioactivity Centres. They allocated special theatre areas for such patients but none of those areas had ventilation to the outside, storage facilities for contaminated water, nor chemical resistant floors, seamless walls for easy cleaning, nor explosion proof electrical fittings.

Have you got a supply of protective clothing, can you use breathing apparatus, are you trained in field work?

Two departments who operated flying squads and had field medical experience had a supply of PVC protective clothing and could use breathing apparatus. One department worked closely with BASIC and the consultant did not go out to site. The department had no PVC protective clothing and breathing apparatus.

Two departments that cooperated with ICI closely were trained in field work but they usually received patients from ICI site teams.

Five departments had no equipment, no breathing apparatus and no training. They were willing to go out to site under the instruction of the Fire Service.

Have you got a protocol for reception, isolation, decontamination and treatment?

Decontamination facilities were already referred to. Four hospitals, all NAIR Centres, had a protocol; six had none.

Do you feel confident to treat toxic gas inhalations, ophthalmic and dermatology complications?

All ten were confident.

Mass disasters—do you understand the organization of such disasters and the role of medical and nursing personnel?

Two consultants attended Civil Defence exercises and understood the organization and the role of medical and nursing personnel, but felt that further training is needed. Two had some ideas; six had none.

SUMMARY AND RECOMMENDATIONS

The arrangements for the reception of victims of toxic hazards are too variable for comfort and I feel that the subject should be reconsidered by the Health Regions and the Accident and Emergency Departments.

I would recommend the following for consideration:

1. All chemical incidents should be documented and departmental files should be kept.
2. The Regional Emergency Planning Officers should be involved in obtaining information of local CIMAH sites and of local chemical industries. They should coordinate meetings between Accident and Emergency consultants, occupational health workers and managers of industries.
3. Hospital pharmacies should be made aware of local chemical hazards and the need for antidotes, if any, for them. They should also consult the CSA's antidote list.
4. Hospital decontamination facilities should be upgraded according to the recommendation of Hospital Building Note 22, 1986. Decisions should be made whether all major District General Hospitals should have such facilities or only NAIR Centres, where the facility could be also used for radioactive decontamination.
5. Chemical incident protocol should be drawn up as appropriate to the designation of the hospital.
6. Training for site work should be instituted and a cadre of Accident and Emergency consultants who wish to act as site officers, or resuscitation officers should be established. These doctors should be trained in the use of breathing apparatus. BASIC should be involved in the training. Field exercises should be arranged with the Services.
7. Protective clothing must be stored in departments whose consultants are trained in field work.

Information from the Accident and Emergency Departments should be collated by the CSA and should be submitted to the DH with recommendations.

REFERENCES

(1) *Health Service Arrangements for Dealing with Major Accidents.* HC(77)1. DHSS, January 1977.
(2) *National Arrangements for Incidents Involving Radioactivity (NAIR) and Arrangements for Dealing with Contaminated and Radiation Casualties.* HC(76)52. DHSS, November 1976.
(3) *Civil Defence Planning in the NHS.* DHSS, 30 July 1984.
(4) *Health Building Note 22—Accident and Emergency Department.* Department of Health and the Welsh Office, 1986, p. 5 para. 2.14; p. 13 para. 4.2; p. 17 para. 4.9; p. 35 para. 6.89.
(5) *Design Briefing System Notebook DBS 22—Accident and Emergency Department.* Department of Health, 1986, p. 3 para. 5.12.
(6) *Guidelines on a Decontamination Procedure for Victims of Accidents Involving Toxic Substances.* CSA Clinical Services Sub Committee, 1984.
(7) *The Early Management of Contamination by Toxic Chemicals.* CSA Clinical Services Sub Committee, January 1988.

Immediate response:
Poison centres: their role in the management of major incidents involving chemicals

P. Kulling

Swedish Poison Information Centre, Karolinska Hospital, Stockholm, Sweden

INTRODUCTION

Information management is a primary theme in disaster management. Timely information can change the entire character of an accident and the Poison Centre has an important role in handling all types of chemical accidents where toxic effects on man can be expected. One very important task is giving information about the toxic substance including toxicity data, risks, first aid measures, hospital treatment, etc., in the very acute situation. Other important tasks for the Centre are to take an active part in the contingency planning for chemical accidents and in education of rescue personnel and disaster medicine planners. By initiating and planning for a close collaboration between different institutions and organizations much experience can be acquired from earlier accidents. This might give guidelines on preventive and therapeutic measures for the future. A Poison Centre is often the only centre in a country or a region which can in this way act on a centralized basis, for example in providing and adapting information for the rescue team, giving guidelines on supplying antidote stores, initiating and coordinating activities for follow-up studies, etc.

POISON CENTRE RESOURCES

Taking into consideration the large number of toxic substances that are handled at industrial plants and working places or transported by road, rail or sea, and the great variety of toxic effects in humans, it is obvious that information on a chemical substance including toxic effects, chemical and physical properties and first aid measures, has to be compiled and that this information must be easily available in case of an accident. In this work Poison Centres play an important role. A Poison Centre's main task is to develop toxicology data bases by compiling information on toxic and non-toxic substances and to disseminate this information, making it easily available in an acute situation.

Most Poison Centres run their information service 24 hours a day. Information resources are in general separate from general library information resources like medical and toxicology textbooks and journals, providing more specific

Major chemical disasters—medical aspects of management, edited by Virginia Murray, 1990: Royal Society of Medicine Services International Congress and Symposium Series No. 155, published by Royal Society of Medicine Services Limited.

information that has been collected, compiled and above all evaluated into specialized and specially adapted documents.

Poison Centres receive from manufacturers, importers, etc., detailed information on ingredients of chemical products. An ambition at the Centres is that risk assessment is added to this information and included in the chemical product files at the Centres' data information banks. Other files in the information banks at the Centres include monographs on chemical substances, drugs, plants, mushrooms, venomous animals, etc. Special files on cases reported to the Centres are most valuable and informative resources.

Most chemicals commonly used in household products or as industrial chemicals are well known, and detailed information is included in the files on chemical substances. In this way they are directly and easily available in the acute situation. For less frequently-used chemicals, however, information is often scarce, lacking or difficult to assess. A great number of chemicals need better documentation. Poison Centres need additional resources for this activity. Much information would become available, and also unforeseen risks might become evident, that would be of value for preventive measures when handling, loading, storing, and transporting such substances.

Industrial plants have gained great experience from accidents with industrial chemicals but this experience is not always available outside the plant. It is of great importance for Poison Centres to obtain this. Activities guaranteeing exchange of information and experience between occupational health services and Poison Centres must be established, if they do not already exist.

Acute information dissemination

When a gas leak from a plant or a hazardous material railroad or road accident has occurred, one of the first acts at the site of the accident should be to contact the Poison Centre giving information about the toxic substance, possible synonyms, etc. This must be included in the check list used at industrial plants, and emergency centres. In this way the Poison Centre has more time to search for relevant information about the toxic substance, if this information should not be easily available at the Centre. Close collaboration with Poison Centres in other regions and countries and with other institutions and experts is important in these situations.

At an early stage the Poison Centre should provide authorities, mass media, i.e. local and the national radio and TV stations and other bodies, with adequate information on the toxic substance regarding its toxic effects, first aid measures and instructions on how to avoid or minimize exposure. This can preferably be done by telefax in order to save time and to minimize the risk of misunderstanding. This information should then be forwarded to the general public as soon as possible.

The Poison Centre itself should also plan for chemical disasters. When necessary its organization should be strengthened. Supplementary staff should be called for and formats for information dissemination to authorities, hospitals, the mass media, etc., should be prepared.

The main task for the Centre in the acute phase is to give information to the medical rescue teams and hospitals, on the toxic substance. Detailed information on medical management is, of course, of crucial importance especially in those situations where specific therapy such as antidote therapy is possible.

The plan at the Poison Centre should also include steps to make it possible, if necessary, to send one or two Poison Centre staff members to the site of accident. Apart from assisting the rescue teams by giving advice, Poison Centre personnel could coordinate activities and prepare and initiate proper follow-up studies. This is of special importance in situations when information on the effects of the toxic substance on humans is inadequate or lacking.

Planning

For rapid and efficient action in the acute phase, proper planning is important. In the planning for chemical accidents Poison Centres play an important role in many ways. Regarding contingency planning for chemical accidents the Poison Centre must accept its responsibility and act in several ways to achieve and maintain effective systems. Disaster medicine plans must be extended to include chemical accidents. A close collaboration between the disaster medicine planners and the Poison Centre must be established. For example the Centre should provide the planners with guidelines including decontamination, first aid, advanced medical therapy and antidote supplies.

Inventory activities must precede the contingency planning and the occupational health services and the toxicologists at industries handling or producing chemicals have a great responsibility in this respect. They must, for example, inform the local hospital about the risk chemicals which are handled at the plant and provide the hospital with relevant information on the toxic substances so that adequate steps can be taken to prepare the hospital in case of an accident.

Another very important task is education of all members of the rescue team. Training programmes and exercises dealing with chemical accidents have to be arranged regularly and the Poison Centre must take an active part in these activities. The rescue team must be provided with information about main risks, first aid measures and hospital treatment and this information should be adapted for these situations.

In the training programmes for medical as well as non-medical rescue team members (doctors, nurses, personnel from the police, the ambulance services and the fire brigade), lectures and courses should be organized. These should deal with different aspects of acute poisoning, organization of rescue work at the place of accident, during transport and at hospital. Training should be geared to the needs and educational level of each group. Poison Centre personnel must take an active part in these programmes.

Close follow-up studies of major as well as minor accidents will provide much valuable information for the improvement of handling accidents, and such activities should be included in the planning. Plans should also be established for research activities. Visiting sites of accidents as observers in order to gather information and experience is of vital importance, not only in the acute but also at a later stage. The Poison Centre should take active part in these activities.

Collaboration

A close collaboration between Poison Centres all over the world and between Poison Centres and other organizations dealing with disaster medicine planning like the World Association for Emergency and Disaster Medicine (WAEDM), the International Programme on Chemical Safety (IPCS) and the World Health

Organization (WHO) is of course of vital importance. Initiating close collaboration between Poison Centres and the chemical industry both nationally and internationally is also of great importance in order to improve the preparedness for and prevention of chemical accidents.

SWEDISH NATIONAL BOARD OF HEALTH AND WELFARE GUIDELINES ON CHEMICAL ACCIDENTS

On behalf of the Emergency and Disaster Committee of the Swedish National Board of Health and Welfare, guidelines are being prepared to meet the demand of the Swedish health care system in case of chemical accidents. These guidelines are based upon experience from activities on the national level but also from recommendations and conclusions from internationally organized meetings (1-4).

As an introduction some examples of toxic chemical accidents are given followed by definitions and recommendations.

Characteristics of a toxic chemical accident

A toxic zone (risk zone) may cover a vast area. The hospital or the route to the hospital may be within the toxic zone, making it impossible to transport victims there.

The rescue personnel may become contaminated by exposed victims when taking care of a non-decontaminated person. Transport vehicles may also be contaminated and so may parts of the hospital, making it unserviceable for a long period.

In a 'pure' toxic accident the damage to the victims is of the same type for all those exposed, only of a different magnitude. Triage systems and treatment measures can therefore be standardized.

Table 1 *Examples of chemicals for which detailed information adapted for disasters might be compiled*

Acetonitrile
Acids
Alkalis
Ammonia
Carbon monoxide
Chlorine
Cyanide
Fire gases
Formaldehyde
Gasoline
Hydrofluoric acid
Hydrogen sulphide
Irritant gases
Inorganic mercury
Nitrites
Nitrobenzene
Nitrogen oxides
Organophosphates
Phenol
White (yellow) phosphorus

Table 2. *Antidotes to be stored at hospitals and on mobile units to be brought to the place of accident in case of major chemical accidents. WHO/EURO Assessor Group rcommendations*

Substance	Indication
Atropine	Organophosphates
Dimercaprol[1]	Arsenic, mercury
Calcium salts	Hydrofluoric acid
for injection	
tablets	
topical (Hydrofluoric acid burn jelly)	
Corticosteroids	Irritant gases
for injection	
for inhalation	
tablets	
Dicobalt edetate	Cyanide
Methylthionine (methylene blue)	Nitrobenzene and nitrites
or	
Tolonium chloride (toluidine blue)	
Obidoxime	
or	
Pralidoxime	Organophosphates
Penicillamine[2]	Arsenic, mercury
Polyethylene glycol 400	Phenol
Sodium thiosulphate	Cyanide

[1]*Newer chelating agents may replace dimercaprol.*
[2]*Not to be stored on mobile units.*

Organization

The aim of organization is to prepare the health care system to take care of a great number of persons exposed to a toxic substance. Existing disaster plans should be extended to include chemical accidents.

Doctors familiar with the specific features of toxic chemical accidents should be included at different levels of the organization.

Planning

When planning for chemical accidents inventories should be made, including lists of which risk chemicals are handled at plants and what chemicals are transported in the hospital region.

Decontamination

Action should be taken so that decontamination can be performed at the site of accidents and at hospitals. The need for hot water at the site of accident and the need for proper decontamination equipment and premises at hospital should be considered.

Information dissemination

Information must be uniform and correct. Information dissemination regarding toxic effects on humans, first aid measures and more specific therapeutic measures should be coordinated. The National Board of Health and Welfare has the overall responsibility for this information dissemination and the Poison Centre is its expert body.

At hospitals, information should be available regarding possible risk chemicals handled at industrial plants and working places in the hospital region. Safety data sheets distributed from the plant or working place might fulfil this requirement. More specific information adapted for these situations should also be at hand at hospitals. Examples of such chemicals are presented in Table 1.

Emergency stores of antidotes

In a limited number of cases, specific therapy like antidote therapy is of great importance. For this purpose antidotes should be stored at hospitals to satisfy the requirements of several poisoned persons. In accidents involving a great number of victims the transportation of victims to hospitals can be delayed for many hours. Therefore a number of antidotes should be stored on mobile units that will be brought directly to the accident location. In

Table 3 *Emergency store of antidotes at hospital. Recommendations in Sweden. Recommended package suffices the requirements for ten seriously poisoned patients for three days. The list is updated every second year*

Substance	Preparation		Package	Indication
Atropine	Atropin	Inj. 0.5 mg/ml	150×20 ml	Organophosphates
Betamethasone[1]	Betapred	Inj 4 mg/ml	75×5×1 ml	Irritant gases
Betamethasone[1]	Betapred	Tablet 0.5 mg	8×100 tabl	Irritant gases
Budesonide[1]	Pulmicort Turbuhaler	Inh pulv 400 µg/dose	2×200 doses	Irritant gases
Calcium glubionate	Calcium-Sandoz	Inj 9 mg Ca/ml	6×5×10 ml	Hydrofluoric acid
Calcium gluconate	Hydrofluoric acid burn jelly	Gel 2.5%	10×25 g	Hydrofluoric acid
Calcium gluconate-lactate	Calcium-Sandoz	Efferv tabl 1 g Ca/tabl	10×10 tabl	Hydrofluoric acid
Cobalt edetate	Kelocyanor	Inj 15 mg/ml	3×6×20 ml	Cyanide
Dimercaprol	BAL	Inj 50 mg/ml	10×12×2 ml	Arsenic, mercury
Dimethylamino-phenol	4-DMAP	Inj 50 mg/ml	10×5 ml	Hydrogen sulphide
Methylthionine	Metyltionin	Inj 10 mg/ml	2×10×10 ml	Nitrites, nitrobenzene
Obidoxime	Toxogonin	Inj 0.25 g/ml	4×5×1 ml	Organophosphates
Penicillamine	Penicillamin[1]	Tabl 250 mg	3×100 tabl	Arsenic, mercury
Polyethylene glycol 400	Makrogol 400	Sol	10×500 ml	Phenol
Potassium permanganate +sodium bicarbonate	Kaliumper-manganat+ Natrium-bikarbonat	Sol 20 mg/ml +100 mg/ml	10×1000 ml	White (yellow) phosphorus
Sodium thiosulphate	Tiosulfat	Inj 0.15 g/ml	40×10×10 ml	Cyanide
Terbutaline sulphate	Bricanyl Turbuhaler	Inh pulv 0.5 mg/dose	2×200 doses	Irritant gases
Tetracaine chloride	Tetracain-hydrochloride	Eye drops 0.5%	1×12×2 ml	Eye irrigation

[1]*Can be replaced by an equivalent substance or preparation.*

Table 4. *Emergency store of antidotes to be transported to the site of accident. Recommendations in Sweden. The list is updated every second year*

Substance	Preparation		Package	Indication
Adrenaline	Adrenalin	Inj 0.1 mg/ml	5×10 ml	Cyanide
Atropine	Atropin	Inj 0.5 mg/ml	75×20 ml	Organophosphates
Budesonide	Pulmicort Turbuhaler	Inh pulv 400 μg/dose	5×200 doses	Irritant gases
Betamethasone[1]	Betapred	Inj 4 mg/ml	10×5×1 ml	Irritant gases
Calcium gluconate	Hydrofluoric acid burn jelly	Gel 2.5%	10×25 g	Hydrofluoric acid
Calcium-gluconate-lactate	Calcium Sandoz	Efferv tabl 1 g Ca/tabl	10×10 tabl	Hydrofluoric acid
Cobalt edetate	Kelocyanor	Inj 15 mg/ml	2×6×20 ml	Cyanide
Methylthionine	Metyltionin	Inj 10 mg/ml	2×10×10 ml	Nitrites, nitro-benzene
Obidoxime	Toxogonin	Inj 0.25 g/ml	2×5×1 ml	Organophosphates
Polyethylene glycol 400	Makrogol 400	Sol	10×500 ml	Phenol
Polyethylene glycol 400 30%	1 part Makrogol 2 parts water	Sol	2×1000 ml	Phenol (eye irrigation)
Sodium thiosulphate	Tiosulfat	Inj 0.15 g/ml	10×10×10 ml	Cyanide
Terbutaline sulphate	Bricanyl Turbuhaler	Inh pulv 0.5 mg/dose	5×200 doses	Irritant gases
Tetracaine chloride 400	Tetracaine[1] hydrochloride	Eye drops 0.5%	2×12×2 ml	Eye irrigation

[1]*Can be replaced by an equivalent substance or preparation.*

Table 2 a list of antidotes approved by the WHO/EURO Assessor Group. In Tables 3 and 4 the recommendations in Sweden are presented.

Place of treatment

The medical team must only act outside the toxic zone. Eye irrigation during transport might be necessary. The hospital should be prepared to take care of a great number of victims with respiratory difficulties or corrosive burns. A great number of people without symptoms may need observation only for one or two days.

If the hospital is in the toxic zone the ventilation system must be closed immediately.

Registration and follow-up

Proper registration of all exposed persons should be carried out as symptoms may be delayed for some time and exposed persons may need to be recalled. Also for the purpose of follow-up studies, proper registration is important. Measures for blood and urine sampling should also be included in the planning to facilitate diagnosis, management and follow-up studies. This is especially of value in those cases where little information is at hand about toxic effects on humans.

Education

Education on the specific features for chemical accidents should be included on all educational levels for nurses and doctors. Also training programmes and exercises should include chemical accidents.

REFERENCES

(1) Report on a joint WHO/IPCS/CEC meeting, *Prevention of acute chemical poisonings: high risk circumstances*, Environmental Health 28. Copenhagen: WHO/EURO, 1987.
(2) Australian Counter Disaster College Report, *Toxic chemical incidents, Mount Macedon*. Australian Counter Disaster College, 1988.
(3) Bourdeau Ph, Green G, eds. *Methods for assessing and reducing injury from chemical accidents*, SGOMSEC 6/SCOPE 40, IPCS Joint Symposia 11. Chichester: John Wiley & Son, 1989.
(4) WHO/EURO Prevention of Accidents, *Assessor group meetings, Finland and Spain, 1988.*

Further reading

Doyle CJ, Little NE, Ulin LS. Acute exposure to hazardous materials. In: Haddad LM, Winchester JF, eds. *Clinical management of poisoning and drug overdose*. Philadelphia, London, Toronto, Mexico City, Rio de Janeiro, Sydney, Tokyo: W B Saunders, 1983: 250–63.

Hines *et al*. Chemical accidents. In: Baskett P, Weller R, eds. *Medicine for disasters*. London: Wright, 1988: 376–90.

Planned response:
Occupational Health Services

John Ferguson-Smith

Occupational Health, ICI Chemicals & Polymers Ltd, Billingham, Cleveland, UK

In this paper, I should like to consider where an occupational health service fits into the planning of an emergency response to a major chemical disaster. I have been asked to describe the provisions in place in ICI's manufacturing complex in Teesside, in the North East of England, specifically those at my own site, Billingham. I should like to share some aspects of our planning, and more especially consider certain fundamental points that we have learned from our own experience in testing our systems.

The first and most obvious difficulty in defining guidelines for this type of contingency planning is the great diversity of occupational health service resource—variations in size, facilities, available expertise and its location, i.e. whether it is locally based or a central resource. The other question reflects the well established controversy associated with the degree of clinical involvement or treatment provision within any individual occupational health service. Whenever this aspect is discussed, of course, the suspicion always remains that a great deal more in the way of treatment, including emergency treatment, is available than is popularly admitted.

In these terms, it is useful to spend a little time reflecting the question 'why does a company, e.g. ICI, have an occupational health service in the first place?' and does it need to have any particular plan in case of a possible major incident or disaster? Companies lay down health and safety policies, and occupational health services develop objectives and guidelines to fulfil these policy statements.

The ICI situation is a good example. ICI Occupational Health comprises of occupational physicians, nurses, toxicologists and occupational hygienists in various groups in the UK and abroad, with the support of a central UK resource in epidemiology and in association with the Company's extensive Central Toxicology Laboratory in Cheshire. Its responsibilities are international and it has derived these agreed objectives.

The primary objective is to support the business by the prevention of adverse effects on the health of employees, customers, and the general public arising out of the Group's operations. Complementary objectives are to manage any adverse health effects which may occur; to review and evaluate trends in, and contribute to the development of relevant legislation, and to provide timely advice on the scope and implications to the business, including action necessary to meet any

Major chemical disasters—medical aspects of management, edited by Virginia Murray, 1990: Royal Society of Medicine Services International Congress and Symposium Series No. 155, published by Royal Society of Medicine Services Limited.

future requirements; to provide competent, professional, independent advice to management and employees on occupational health matters; to plan and execute programmes of health based research of relevance to the Group's operations; to provide general health care resources, in appropriate circumstances, where it is necessary to supplement the local general medical care facilities; to promote cooperation and good relations with government, regulatory agencies, relevant professional bodies and local communities.

In reviewing these, I have highlighted several points. The primary objective refers to '. . . the prevention of adverse effects on the health of our employees, customers and the general public arising out of the Group's operations'. The emphasis here is *prevention* and that, I suggest, is the way that the majority of occupational health services now see themselves, and perhaps how they gear their resources. Clearly we have a role 'to manage any adverse health effects which may occur' and the objectives also refer to the provision of 'general health care resources, in appropriate circumstances, where it is necessary to supplement the local general medical care facilities'. This reminds us in this discussion of medical management of major chemical accidents to consider the situation of remote sites, particularly overseas. ICI for example has hospitals in isolated sites in three countries (India, Pakistan, Kenya) and here might expect to provide total care of all casualties of a chemical accident.

Thus the planned response in the case of major chemical disaster will not only vary from company to company, or country to country, but it is also liable to vary significantly within the parts of a large or multinational Company. This emphasizes the point that the organization of an occupational health service response to a major chemical incident is commonly based on *local* planning.

The place of an occupational health service within the framework of planned response is therefore not always clear, and this is well illustrated by a slide used in presentations by a colleague in our local county emergency services. This shows a bold structure of the inter-relationship between Police, Fire Service, Ambulance, Hospitals, Public Utilities and County Council Emergency Planning. There is a little box at the periphery of this diagram for 'Occupational Health', which is joined to the rest of the structure by a broken line labelled with a '?'. This typifies what is often the perception from outside the industry (and perhaps sometimes within!).

If we look at our own circumstances on Teesside, ICI Chemicals & Polymers Limited have three principal sites north and south of the River Tees—two of which are adjacent to residential areas. There are two Occupational Health departments based at (i) Wilton and (ii) the department with which I am associated at Billingham. The department at Billingham consists of three medical officers, ten nurses (five of whom are on shifts), paramedical and secretarial staff and first aid back-up from the Site Emergency Services operators (firemen) who have additional training in the specific occupational hazards associated with the chemicals on site. The Billingham Occupational Health department has the support of a regional science resource of six toxicologists and occupational hygienists, and services ICI C&P's Billingham and North Tees Sites, and provides an occupational health service on contract to a group of different chemical processing and chemical storage companies in the Seal Sands area, which are largely built on reclaimed ground towards the mouth of the river. In addition to the large inventory of chemicals held within the area in storage as well as in process, there is also the regular transport of imported materials for process and exported products by road, rail and sea.

The CIMAH 'safety cases' for the Billingham site—ammonia, ammonium nitrate, hydrogen cyanide, acetone cyanohydrin, arsenic, amines, phenol—reflect this variety, and in addition to the toxic hazards associated with fertilizer, cyanide and acrylics, or phenol and amine derivatives production in the Billingham complex, there is the flammable potential of the petroleum products and aromatics at the other ICI site.

Due to the extent of the area, our staff will have the opportunity to deal with minor incidents periodically and we have a number of ambulances deployed across the area and driven by our own firemen/first aiders. Outside of normal day hours, there is a Shift Nursing Officer on duty in the main medical department with a Medical Officer on call 24 hours of every day.

Procedures are laid down for occupational health departments to deal with major incidents and these are part of the general site emergency procedures, and are also tied in with the procedures for the designated receiving hospitals, county emergency services—particularly the ambulance service—and the local authority.

The procedures for major accidents and for toxic releases are practised at regular intervals (usually yearly for a major incident with additional exercises through the year for testing the responses to a toxic release alarm). The major exercises are carried out 'live' in conjunction with the Police, Fire Brigade and Ambulance services. Various scenarios are envisaged. As an example, major plant structural damage or failure is presumed with a 'script' which escalates as time goes on, introducing additional complications to the emergency response teams in control of the incident and those on the ground. 'Casualties' are enlisted and behave (and are made up) in a realistic fashion. In this type of situation, the occupational health staff are entirely involved. We see ourselves as the first-line medical response and we expect the first casualties on site will be assessed and given necessary emergency treatment by occupational health staff with the Site Emergency Services first aiders. Depending on the time of day or night, the initial reaction may be controlled by a nursing officer while the duty medical officer and additional medical/nursing staff are called. The site medical centre acts as the casualty clearing station. With the declaration of a major accident, an ambulance service liaison officer moves into the medical centre as part of their deployment at the site.

In this paper, I shall not go into further detail of 'who does what and where'. The detail of this has to be worked out individually according to the type of establishment and available resources. At the end of our major exercises, we have a debriefing session—usually the next day—when all involved site departments, and the county emergency services, local authority officers and also the organizers of the 'casualties' discuss their views on what went well and what requires improvement.

An example of a development from this debriefing session is that the ambulance service now control all transportation of casualties whether in their own or ICI's ambulances. The provision of personal protective equipment and decontamination procedures within the ambulance service has lent itself to this interchangeability of resource.

It is clear that advice on planning an occupational health service response at site level has to be in a rather general form. The wide variation of in-house resources and local facilities, e.g. hospitals, do not allow a more detailed prescription, and I should like to concentrate on two main aspects:

1. Triage and treatment
2. Information and communication

When the function of a particular occupational health service is examined in the overall plan to manage a major incident, there may or may not be a practical role in performing triage or providing treatment. However, there should always be a role in providing good information, and communicating that information to the relevant areas and authorities.

If there is involvement in the treatment of initial casualties, or triage in the multi casualty situation, the overriding consideration is to match the expected performance of the particular occupational health team with the abilities and capabilities of its personnel, equipment and resources, given that there is perhaps often a natural temptation to be overambitious. In this vein, there are three broad aspects to consider—equipment, training and control communications. It is perhaps stating the obvious to say that equipment has to be appropriate, accessible and provided in adequate quantities. This is particularly true in the case of emergency medical equipment; from dressings, drugs, intravenous fluids, and infusion sets to resuscitators and defibrillators. Provision of equipment of any level or degree of sophistication, from basic to complicated, must go hand in hand with comprehensive instruction of occupational health service staff and the opportunity for regular training. There is absolutely no point in having the necessary equipment if, in any emergency, personnel are not immediately clear how to use it. The same goes for personal protective equipment and self contained breathing apparatus. Personnel must be conversant with the equipment and practised in its use. Staff in our department, for example, have breathing apparatus as a standard part of their emergency gear and they are periodically given refresher training and tested in their use of it.

The question that arises time after time in major emergency exercises is the adequacy of communication and I make no apology for belabouring this essential subject. In the initial stages of a major incident, alerting and calling-out additional medical and nursing staff may be a priority. A call-out procedure must be established and known to all personnel who may be involved. In our areas this takes the form of lists which work either in cascade fashion (each person phones the next available doctor/nurse down the list before leaving home themselves) or personnel are called out by duty staff in the other main site not affected by the incident, again in a specified order. In planning an occupational health service response, a practical approach has to be taken to the number of staff that one might expect to alert at any particular time. When we test our own call-out systems out of hours by a telephone exercise, we get a marked variation in the number of staff who would have been available. For example, early on a Sunday morning there would probably be a high percentage available, whereas mid evening on a Friday might yield a low response.

Good communications are paramount for those managing an incident in the control of those 'at the front', mobile units for example, and for the return flow of adequate up-to-the-minute information to the centre. A breakdown of communications soon leads to restriction in efficiency of emergency response. Like all aspects of a planned response, this has to be anticipated and tested. Examples of problems are radio 'dead-spots' on a chemical works due to buildings or plant structures, or congestion of emergency radio channels when an incident gets into full swing. These types of potential problems must all be foreseen and tested and adequate provision, whether telephone lines, radios, messengers or whatever, made to deal with any scale of incident.

The Occupational Health function during a major incident requires a direct line of communication with the Site Emergency Control Centre or its equivalent. This is the designated centre where those senior mangers who are dealing with the incident are based, with the appropriate back-up staff and resources. Here also the local authority emergency services—Fire Brigade, Police, Ambulance Service—

set up their control centres in close proximity to one another. This entire group requires ready, accurate information on the (initially acute) toxic effects of chemicals that may be released or generated (e.g. by combustion) and which may be encountered, and also feed-back information on casualty numbers, health effects already observed, etc.

Central coordination with the emergency services as part of overall control of an incident has just been described, but liaison directly between Occupational Health and particularly the Ambulance Service may be logistically appropriate. For the reasons outlined earlier, we now have permanently installed Ambulance Service radio equipment in our own department. An ambulance liaison officer moves into the department when a major emergency is declared and the overall control of ambulance transport, whether local authority or company vehicles, would be coordinated through this officer.

During a major chemical incident, the other essential area where there is a need for the communication of information, at as early a stage as is practicable, is to the hospitals who may receive patients who have been, or believe they may have been, affected. This information should also be passed to the community functions, for example the Environmental Health Medical Officer, and made available for general practitioners on-call, particularly where an incident is not restricted or contained well within a plant area. Occupational health services have a clear and vital role in providing the clinicians who have to assess and treat patients who may result from a chemical incident with the available toxicological information and existing knowledge on expected human health effects and modes of treatment.

This aspect was well illustrated by an actual incident which occurred a couple of years ago in a fertilizer production area. There was a fire with thermal decomposition of a compound fertilizer material, with emission of a cloud containing a percentage of nitrogen oxides which moved across the adjacent river. A major emergency was declared as the incident had the potential to affect the public outside the factory. The number of people affected was limited. A total of 17 people were admitted to hospital for treatment or observation at various times during and after the incident, and 14 were discharged the next day. These were predominantly company employees, policemen, seamen from a ship berthed close by, and later the following day, two firemen. Three of the employees were admitted to Intensive Care, and, sadly, one subsequently died. In addition to the duty medical officer who was called in to the incident, two other medical officers were contacted and also came in. The immediately affected persons who were on the plant had been treated and transferred to hospital within a short time, and there was no further 'clinical' need. However, the three medical officers established liaison with the hospital consultants which was maintained during the duration of the incident and continued subsequently while patients remained in hospital. The local Accident and Emergency departments and the general practitioner deputising service were briefed on the extent and possible effects of the emission. As soon as an environmental and analytical evaluation was made, this was shared with the medical officers, who were able to pass on an assessment of any potential medical effects in the community. This communication was clearly valuable and for example contributed to the rationale of whether individuals were admitted to hospital for observation or not. Doctors in the community who might encounter anxious patients were much better informed and able to make an assessment, and offering reassurance where appropriate.

This incident, though very limited in its extent, is described to underline from a practical viewpoint the importance of establishing communication and expeditiously passing on all relevant information. Occupational health services are multi disciplined, but as I said at the start, vary a great deal in their composition and resources. The roles of occupational physicians, nurses, toxicologists and occupational hygienists in managing this aspect of a major chemical incident has to be separately assessed and defined for each location.

I have described aspects of a scheme organized on the basis of a manufacturing complex with a large employee population, which involves the occupational health service in first-line response on site to a major chemical incident. I have emphasized the importance of occupational health staff being trained to use, as well as possessing, appropriate equipment and being given the regular opportunity to demonstrate that ability. Nevertheless, whether that all forms part of another occupational health service's planned response or not, the role of the occupational health service in providing good information on the potential health implications of a major chemical incident is beyond question. Information has to be passed to emergency services, local authorities and company managers and be expressed in an understandable way, and close liaison with outside medical colleagues has to be established. The question already raised in this symposium is the quality of that information and whether it is adequate to meet for example the emergency physician's needs. Limited information is better than no information at all, but the resources to hold or obtain adequately detailed information must be part of the planned response.

In terms of the future, occupational health services may be reviewing their role within major accident procedures, particularly the initial medical role on site, and this is currently under reconsideration in our area. The facilities of local Accident and Emergency departments coupled with local ambulance resources—including the aspects of training of staff, provision of specific treatments and stocking of (the limited number of) appropriate antidotes—will feature highly in these reviews and influence their outcome.

Further reading

Health & Safety Executive. *The Control of Industrial Major Accident Hazard Regulations 1984* (CIMAH): *further guidance on emergency plans.* Health & Safety series booklet HS(G)25. London: HMSO, 1985.

Pocchiari F, Silano V. Contingency planning for and response to emergencies and accidents involving toxic chemicals. *Chemosphere* 1983; **12**: 745–8.

World Health Organization. European Co-operation on Environmental Health Aspects of the Control of Chemicals—Interim Document 1. *Planning emergency response systems for chemical accidents.* Copenhagen: IPCS, 1981.

Planned response:
Local Authority

Martin Sibson

Essex County Council, Chelmsford, UK

INTRODUCTION

I have been invited to describe the Local Authority responsibility for the preparation of a planned response to a major chemical disaster. I will approach the subject in the following way:

1. Describe the job of an Emergency Planning Officer against the background of the All Hazards Approach
2. Describe briefly what a Local Authority is—and what it is not
3. Identify the statutory powers of a Local Authority for civil emergency planning—or lack of them
4. Examine the task of preparing a plan with examples of 'best practice' and some obstacles to our efforts
5. Give some impressions of the recent Home Office Review and other initiatives which may make a positive contribution to effective response to major disasters, including those with chemical or pollution consequences

ROLE AND RESPONSIBILITY OF AN
EMERGENCY PLANNING OFFICER

A Principal Emergency Planning Officer is usually responsible to his Chief Executive for the preparation of plans for Civil Defence in the event of hostilities and for Civil Emergencies in peacetime under the umbrella title of Civil Protection.

This is epitomized by the All Hazards Approach in which it is now acknowledged that many of the skills and resources needed for a planned response are common to both requirements.

The nature of the risk and the consequences of the event can be similar whether the chemical or biological hazard is caused by a deliberate act of war or terrorism, or by accident. Only the reasons and, perhaps, the scale would be different.

Major chemical disasters—medical aspects of management, edited by Virginia Murray, 1990: Royal Society of Medicine Services International Congress and Symposium Series No. 155, published by Royal Society of Medicine Services Limited.

THE LOCAL AUTHORITY—WHAT KIND OF ANIMAL?

The term 'local authority' is used to describe an organization which is separate from some of the principal emergency services. This is not so. Most policemen and firemen belong to forces or brigades which are part of their own local authority at County or equivalent level, although the unique constitutional position of the police is recognized. The Ambulance Service is, of course, a Department of Health responsibility.

Here it is essential to distinguish between the two tiers of local government in England and Wales, those of County and District (inc. Borough) Councils and the division of functions between them.

The County Council is responsible for the provision of education, social services, libraries and maintaining highways (unless there is a District Agency). It is also the principal Civil Defence authority. Equivalent bodies have succeeded the former Metropolitan Authorities (e.g. London, West Midlands, Greater Manchester and Merseyside) and their emergency planning is carried out by Fire and Civil Defence Authorities.

District Councils are responsible for housing (and the homeless), household waste disposal, environmental health and local planning and development controls (a most important function when considering the location of premises handling hazardous substances).

When commencing duties in my present post, I was impressed by the professional attitude, skill and goodwill of many staff and the wide range and scale of operation of local authority services; matters which are often taken for granted.

Another important consideration is that it is elected Members who make policy decisions and it is advisable to keep them informed about the plans we commend to them. They represent a vital link with the community and their support is to be preferred to disinterest or opposition based upon lack of knowledge of the facts.

ROLES AND RESPONSIBILITIES—COORDINATION AND CONTROL

There has been very limited statutory authority on the question of coordination and control of action by emergency services and others at the scene of major accident or natural disaster. Exceptions include the CIMAH Regulations 1984.

Different organizations have their own arrangements for the most effective performance of their functions. For example, Fire Service Acts have always been most specific in describing the powers and duties of firemen in relation to fire prevention and fire fighting.

The police have tended to rely upon one or more of their general responsibilities for the protection of life and property, the preservation of law and order and maintaining the free passage of the highway.

The local Government Act 1972, S138 (as amended) provides *powers* (not duties) to County and District Councils so that where an emergency or disaster involving destruction of, or danger to, life and property occurs or is imminent or there is reasonable ground for expecting such an event which may affect their area or inhabitants, the Council *may*:

1. Incur expenditure . . . calculated to avert, alleviate or eradicate the effects or potential effects of the event; and
2. Make grants or loans in certain circumstances.

Where such action has been taken and expenditure incurred the Secretary of State for the Environment must be notified.

In this brief selection of legislation touching arrangements in the event of emergencies I must include the Health and Safety at Work Act 1974, the full purpose of which is to promote the health, safety and welfare of people in the workplace and control of dangerous substances and certain emissions into the atmosphere, and the Food and Environment Protection Act 1985.

Finally, there is the Civil Protection in Peacetime Act 1986 which allows the use of resources and facilities provided for Civil Defence purposes in the event of civil emergencies.

However, there is very little help if we are looking for statutory guidance on the question of defining roles and relationships when more than one service or organization is involved.

The Home Office Consolidated Circular entitled Emergency Planning Guidance to Local Authorities (EPGLA) 1985 SS22–24 recognizes and describes well the respective roles of the principal emergency services, local health or other authorities, other essential services and voluntary associations as well as how to obtain military assistance, as shown in this abstract:

> 'Local authorities have a primary role to maintain their own services and help people in distress; secondly, a general duty to *co-ordinate* what is being done by the various organizations which are giving help.
>
> The appropriate emergency services would direct operational activities at the scene. In general officers of the local authority would obtain additional manpower or specialized equipment; provide temporary accommodation; meals and other forms of relief . . . .
>
> The police would have an operational role in such matters as evacuation, crowd and traffic control, public safety and advice and facilitating the activities of other services. Consultation with the police will be an important aspect of planning by local authorities.'

Why should any Local Authority make plans to cope with civil emergencies in their area when there is no statutory duty or funding to do so?

You will recall that the Local Government Act 1972 S138 was loosely worded, providing *powers* which are rarely used. On the other hand, most authorities recognize that they have a moral obligation to do so—it is an extension of their normal responsibilities to:

1. *Prevent* or reduce the probability of accidents
2. Mitigate the effects should a major accident occur
3. Restore normality and rehabilitate as soon as possible

These obligations coincide with the phases of any major disaster as follows:

Before—prevention

1. Planning and developmental controls
2. Consultation and liaison with site and transport operators
3. Preparing, maintaining and exercizing emergency plans

Response—mitigation of the effects at the time

1. Early alerting to assist mobilization and coordination of support by other essential services, military assistance and contribution from voluntary associations
2. Close support for the emergency services at the scene as required, e.g. resources to assist direction/diversion of traffic
3. Provision of care and welfare for those affected e.g. through Reception and Rest Centres, liaison with Police Casualty Bureau

After—restore and rehabilitate

1. Short and long-term measures including rehousing—drying out premises/stock, clearance of roads, repair/demolition of property
2. Counselling and other social support

THE PLANNED RESPONSE TOWARDS ACHIEVING THESE OBJECTIVES

Before embarking upon the task of planning a response to major accidents we need to ask questions such as:

- *What* is the *purpose* of the plan?
- *Who* is it *for*?
- *When* will it be *activated*?
- *How* will it be *implemented*?

The answers will help us to determine whether it is to be an 'on-site'; or an 'off-site' plan or both and whether it will be in generic form or specific to the site or event. Whatever the answers—there are factors common to each.

Many different interests may be reflected in the need for making contingency plans and will, quite properly, be primarily concerned to meet their own responsibilities and requirements.

However, there is the very real danger that such planning could take place in isolation with the result that the overall plan is not integrated but merely a collection of individual interpretations of respective roles. Under those circumstances effective coordination at the time of need is virtually impossible.

One plan?

The combined approach offers the preferred course to achieve the concept of 'one plan', that plan having component parts which can respond in accordance with a developing or changing situation. It is a plan where the roles and relationships have been discussed and where interfaces have been identified. Only through consultation and liaison between all participants can there be better understanding of the whole picture—rather like putting the last piece in a jigsaw puzzle. Coordination at the scene of the major disaster can only be achieved through writing it into the plan from the outset.

An example of how this approach has been used in response to the requirements of the Control of Industrial Major Accident Hazards Regulations 1984 is given in a Case Study on the North East Thames Combined Accident Plan (NETCAP) (Appendix A together with a profile of the area and an account of the 'decade of scrutiny').

The Thameside between Corringham and Purfleet has been covered in a similar manner with some 16 sites included in NETCAP II.

The medical aspects of Local Authority response to major chemical hazards

The site operator is responsible for taking measures to educate and train his workers in respect of the risks and the consequences should things go wrong such as the method of warning those who are likely to be effected and of the action to be taken—to 'shut-down', to shelter or to evacuate and to give advice as to medical precautions or treatment, including details of designated hospitals.

This information should be published in the 'on-site' and the 'off-site' plans for the benefit of the emergency services to (a) protect them in the course of their duties and (b) provide the basis for advice and guidance to the public, whether residential, working nearby or passing through.

Some advice may have already been given to those who live within a stated distance of a specified site. This would be given by notices displayed on the site perimeter and by letter (as required under CIMAH Reg 12—examples given) and be reinforced by personal delivery which provides the opportunity for further explanation if required.

Public alert or warning systems

There are some instances of site warnings which are also capable of alerting the public in the close vicinity of the installation and information on this would be included in the letter referred to earlier.

Here it is worth referring to a publication of 1978 entitled *Canvey Island—Advice to Householders* where an alert can be given by way of a varied signal over the Wartime Warning system (in the event of flooding or industrial accident). The prevailing situation with regard to Public Alert Systems is the subject of research by a CEPO Society Working Group and by the Society of Industrial Emergency Service Officers (SIESO). A Government review of the United Kingdom Warning and Monitoring Service has referred to the possible application to civil emergencies.

However, it may well be that, to avoid confusion, the best standing advice should be simple, unambiguous and reinforced by police warnings especially through the media, local and national giving the most up-to-date advice such as to shelter by staying put unless or until told to the contrary, using basic words like 'Go-indoors, close doors and windows and wait until you hear further'.

What are the sources for the most reliable information in a chemical incident?

In the case of an incident at a 'notifiable' site it is relatively straightforward. We should already have an inventory of substances, quantities, processes used and the measures to be adopted in the event of an accident. It is not quite so easy with a hitherto unidentified operator, whether *in situ* or in a linear example. Then we need early information from the scene to assist in the assessment of the risk and identification of the best measures to be applied.

Fortunately, we are often able to draw upon schemes such as Hazchem or Chemsafe and legislation that requires tankers, drums or containers to be marked in accordance with a Code which identifies the substance and the appropriate response. There is also the contribution made by the experience of local authority scientific officers who, in some areas, advise the Fire and Rescue Services.

Another valuable aid is a relatively new facility known as Chemet which is a scheme introduced by the Meteorological Office to provide advice on patterns of expected behaviour of plumes following a toxic release into the atmosphere.

CONCLUSIONS

Finally I would like to give some brief impressions of the recent Civil Emergencies Review arranged by the Home Office and held in November 1988.

The emphasis was on the response phase and examined the present arrangements of the emergency services, local authorities, government department and other public agencies and the voluntary services. The Health Service was represented by Ambulance Officers, an Emergency Planner and a doctor from an Accident and Emergency Department of a London Hospital.

The Home Secretary has made a statement in the House of Commons but most of the salient issues have already been touched upon in my paper and it is probably an opportune moment to repeat them:

1. Liaison, coordination and control at Local Government level
2. Involvement of all participants, including voluntary associations, in the planning process from an early stage
3. Casualty Bureaux
4. Databases
5. Training and exercises
6. Legislation needs?
7. Counselling

Other initiatives

1. The appointment of a Civil Emergencies Adviser by government.
2. Implementation of further amendments to the CIMAH Regulations.
3. Further developments through the European Commission including the recognition of the concept Civil Protection.
4. Interest expressed by the Organisation for Economic and Cultural Development in the subject of public safety and information to the public.

Most of what we need to carry out our responsibilities to prepare emergency plans so that we can respond effectively in the event of a disaster is already known or available. What is sometimes lacking is recognition of the need to work together in a positive manner in what is a joint enterprise. I hope that this paper provides the reader with an insight into how Local Authorities should be responding to this worthwhile and rewarding task.

Appendix A

CASE STUDY

Control of Industrial Major Accident Hazards Regulations 1984
Preparation of Off-site Emergency Plans. (Reg 11)
The North East Thames Combined Accident Plan (NETCAP)

The County Emergency Planning Officer for Essex describes the approach by his County towards the preparation of off-site emergency plans for a specific area for reasons which were geographical, historical and because of the similar nature of the risks arising from the hazardous substances handled and the industrial processes used.

In Essex almost half of the sites identified by the response to the Notification of Installations Handling Hazardous Substances (NIHHS) Regulations 1982 are to be found along the Thames between Canvey and Purfleet. The close location of a number of industrial sites in the area of Canvey Island and part of Thurrock, on the north east bank of the Thames which are likely to be classified as 'top tier' under the CIMAH Regulations and the publication of the Report on the Inquiry into the British Gas Methane Terminal in May 1983 afforded the opportunity for a 'combined approach' to the task.

Over the past decade, the risks associated with industrial processes and development on Canvey Island have been the subject of close scrutiny and several reports including those by the Health and Safety Executive of 1978 and 1981 so that when the Inspector recommended, in the most recent case, that the emergency arrangements for the area should be reviewed the task was justifiably given high priority.

A Member Working Group of the County Council with representatives from Castle Point and Thurrock District Councils required that this review be undertaken. However, it was accepted that this could be carried out concurrently with the duties to be laid upon the local authority to make off site emergency plans under the provisions of the then forthcoming CIMAH Regulations as five of the six industrial sites on Canvey and in the Corringham area of Thurrock would be designated 'top-tier' sites whilst another agreed to take part on a voluntary basis.

A Steering Group was established in December 1983 which consisted of senior officers from the County and District Councils, the principal emergency services and other public authorities as well as from industry, whose goodwill and cooperation from an early stage was vital.

A high degree of commitment to the need to work for a unified emergency plan for the area was agreed in accordance with the following aim:

'To achieve a combined approach on emergency planning between the emergency services, industry, local authorities and other public services in the event of a major accident involving hazardous substances at one or more of the specified industrial installations on Canvey Island or in the Corringham area of Thurrock in which the consequences may not be contained within the site boundary of the installations.'

The principal objectives were stated as:

1. to define the area and identify the sites
2. to define the roles of participants
3. to establish procedures for implementing the Combined Accident Plan

The Plan was to be North East Thames Combined Accident Plan (NETCAP) and it would have two parts.

Part I is descriptive and the information would be available to be seen by the public. It includes a profile of the area and of the industries involved and a section dealing with the management of risk in which the nature of the hazards present and their possible consequences off-site in the event of an accident are described together with information on advice/warnings for the public. The roles of the emergency services and the other public authorities which could be involved are described.

Part II contains the procedure for implementing NETCAP operationally and consists of three stages:

1. NETCAP—Alert
2. NETCAP—Confirmed
3. NETCAP—Cancel

Supporting information includes:

1. Cascade 'call down' system for alerting key personnel
2. Maps showing details of advance direction signing of routes for emergency service vehicles and of rendezvous points which have been designated on a County wide basis
3. Matrix giving details of resources available on a mutual aid basis for use by other industrial installations and/or emergency services

Plans of a site-specific kind have not been overlooked—from Harwich Harbour down to isolated 'one man and a boy' outfits which handle agrochemicals in quantities over the threshold level.

The nuclear industry deserves a special mention in the light of developments post Chernobyl (quote from the County Emergency Planning Officer (CEPO) Society Nuclear Site—Emergency Arrangements 2nd Report and Addendum July 1988).

APPENDIX A.1

Profile of Canvey Island and part of Thurrock

This area of low lying salt marshland extends for about nine miles along the north bank of the Thames and is about two and a half miles at its widest across Canvey Island. Canvey Island is divided from the mainland on the Thurrock or west side by Holehaven Creek whilst two other linked creeks complete the separation to the north. It was reclaimed from the sea during the 17th Century by a Dutch engineer after having been split off from the mainland through the effects of successive high tides.

The island has a long history of severe flooding—the 'Great Tide' of 1953 being the cruel climax. An extensive programme of improved sea defences has just been completed and includes 21.5 kilometres of raised sea wall and three movable barriers, which are part of the Thames Barrier scheme, are located between the island and the mainland.

The population of some 3500 before 1939 has risen to about 35 000 with new housing still being built and further proposed industrial and leisure development. It is a seaside resort with a number of caravan and holiday camp sites.

Residential areas are to the eastern half of the island, light industry is sited towards the southwest and the tank storage installations of Texas Limited, London and Coastal Oil Wharves Limited and The British Gas Methane Terminal are located beside the Thames, where the deep water shipping channel passes close to the bank and large ships can be moored at the jetties there. Two roads link the island to the mainland; the original road over Benfleet Creek to the north and the more recently built Canvey Way over to Pitsea.

The part of Thurrock covered in this profile is almost entirely used for industrial purposes and there is no residential development in the near vicinity.

The two large oil refineries of Shell UK and Mobil Oil Company Limited are located on the riverside; a major extension has recently been completed at the latter site. The liquified petroleum gases cylinder filling plant of Calor Gas Limited is located at Coryton to the north of the refineries. There are good road and rail links direct to the refineries.

With acknowledgment to the HMSO publication *Canvey-summary of an investigation of potential hazards from operations in the Canvey Island/Thurrock area* (as amended).

APPENDIX A.2

Canvey—a decade of scrutiny

Over the past decade industry on Canvey Island has been subject to a series of investigations and four Reports have been published in the five years up to 1983. The events are summarized below:

1972

Construction of the Occidental Oil Refinery commenced but stopped in 1975 to allow for a major design study review which was concluded during the period of the investigation carried out by the Health and Safety Executive between 1976–78. Meanwhile the local planning authority refused permission for additional refinery facilities on their site. Storage tanks and a jetty which have not been used can be seen there.

1973

United Refineries Limited were granted planning permission to build an oil refinery on two areas of land on the west side of Canvey Island but construction was not commenced because of an enquiry into the possible revocation of planning consent.

March 1976

The Secretaries of State for the Environment and Employment requested that an investigation be carried out into the risks to health and safety associated with various installations, both existing and proposed, on Canvey Island and the neighbouring part of Thurrock.

June 1978

The Health and Safety Executive published its Report on an investigation of potential hazards from operations in the area.

March 1981

Report of the enquiry into the proposed United Refineries Limited Oil refinery at Canvey Island published. The Secretary of State for the Environment announced that there would be an urgent public enquiry into the British Gas Methane Terminal on Canvey Island.

September 1981

Report on the Safety of Operations and Management Arrangements at the British Gas Methane Terminal published.

May 1983

Report on Canvey Island-British Gas Methane Terminal published. The Secretaries of State for the Environment and for Energy announced that the Methane Gas Terminal should be allowed to continue in operation at its present capacity. At the same time the Secretary of State for the Environment stated that he did not propose to revoke a planning permission granted in 1973 to United Refineries Limited for a new oil refinery west of Canvey Road, Canvey Island.

July 1989

Site sold with a view to major residential and leisure development.

Planned response:
Civil Defence

John Stealey

Home Office, London, UK

The Civil Defence Act of 1948 includes in its definition of civil defence '. . . provision of any measures not amounting to actual combat for affording defence against any form of hostile attack by a foreign power, or for depriving any form of hostile attack by a foreign power of the whole or part of its effect, whether the measures are taken before, at or after the time of attack . . .'.

This is very specific legislation and relates directly to war (or hostile attack). In recent years there have been considerable additions to the Act in the form of Regulations to widen the powers of local authorities in interpreting their responsibilities for civil defence planning. In 1983, Regulations placed duties on local authorities to carry out a number of duties including to provide and equip emergency control centres, train their staff and make a variety of plans.

The Civil Protection in Peacetime Act, 1986, allows local authorities to make use of any of their civil defence resources in taking action which is calculated to avert, alleviate or eradicate the effects of any event even if unconnected with any form of hostile attack. In addition, authorities may make, review and revise plans so as to allow the use of their civil defence resources in connection with any emergency or disaster which may occur or become imminent. No single organization is responsible in the United Kingdom for dealing with major accidents or natural disasters. Governments over many years have decided that a national disaster force or organization would not improve existing arrangements which rely on immediate assistance being given by the emergency services such as police, fire and ambulance. These services could be supplemented where necessary by local, health and other public authorities. If assistance is required it is drawn in from surrounding areas; perhaps this might be viewed as a series of concentric circles, each one having a larger area from which to draw resources. Central Government coordination is available if necessary and this is a task which falls primarily to the Cabinet Office; the principle there is that a Central Government Department acts as 'lead Department' with further resources being mobilized and coordinated through Cabinet Office if needed. This is the framework on which all planning has been based so far.

Major chemical disasters—medical aspects of management, edited by Virginia Murray, 1990: Royal Society of Medicine Services International Congress and Symposium Series No. 155, published by Royal Society of Medicine Services Limited.

There are a large number of people involved in civil defence planning today and therefore there is a very marked requirement for coordination. Central Government role in coordination is through the Home Office and Cabinet Office then on to the local authorities, the emergency services, who are necessarily in the front line of dealing with emergencies, the public utilities, armed services and voluntary bodies. One of the volunteer groups for whom Home Office has responsibility in their training are the scientific advisers. Local authorities are encouraged to recruit scientific staff from a wide range of disciplines and who are employed in a variety of professional and academic posts. They are trained in aspects of wartime duty particularly in looking at weapons effects, analysing data on damage and casualties and the development of operational research techniques which can be applied to decision making and evaluation of post-attack options such as mobilization and utilization of vital resources. The Home Office also appoints a number of Regional Scientific Advisers, many from senior academic posts in Universities, who would have a wartime role somewhat akin to that of the local authority Scientific Adviser but who would be stationed at Regional Government Headquarters throughout the country.

One of the main areas of civil defence planning, which might be linked to large toxic chemical releases such as Seveso and Bhopal, is that of chemical warfare and protection. Much of this is in the process of current policy development; nevertheless, there are lessons already learnt from which to draw some experience and knowledge at least to help frame the sorts of questions which need answering. Furthermore, the planning assumptions on which civil defence is based are changing rapidly, moving away from a singular stance on a nuclear threat to include a period of tension and conventional war. This type of conventional attack, in which high explosive is used, could result in the disruption of chemical plant and storage sites and the release of large quantities of toxic chemicals into the atmosphere. It should also be noted that a period of conventional war may well include attacks with chemical warfare agents and whilst this is not a major threat against city targets its use in certain areas cannot be ruled out.

The chemical agents could be delivered by bombs, missiles or spray and their effects would be to kill or incapacitate when inhaled or picked up in contact with the skin. Once released into the atmosphere they can drift downwind and contaminate large areas several miles away from initial targets. It is important to state that the Government believes the best way of dealing with this threat is through a comprehensive international ban on chemical weapons; however, it is examining ways of detecting and monitoring the presence of chemical agents and warning the population who may be in danger. It is also considering what protective measures can be taken and advice to the population sheltering in their homes. The Government is actively considering the problems of chemical warfare but much has still to be done.

In addition, there are aspects of the 'all hazards' emergency planning which the Home Office is considering. The broader context of emergency planning links between planning for peace and war and particularly with the focus on the kinds of disasters which can occur such as industrial accidents and natural disasters. The Civil Protection in Peacetime Act, 1986, enables civil defence resources to be used in the mitigation of peacetime disasters allowing dual use of planning, staff facilities and equipment in local authorities. This Act must be seen in a realistic context for there are differences of scale and dimension in planning for wartime and peacetime emergencies and one cannot be extended indefinitely into the other. Mention should also be made of the public information programmes which have been carried out and, particularly the production of a quarterly magazine, *Civil*

Protection, which is edited by the Home Office. It has a growing circulation of about 50 000 copies per print run. It gives a good flavour of current development in civil defence and civil protection.

In the last few years this country has witnessed a catalogue of major disasters ranging from the Bradford fire and Zeebrugge through to Piper Alpha, Lockerbie and the recent air crash on the M1 near East Midlands airport. The most important point in this catalogue of disaster is the operational response and there is general public agreement that this response is very well organized in this country and reflects how the emergency services, sustained and supported by local authorities and voluntary organisations, carry out their tasks.

There has been a great deal of thought within the Home Office in recent months on how to draw out full lessons from the disasters and to review the structure which exists at present for handling these disasters. Much of the study has looked at the balance between local and national responses and this is a crucial area being considered by Central Government. Some of the thoughts were put together in a consultation paper, issued by Home Office last year. It was discussed with a variety of operational services and culminated in a seminar at the Civil Defence College (recently re-named the Emergency Planning College) in November last year, where about 70 senior officers concerned with handling disasters debated the present position. Ministers are now considering the conclusions to be drawn from the exercise*.

To summarize the position to date: the UK has no national disaster squad and the range of disasters which have occurred in recent years have been handled by the appropriate emergency services who direct operational activities at the scene and who have shown this to be a working system. It must also be remembered that Police, Fire services, and local authorities make plans for dealing with major accidents which are exercised and revised on a regular basis. It is not a case, therefore, of trying to put together a system as and when emergencies arise. And, of course, part of the planning includes the involvement of local health authorities and the arrangements they have for handling mass casualty inflow.

Most of the disasters so far considered are bounded geographically into a relatively small area and that once the disaster has struck the problems are concerned more with clearing the area, identifying injured and dead and organizing casualty bureaux, maintaining communication data on update reports for people making enquiries, keeping routes for entry and exit open to emergency services and liaising with local authorities, voluntary bodies and other services to provide support. The disaster incident tends to be a relatively short timescale where the major problem is clearing up after the event. There is, however, one group of accidents which are time displaced and these concern the spread of toxic materials by the wind over large areas. This may, of course, be on an international scale such as Chernobyl but is more likely to be spread over a few miles from a site. Once a release of toxic agent has occurred it poses a threat for a considerable time thereafter.

The Bhopal and Seveso incidents certainly focused attention on the problems of toxic chemical release and the latter led to an International Study and the Seveso Directive. This was taken up in the development of regulations in the UK known as the Control of Industrial Major Accident Hazards (CIMAH) Regulations 1984, which require local authorities to draw up emergency plans in conjunction with the operators of the sites (1,2). Under these Regulations industry is required to prepare safety cases related to the substances it stores on site which is a time

---

*Since this lecture was given the Home Office has appointed Mr David Brook to be the Civil Emergencies Adviser reporting directly to the Home Secretary.

consuming and skilled task. However, as our society becomes more complex, relying on industrial processes then the opportunity for accidents increases. It is the essence of the CIMAH Regulations to apply risk analysis which takes into account a probability factor and aims to reduce both the probability of accidents happening and the hazard they present if they do occur.

Knowledge of meteorology is an important aspect in determining the spread of toxic vapours. Recently, the Meteorological Office has developed a scheme for providing meteorological data appropriate to peacetime chemical incidents. This is known as CHEMET. The system describes downwind threat territory using data on cloud cover (and hence sunlight), temperature and humidity, rainfall, wind speed and direction together with an atmospheric stability rating based on the Pasquill determinations. Although this is, of course, important information it should be borne in mind that under neutral meteorological conditions wind speeds might vary between say 3.5 and 7.0 metres/second. Taking an average of 5.0 metres/second the leading edge of a cloud will have travelled three kilometres in 10 minutes. This is not a long time for decision making. Warning is paramount in this situation. Precise details of the toxic material, its persistency, toxicity and physical characteristics may have to wait until later. CHEMET is a good service for providing information to police and fire services who have to approach a contaminated area and will be useful for identifying risk areas and possible evacuation areas. However, there are errors in any such system. For example, defining the type of chemical agent used is very difficult. Precise measurements on meteorological conditions are more reliable but up-to-date forecasts are important. Finally, the models used to assess downwind distance are usually those for dispersion of neutral buoyancy gases over flat, grassy terrain. Increased ground roughness lengths and heat island effects of cities both contribute to greater turbulence but also lead to still, stagnant areas and pockets where dilution may not occur.

One of the best ways of providing protection is to evacuate the area downwind of the hazard. Often these types of hazard might require great numbers of people to be evacuated. The US Civil Defence Organisation (FEMA) reviewed cases of evacuations due to chemical accidents in the period of 1980–1984 (3). Such events were not rare; they reviewed some 300 cases and found the frequency was about one event per every six days. However, this was a skew distribution on geographical basis where industrial cities had a higher frequency than the more rural areas. However, train and truck spills contributed quite highly. Nevertheless, all accidents were handled as state or local emergencies.

Closer to home there was a large release of noxious nitrogen oxide vapour at Nantes in France in 1987 (4). Here some 850 tons of solid fertiliser caught fire which spread a toxic cloud 13×5 kilometres downwind. At least 25 000 people had to be evacuated.

The Bhopal incident in December 1984 was a release of methyl isocyanate in gaseous form (5). This was a non-ignition source in which four major safety systems either failed to operate or were ineffective. The expected number of deaths from this disaster were thought to be around 2600 and over 170 000 people had to receive treatment. A number of factors contributed to this disaster. Firstly, the safety systems did not operate. Secondly, the meteorological conditions at the time of the incident (0030–0130 hours) may have produced still, or static, air very characteristic of a stable inversion layer which often occurs after sunset when there has been highly daytime insolation. Furthermore, the areas where most victims lived were shanty towns with high population densities and poor quality houses having high rates of ventilation. Therefore, inside concentrations soon reached those of the outside and lethal dosages were quickly reached.

In January 1987 a chemical tanker spill in Southampton resulted in the evacuation of 500 people (6). Again, the local problem was dealt with by local people and the emergency services.

These incidents can be used as a background to chemical warfare although the levels of toxicity are generally much higher. Primary chemical warfare agents are the nerve agents, the blister agents and blood gases. Of these, the nerve agents are the most toxic both by inhalation and skin absorption and their mode of action is to block the action of acetylcholine esterase by irreversible inhibition. A few small drops on the exposed skin is enough to give a lethal dose. As an inhaled exposure hazard it is the total dosage, denoted as the Ct (the concentration/time integral), which is important and a Ct of about 100 mg min/m³ is a lethal dosage of nerve agent sarin (7).

Blister agents such as mustard gas are lethal both through inhalation and cutaneous absorption. A further problem, however, is that they form very large watery blisters on any exposed skin and exposure to vapour is capable of causing injuries which require considerable hospital support and nursing.

Hydrogen cyanide, a blood gas, is very volatile and is quickly blown off into the atmosphere.

A further way of classifying chemical warfare agents is by their persistence, which refers to the length of time they present a hazard, not the duration for which the injury would last. The non-persistent agents, of which hydrogen cyanide is a marked example, dissipate into the atmosphere within a few minutes. In contrast, persistent agents, mustard gas and some nerve agents are classic examples, will evaporate very slowly giving off vapour which travels downwind. It is possible to modify agents chemically such that they evaporate slowly. Chemicals which evaporate slowly will cause disruption on a massive scale to any area in which they are used. Personnel will be forced to take shelter or wear protective clothing, the latter action slowing down considerably the normal working rate of people having to wear this clothing.

Evaporation rates will be altered by the density of agent spread, the temperature and wind speed. Rain can also affect evaporation rate. However, for mustard gas it may not be unusual to find agent present some five days after attack and nerve agents for three days. Cold weather could increase these durations by a factor of three or four. Therefore, the factors which modify the downwind hazard area are density of deposition, physical characteristics of agent, meteorological conditions and the toxicity.

It is reasonable in peacetime incidents to over describe threat areas and move great numbers of people. It is unlikely that the source will be very large, in comparison with that of a chemical warfare attack.

Physical protection systems can be considered by two distinct methods. Individual protection, is very effective but, as already stated, for some chemicals it is not only the respiratory tract but also hands, feet and exposed skin which will require protection.

Secondly, collective protection systems may be able to offer a high degree of protection where doors and windows are sealed to prevent ingress of vapour. However, unless the room is completely sealed, i.e. it is airtight, there will be some inboard leakage of vapour and given that dosage is the integration of concentration over time it is found, at least by theoretical modelling, that a dosage inside can reach that achieved outside. Therefore, it is important to alert people to open windows or move outside once the outdoor concentration has fallen below that indoors.

The Home Office is at present considering measures for detection, warning and means of protection for chemical warfare. The results will reflect and integrate with the overall planning assumptions within civil defence preparedness which includes protection against conventional and nuclear weapons.

Therefore, to summarize: There is no Central Government responsibility to handle major chemical accidents in peacetime. The Seveso and Bhopal incidents showed the potential for massive disaster but the CIMAH regulations are a precise set of rules governing both the operation of chemical plant and the interaction with local authorities on plans for dealing with accidents. They include keeping the local population informed and aware. The emergency services regularly review their plans for handling chemical accidents and there have been a number in this country from which to learn lessons. The meteorological office has developed a chemical forecast method on which decisions for entering contaminated areas and evacuating people can be made. All of these functions are reviewed in the light of risk factor analysis and obviously will be updated as new systems come into play and risks change.

Chemical warfare in the UK could potentially put many thousands of civilians at risk from downwind spread of toxic vapour. However, whilst working towards an international ban on chemical weapon systems, the Government is actively reviewing the nature of the hazard from chemical agents and considering methods and advice for protecting the population.

REFERENCES

(1) *Guide to the Control of Major Accident Hazard Regulations (CIMAH)*, Health and Safety Series Booklet, HS(R)21, 1984.
(2) CIMAH Regulations 1984. *Further guidance on emergency plans* HS(G)25.
(3) Sorensen John H. *Evacuations due to chemical accidents: Experience from 1980 to 1984*. ORNL, Oak Ridge, Tennessee, USA, January 1986.
(4) Genesio M. Emergency and intervention plans: the French experience. In: Gow HBF, Kay RW, eds. *Emergency planning for industrial hazards*. Elsevier Applied Science, 1988.
(5) Personal Communication: Safety and Reliability Directorate, UKAEA, Culcheth, Warrington.
(6) Rafalowska Helena (ed). *Civil Protection*, Spring 1987. London: Home Office.
(7) *Health aspects of chemical and biological weapons*, WHO, 1970.

Planned response:
Inter-services communication and coordination

B. P. Bleasdale

Emergency Planning, Nuclear Safety Operations Branch of the Central Electricity Generating Board, London, UK

INTRODUCTION

A nuclear power station has many features in common with other large scale industrial installations. It is concerned with carrying out physical and chemical processes on a large scale and, in certain areas, these processes involve the safe containment and management of materials which could present a hazard to staff or, under extreme circumstances, the public. The experience of the accident in 1957 at a military pile at Windscale ensured that at a very early stage in the development of nuclear power in the UK the importance of maintaining well planned, practical and regularly rehearsed emergency arrangements was recognized by all involved. Thus, ever since the Central Electricity Generating Board (CEGB) first nuclear power station was licensed for operation in 1962, it has been a condition of each licence that there should be emergency arrangements. These arrangements parallel those that are now required for other, non nuclear, hazardous industries under the Control of Industrial Major Accident Hazards (CIMAH) Regulations of 1984 (1).

In order to remain effective it is essential that emergency arrangements are continually reviewed, refined and updated in the light of experience gained from exercises, developments both in the UK and abroad, and from close collaboration with all those professionally involved. Over the years the emergency arrangements have evolved and, for example, now incorporate a number of improvements which arose from analysis of the events at the Three Mile Island accident in 1979 (2).

The development of effective emergency arrangements involves collaboration between a number of organizations whose expertise or facilities may be required. Whilst the CEGB is responsible absolutely for the safe operation of its plant, it must rely on many other organizations for actions to be taken off-site in the event of an emergency. For example the Board has no authority to instruct the public to take protective action or to impose restrictions on foodstuffs; these are matters for the Police and Ministry of Agriculture, Fisheries and Food, respectively. Thus the emergency arrangements for the CEGB's nuclear power station are made up from interlocking plans and procedures of many different organizations, each of which has specific areas of responsibility. An essential part of planning for emergencies is that the plans must provide a firm framework on which a flexible

Major chemical disasters—medical aspects of management, edited by Virginia Murray, 1990: Royal Society of Medicine Services International Congress and Symposium Series No. 155, published by Royal Society of Medicine Services Limited.

response can be mounted to events whose detailed features are not foreseeable, rather than being rigidly constrained to respond to one particular incident. It is equally important to ensure that all those who have a role in planning and implementing the arrangements understand where their responsibilities begin and where they end. Coordination and communication between the groups is vital, both during planning and in implementation and requires extensive consultation. The importance of this aspect is recognized in the nuclear site licences granted to the CEGB which impose a requirement for such consultation.

In the past each station had a Local Liaison Committee which acted as the link between the CEGB and groups and its Local Parish Councils. Consultations on emergency arrangements formally took place at the time they were first drawn up and submitted to the Nuclear Installations Inspectorate for Approval and continued subsequently on an *ad hoc* basis with meetings between the professional staff involved.

In 1987 the Local Liaison Committees were restructured and re-formed as Local Community Liaison Councils and at the same time Emergency Planning Consultative Committees (EPCCs) were established at each site. The EPCCs put the consultation on a more formal basis and have a membership consisting of professional representatives from all those bodies with defined roles in the emergency arrangements for the power station. Bodies represented include:

- Regional Health Authority
- County Council
- Local District Council
- Regional Water Authority
- County Fire Service
- County Police
- Ministry of Agriculture Fisheries and Food

In addition the Department of the Environment and Nuclear Installations Inspectorate may send representatives to meetings as observers. The EPCC meets at least once a year, and often more frequently, and keeps under review the adequacy of communications, arrangements, and resources to enable the emergency plans to be put into operation effectively should the need arise. Members of the Committee may attend and will review exercises of the station emergency plan. The EPCC considers the report of each exercise and advises the Local Community Liaison Council of its conclusions. The EPCC also provides advice and information to the LCLC on emergency planning matters. Apart from the formal consultation which takes place through the EPCC there is a constant dialogue and interchange between the Board and other organisations. For example Local County Fire crews regularly attend CEGB sites for familiarization and drills, whilst CEGB members of station Fire Teams have undergone training at Fire Service training courses.

In addition to consultations at a local level there is also contact at a national level between the Board and the various organizations involved. This allows for an exchange of ideas and ensures that, as far as is practicable, a uniform approach is adopted throughout the county. The Board therefore has established contact with groups such as the Association of Chief Police Officers and the society of County Emergency Planning Officers and has been represented on the Central Fire Brigades Advisory Council's Working Group on Chernobyl.

EMERGENCY PLANNING

Emergency planning is concerned in the first instance with non-routine actions to be taken on the site following a serious fault, including measures taken on-site to protect staff and the arrangements provided to ensure that the public off-site are safeguarded.

Clearly the first responsibility of the CEGB is to recognize that a situation exists that requires implementation of the emergency arrangements and to set in motion the necessary notifications and actions. Within the CEGB's emergency plans (3) the term 'Emergency' has a specific, clearly defined meaning; i.e. 'A hazardous condition the effect of which is to cause, or is likely to cause a radiological hazard to members of the public in the vicinity of the site'. A hazardous condition which is confined in its effects to within the site security fence is defined as a 'Site Incident'. If either of the above conditions were to arise the CEGB's site emergency organization would be set up and this would have the following basic objectives (4):

1. Managing the event on-site so as to ensure that a safe and stable plant condition is re-established
2. Determining what the situation is on site and the extent of any hazard to staff
3. Protecting the staff (if this should be necessary)
4. Notifying those off site who have to be informed; (Figures 1 and 2 show typical initial communication chains for a Site Incident and an Emergency, respectively)
5. Determining what, if any, is the hazard to people off site
6. Providing advice to those off-site organizations who have the responsibility for the protection of the public and the need for protective measures to be taken, if any; and
7. Providing information about the Emergency to the public via the media

The above list is not drawn up to indicate any judgement about relative priorities attached to the objectives but it will be noted that items (1) to (3) are chiefly concerned with the site whilst (4) to (7) extend to off-site aspects. It can be seen that the CEGB's responsibilities for taking action are chiefly confined to the on-site aspects of the incident. Its responsibilities off-site are concerned with providing accurate information and advice to those who are charged with taking action off the site.

For either a Site Incident or an Emergency the same on-site response would be initiated under the overall charge of an Emergency Controller who would be based at the Station Emergency Control Centre (5). However, for an Emergency state—i.e. one with a potential radiological hazard to members of the public—two off-site centres would also be set up. These are the Operational Support Centre (OSC) and the Press Briefing Centre (PBC). One of their functions is to relieve the staff on the site of the responsibility for considering the off-site aspects of the situation, thus freeing them to concentrate on dealing with the situation on-site. The OSC also coordinates support to the station from within the CEGB and the nuclear industry as a whole. It would however be some four to six hours after declaration of an emergency that the OSC would be declared operational and during that time the station staff would be acting as a focal point. It is appropriate therefore to consider the interactions between the various services and organisations as being in two separate phases.

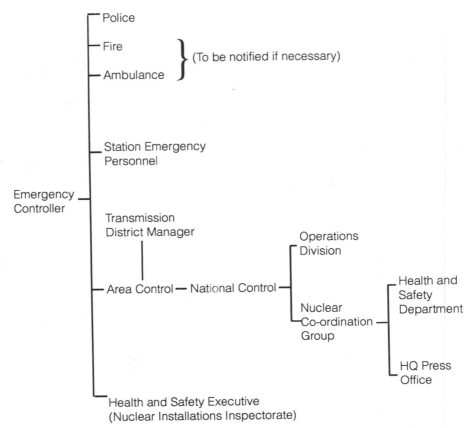

Figure 1 *Notification chain for a site incident.*

Phase 1

In Phase 1, which starts with the declaration of an Emergency, trained station staff will form the site emergency organization under the command of the Station Emergency Controller. The Station Emergency Controller is responsible for initiating the emergency actions to be taken by CEGB staff, and for alerting the off-site organizations which have responsibility for taking counter-measures to protect the public.

The station is permanently manned in such a way that a site Emergency Organization can be set up immediately with key additional staff being available on-call.

During this phase the Station Emergency Controller's responsibilities include the monitoring and assessment of the level of radioactivity on-site and off-site. Advice to the police on any immediate action to protect the public would be given by the Emergency Controller.

In addition to CEGB staff, members of the emergency services will attend the site and the Emergency Controller is responsible for ensuring that they are properly received at the gatehouse and escorted on-site by safe routes to where they are needed. Proper radiological control would ensure the safety of these personnel. A police liaison officer would go to the station Emergency Control Centre where he would remain in close touch with the developing situation and

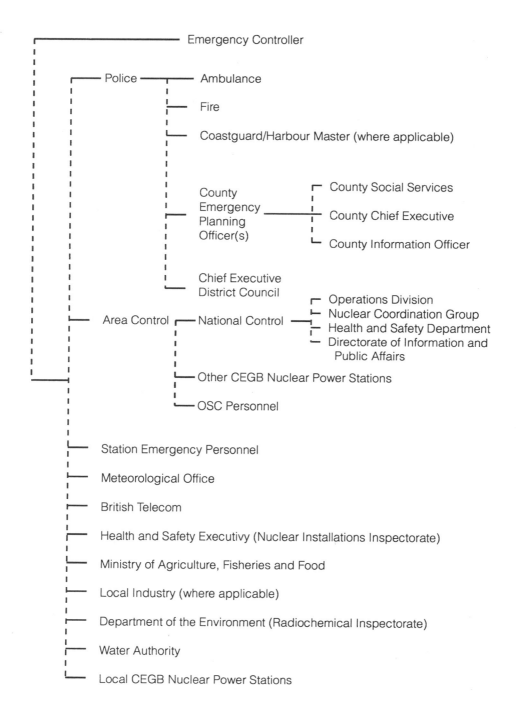

Figure 2 *Notification chain for an emergency.*

receive any advice regarding the need for countermeasures (such as evacuation) to protect the public. The police liaison officer would, via a direct link with police control, act as the prime interface between the Board and other bodies such as Local Authorities. Where necessary the Fire Brigade would also provide a Liaison Officer in the Station Emergency Control Centre.

During this period the cascade of the notification chain would be progressively alerting other sections within the CEGB and in local and national authorities. These would in turn implement their own emergency arrangements as part of the overall plan. The CEGB's Nuclear Emergency Information Centre located at CEGB headquarters in London would assist by coordinating the resources of the Board and nuclear industry in support of the affected station, and the Department of Energy's Nuclear Emergency Briefing Room (NEBR) in Whitehall would provide the link with central government and national resources.

Figure 3 shows the key centres during this phase and how they interface with each other.

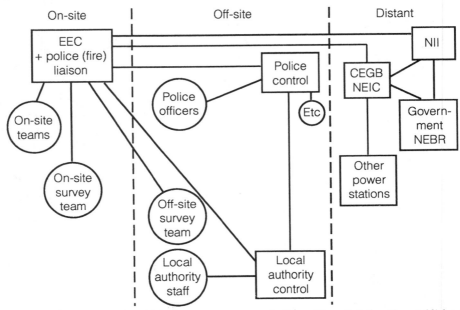

Figure 3   *Key centres and activities in emergency organizations. Phase 1: before the establishment of the Operational Support Centre and the Press Briefing Centre. ECC, Emergency Control Centre; NII, nuclear installations inspectorate; NEIC, nuclear emergency information centre; NEBR, nuclear emergency briefing rooms.*

Phase 2

Once the OSC was operational (i.e. fully manned and set up) it would take over the responsibility for advising all bodies with off-site responsibilities on technical aspects (such as the need for countermeasures). It would provide a focal point for liaison between representatives of the CEGB and Central and Local Government Departments and Agencies and therefore assist in ensuring that technical advice was available to all and was understood. The OSC would be the primary source of information for the Press Briefing Centre (PBC), providing a single authoritative source of information for the news media and, through them, the public.

The OSC and PBC are specially equipped facilities located close to each other at some distance from the site and each is under the control of a senior CEGB manager.

In addition to CEGB staff, the following organizations would have representatives at the OSC:

- County Police
- Local Authority
- Health Authority
- Water Authority
- Nuclear Installations Inspectorate
- Ministry of Agriculture Fisheries and Food
- Department of Environment
- Department of Energy
- National Radiological Protection Board

The representatives from these bodies are provided with accommodation and the necessary infrastructure such as telecommunications, within the CEGB's OSCs. In order that these staff can operate satisfactorily and, particularly, that there is a proper interchange of information among them, extensive preplanning and exercising of the facilities and procedures is necessary.

A Government Technical Advisor (GTA) would be sent to the OSC within a few hours of the emergency being declared. The GTA would be formally appointed by the Secretary of State for Energy and would become the authoritative source of *advice* to police, local authorities and central government on important technical issues and would act as the principal spokesman at press conferences. The GTA has no executive responsibility. In making his assessments and arriving at his advice the GTA would consult with, and call meetings of, those organizations represented at the OSC. The functions of those organizations can be summarized as follows:

Police: The responsibility for taking action, including evacuation, to protect the public rests with the police as in any other type of civil emergency. A senior police officer attends the OSC and acts as the link between the GTA, OSC Controller and the Police Control Centre, where all executive actions are taken.

County Council: Local Authorities would be mainly involved in the provision of accommodation, food, transport and information for members of the public. The County Council has a liaison officer at the OSC who communicates with the Local Authority Control, who in turn communicates with District Councils.

Health Authority: An emergency could result in demands being made on NHS hospitals and the Health Service generally. These demands would fall into two main categories: an immediate need for treatment of casualties, and a possible demand for medical advice from people who had been exposed (or thought they had been exposed) to radioactivity. Additionally the ambulance service may be required to assist in the evacuation of elderly or infirm members of the public. A senior representative of the Health Authority would attend the OSC.

Nuclear Installations Inspectorate (NII): The NII advises on the management of the emergency and the measures taken to rectify the fault and to protect the public. They also consider and give advice on safety measures to be taken at other operating nuclear sites. In addition to attending the OSC and the affected station, they also set up an emergency centre in their headquarters in Bootle.

Ministry of Agriculture Fisheries and Food (MAFF): A release of radioactivity following an accident could contaminate grass, crops, and produce. MAFF has the responsibility for deciding what countermeasures, such as restriction of milk supplies, are required and the statutory powers to implement restrictions. In determining what range of restrictions to impose MAFF would utilize the monitoring results coordinated at the OSC and the advice of the GTA.

Department of the Environment: The Department of the Environment has special responsibility for advising water authorities on the control of potable water and for arranging the disposal of waste arising from the accident. One of Her Majesty's Inspectors of Pollution would attend the OSC.

Department of Energy: The representative of the Department of Energy at the OSC provides a link between the OSC, the Press Briefing Centre and the Nuclear Emergency Briefing Room (NEBR). The NEBR is the central briefing point for Central Government Departments in London.

National Radiological Protection Board (NRPB): The NRPB is responsible for advising the GTA on the significance of radiological conditions in the affected area, and for coordinating the long-term monitoring over a wider area than that covered by the CEGB (i.e. beyond 40 kilometres from the site). Officers from NRPB would liaise with the Emergency Control Room at Chilton passing them data which would be used in computerized modelling of the potential consequences of the emergency.

It can be seen that the OSC is one of a number of off-site centres. Actions taken by organizations such as police, local authorities, etc., would be controlled from their own centres, just as they would in the event of any other civil emergency. The role of the OSC is therefore to provide a centre where the CEGB can provide off-site organizations with the technical information and advice they require to respond adequately. It also provides a focus for liaison between those involved and so allows for more effective communication on technical aspects. Figure 4 shows a simplified representation of the key centres of activity during Phase 2.

Nature of the hazard

One of the prime purposes of the emergency arrangements would be to safeguard the members of the public in the vicinity of the affected site. The National Radiological Protection Board recommends Emergency Reference Levels (ERLs) (6) of dose for instigating countermeasures to protect the public. The ERLs cover a range of dose, the lower level being set at a point where consideration should be given to implementing the countermeasure and an upper level of dose at which the countermeasure should be introduced whatever the circumstances. Between these two levels of dose, judgements can be made depending on the circumstances that prevail at the time. For example in severe weather conditions it may be more hazardous to evacuate people than to leave them at home.

Unlike some situations in the chemical industry where countermeasures are required to avoid immediate life threatening situations, actions would be taken in the event of an accident at a nuclear plant to avoid a small increment in long-term risk of detrimental health effects. The level of hazard which corresponds to the dose at which the evacuation countermeasure would be advised is very small and can be illustrated as follows (7). Every individual in the UK is subject to a lifetime risk of fatal cancer of about 0.2 (one person in five dies from cancer). The additional risk of fatal cancer which would correspond to advice from the CEGB to evacuate members of the public is a lifetime risk of about 0.0001. Put another way, the CEGB advice (based on national guidelines) would be to evacuate members of the public in order to prevent their risk of death increasing from 0.2 to 0.2001.

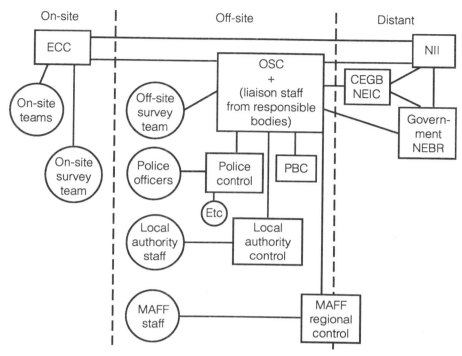

Figure 4 *Key centres and activities in emergency organizations. Phase 2: after the establishment of the Operational Support Centre and the Press Briefing Centre. NEBR, nuclear emergency briefing room; NEIC, nuclear emergency information centre; NII, nuclear installations inspectorate; ECC, emergency control centre; OSC, operational support centre (CEGB); PBC, press briefing centre (CEGB); MAFF, Ministry of Agriculture, Fisheries and Food.*

It is important that the potential effects on the health of the population should be accurately assessed and to this end the CEGB has set up an Emergency Dose Assessment Service (EDAS) based at its Berkeley Nuclear Laboratories in Gloucestershire. The main role of EDAS would be to provide an assessment of the radiation doses to members of the public and to the population as a whole following an emergency. It would also assess the doses to individual members of the Emergency Services attending the incident. To carry out this assessment EDAS would receive information from:

1. Perimeter fence gamma monitors which continually measure the radiation levels around each site
2. A large number of radiation detectors (TLDs) predeployed at distances of up to 30 kilometres from each site and which would be collected and analysed after the event.
3. Results from mobile survey teams, and including the analysis of food and environmental samples

As well as providing short-term estimates of the possible consequences of the emergency they would, over a period of a week or so after the accident, also provide detailed assessments of doses from which potential health effects could be determined.

CONCLUSION

For more than 25 years the CEGB has been responsible for operating nuclear power stations in England and Wales. During that time there has not been a single accident at a CEGB nuclear station that has required the emergency arrangements for the protection of the public to be implemented. This is not surprising; it is the overriding objective that accidents should not occur. Nevertheless the CEGB has always recognized the sense in providing emergency plans and, together with the responsible off-site authorities involved, has maintained and rehearsed emergency arrangements throughout the past 25 years. Our experience has taught us that there is no substitute for careful preplanning to provide flexible and workable arrangements and that the interaction between the individual plans of the various organizations, must be regularly rehearsed and tested. Only in this way can there be confidence in the emergency arrangements. In the immortal words of Lord Baden Powell, 'Be prepared'.

REFERENCES

(1) *Control of Industrial Major Accident Hazards Regulations 1984*, Health and Safety SI 1984/1902 London: HMSO.
(2) Goldfinch EP, Orchard HC. A Review of the emergency arrangements for CEGB Nuclear Power Stations following the accident at Three Mile Island. In: *Proceedings of the 14th Joint Conference of the Fachverbandes for Strahlenschutz eV and Societe Francaise de Radioprotection.* 1981: 650–660.
(3) *CEGB Nuclear Power Station Emergency Plans and Handbooks.* Central Electricity Generating Board 1986.
(4) Western DJ. Emergency planning. Proof of Evidence CEGB 12 to the Hinkley Point C Public Inquiry 1988.
(5) McDonald HF, Harte G, Corbett J. Developments in emergency monitoring arrangements at CEGB Nuclear Power Stations since the Three Mile Island Accident. *Nuclear Energy* 1987; 1: 31–40.
(6) *National Radiological Protection Board ERL2.* London: HMSO, 1981.
(7) Western DJ. Potential off-site effects of radiation. Proof of Evidence CEGB 10 to the Hinkley Point C Public Inquiry 1988.

Planning for chemical incidents at sea— the role of the Lifeboat Service

Wilson Adam, William J. Guild, Sir George Smart and Glyn N. Volans

Hazardous Chemicals Subgroup, Medical and Survival Committee, Royal National Lifeboat Institution, Poole, Dorset, UK

INTRODUCTION

The Royal National Lifeboat Institution (RNLI) has existed for 165 years with the primary objective of saving life at sea. It is a charity which needs £36 million a year from voluntary contributions to function efficiently and to replace boats as necessary. It operates 203 lifeboat stations around the entire coast of Britain including Ireland, its lifeboats being crewed mainly by volunteers. The total of lives saved between 1824 and 1988 is more than 117 000 and in 1988 alone 1338 lives were saved on 4185 operational launches.

Over the years lifeboats have become faster and more efficient and medical knowledge about survival at sea has increased. All RNLI Lifeboat Stations have an Honorary Medical Advisor (HMA) and the Institution has formed a Medical and Survival Committee to advise on all medical questions related to survival and personnel protection.

To date, chemical incidents in RNLI operations have been uncommon and thankfully minor. Nevertheless, there have been incidents elsewhere where hazardous chemical containers have been on board vessels in distress (including vessels on fire). In addition, chemical containers have also been washed ashore and one report detailed 130 containers of 41 hazardous chemicals washed on to the shoreline of England and Wales during 12 months (1).

Against this background, the Medical and Survival Committee of the RNLI formed a Hazardous Chemical Subgroup with the following remit:

1. To assess the potential hazards of chemical incidents in RNLI operations.
2. To advise on appropriate measures to minimize the risks to both the shipwrecked and the lifeboat crew.

METHODS

Hazard assessment

1. An enquiry was made into the movements of chemical carrying vessels around the coasts of the United Kingdom and Eire.

Major chemical disasters—medical aspects of management, edited by Virginia Murray, 1990: Royal Society of Medicine Services International Congress and Symposium Series No. 155, published by Royal Society of Medicine Services Limited.

2. A review of records at the RNLI and the National Poisons Unit (NPU) was undertaken to detect significant incident reports during the previous three years.

Advice on appropriate measures

1. A chemical incident was programmed into the annual RNLI exercise MEDEX 1986.
2. The subject was considered as part of the general on-going review of equipment carried on board lifeboats and the first-aid training offered to lifeboat crews.

RESULTS

Could accidents occur?

A survey undertaken by one member of the working group (WA) demonstrated that in total British ports handle approximately 400 million tonnes of goods each year. The import to export ratio is close to 1 : 1 and 60% of the tonnage relates to petroleum products.

The traffic movements could be seen to vary between regions and within each region the major ports were identified (Table 1).

The ten largest ports handle 70% of the total traffic and when bulk traffic is analysed by commodity, 'chemicals' were seen to account for approximately nine million tonnes or 3% of the total annual traffic.

Table 1 *Major shipping movements*

Traffic movements, geographically	Fuel	Non-fuel
South Coast	8%	15%
West Coast	24%	29%
North East Coast	53%	29%
South East Coast	14%	26%

Major port analysis by size of movements
1. Shetlands E
2. London SE
3. Tees NE
4. Milford Haven SW
5. Grangemouth NE
6. Immingham E
7. Southampton South

Major areas of chemical movements
Tees
Forth
Immingham
Harwich/Felixstowe (rail/ro-ro)
Dover (road/ro-ro)
Southampton
South Wales
Liverpool Bay

The River Tees carries the largest chemical cargo load (approximately three million tonnes annually) because of the large manufacturing and storage facilities within the estuary. Approximately 100 chemicals account for most of this load, divided almost equally into four categories:

1. Toxic and/or inflammable
2. Inflammable
3. Corrosive
4. Others

The 'average' chemical ship size in the Tees is about 2000 tonnes, from which it can be calculated that there are approximately 1500 chemical movements annually including 350 classified as toxic. Looked at another way, there are approximately 5 chemical movements per day, every day and there are often 8–10 tankers 'parked' waiting for entry to the port. The most toxic chemicals used were nitrites, cyanides and phenols. 'Other chemicals' are those associated with the increasing trade in petrochemical products.

The Firth of Forth has a major petrochemical complex at Grangemouth and a recently established terminal for compressed gas tankers at Mossmorran.

Have accidents occurred?

Two major chemical incidents had been recorded by the RNLI during three years.

1. A ship wrecked off the South-west coast of Scotland had lost dangerous chemicals overboard. Some containers were washed up on the shore. The lifeboat crew were referred to hospital to check for contamination but no obvious effects were found.
2. A compressed gas tanker grounded on a reef in the Forth. An alert was called but the gas cargo was safely transferred over four days. Fortunately, there was no leak and no explosion.

The NPU had not been called in these incidents but responded to several theoretical enquiries from HMAs and in one instance had been called in a 'paper exercise'.

Could the RNLI respond effectively to an accident?

As part of the Medex '86 exercise, a chemical carrying vessel caught fire. Drums of a chemical were breached with the formation of a red gas/smoke cloud. The victims of the accident were suffering from burns plus the effects of toxic fumes. They varied in severity from mild to one fatality and included several crew members trapped in a hold.

The lifeboat was called out by HM Coastguard and was warned from the outset that dangerous chemicals were involved. The Coastguard obtained information on the cargo from the owners and advice on the risks was sought from the NPU and an on-line hazardous chemical database. The possibility that the cloud contained nitrogen dioxide was recognized by the Information Scientist on duty at the NPU and information on toxic risks was provided, together with advice on first aid. The information and advice was adapted to the needs and skills of the lifeboat crew managing the incident using reference sources which included the Chemical Supplement to the Ship Captains Guide (2).

The lifeboat arrived on the scene and would have boarded the vessel without hesitation had the advice not been received, via the coastguard, to wait until the fumes had cleared. The subsequent first aid/rescue was undertaken with considerable skill.

What improvements in response are required?

A review of the RNLI First Aid Training Programme was already in progress and it was recognized that some instruction relevant to chemicals carried at sea was already contained in a section on burns and chemical accidents. The Hazardous Chemicals Subgroup considered this section in detail and recommended additional material to give a wider awareness of chemical hazards and appropriate return for safety and first aid.

CONCLUSIONS

1. Carriage of chemicals at sea is increasing and sailings/landings are concentrated at certain ports. Nevertheless, accidents involving chemicals could occur anywhere at sea.
2. Accidents involving chemicals at sea are infrequent and to date the RNLI has encountered only two major incidents, both fortunately without serious toxic effects. The material of the existing routine protective clothing is already resistant to many chemicals. New protective clothing is currently under test by a separate working group and should by design offer further protection.
3. At the present time, the provision of special equipment on board the lifeboat for chemical incidents cannot be justified on grounds of cost or use of the limited space aboard such vessels.
4. The existing safety equipment and first aid training should meet the basic needs of the lifeboat crew in a chemical incident, however, further action is planned to ensure:

   (i) that all lifeboat crew will recognize situations where chemical hazards are present;
   (ii) that there will be good communication between the RNLI, the Coastguard and chemical hazard/poisons information services such as the NPU in the event of any chemical incident;
   (iii) the first aid training programme includes advice on the risks of poisoning and appropriate treatment;
   (iv) the RNLI is kept informed of all relevant developments in disaster planning.

In time, the first aid training programme will be strengthened by the production of a video film and in future any chemical incident involving a RNLI response will be fully evaluated.

REFERENCES

(1) Davies GH. Chemical peril on beaches. *Sunday Times*, 18 November, 1984.
(2) Department of Trade. *The chemical supplement to the ship captain's medical guide*. London: HMSO, 1983.

SESSION IV

PROBLEMS RELATING TO MAJOR CHEMICAL DISASTERS

Chairman: Dr D. A. D. Slattery

Definition of a major incident involving chemicals

M. Govaerts-Lepicard

Centre Anti-Poison, Brussels, Belgium

INTRODUCTION

Although a definition has been given in a directive of the Commission of the European Communities:

> 'Any incident connected with an uncontrolled development (such as a leak, fire and/or explosion) of an industrial activity involving a serious immediate or delayed hazard to man and/or the environment'

it is not easy, and perhaps not possible, to summarize in a few lines the characteristics of incidents that are so different in their origins and their implications, even if they present common elements.

Poison Centres fortunately deal most often with chemical accidents involving one or a small number of potential victims, corresponding to a limited danger for the community (1). However, the number of victims is not the only criterion and certainly not the prime one in deciding that a major rather than a minor situation is faced. Moreover, in many cases the alert is given when there are no actual victims, but only potential ones. A chemical disaster can be defined as a chemical hazard for a large number of people.

Criteria of appraisal can include: the extent of the contaminated area, the size of the exposed population; population density in the contaminated area for volatile chemicals; the amount of chemicals involved and their toxicity.

At least two of these criteria have to be combined for this first estimation. In this respect, it is interesting to look at the table given in the chapter 'Major hazards control' by R. Raimondi in the last edition of the *Encyclopedia of Occupational Health and Safety* (2).

Table 1 lists all the major industrial accidents recorded from 1975 to 1977 inclusive. Although most of them include an explosion and are not exclusively or not at all toxic, we found that in general few deaths were involved (more than 10 in only three accidents) and in some cases very few injuries. It is, therefore, more the potential risk than the real consequences of the event that is taken into account.

Major chemical disasters—medical aspects of management, edited by Virginia Murray, 1990: Royal Society of Medicine Services International Congress and Symposium Series No. 155, published by Royal Society of Medicine Services Limited.

Table 1 *Major industrial accidents (1975–77)*

Year	Location	Description	Killed/injured
1975	Belgium	Ethylene from polyethylene plant explosion	6/15
	Beek, Netherlands	Propylene explosion	14/104
	Germany (FDR)	Naphtha plus hydrogen exploded	0/4
	California	Hydrogen explosion	0/2
	Louisiana	Butadiene escaped without ignition	0
	Louisiana	270 tons propane escaped but failed to ignite	0
	Czechoslovakia	Explosion of light hydrocarbons	14/?
	Netherlands	Ethylene explosion	4/35
	France	Large confined vapour explosion	1/35
	South Africa	Methane explosion	7/7
	Philadelphia	Crude oil explosion	8/2
	United Kingdom	Electrolytor plant explosion	1/3
1976	Texas	Ethylene explosion at alcohol plant	1/15
	Texas	Natural gas leakage ignited	1/4
	Puerto Rico	C_5 hydrocarbons ignited	1/2
	New Jersey	Propylene explosion	2/?
	Lake Charles	Isobutane explosion	7/?
	Baton Rouge	Chlorine release: 10 000 evacuated	0
	Norway	Flammable liquid escaping from ruptured pipe explosion	6/?
	Seveso, Italy	Escape of TCDD resulting in evacuation of entire area	0
1977	United Kingdom	Fire and explosion involving sodium chloride plant	?
	Mexico	Ammonia escaped and leaked into sewer system	2/102
	Quatar	LPG explosion damaging villages distant from source and closing airport	7/many
	Mexico	Vinylchloride release	0/90
	Cassino, Italy	Propane/butane explosion	1/9
	Jacksonville	LPG incident resulting in evacuation of 2000	?
	Gela, Italy	Ethylene oxide explosion	1/2
	India	Hydrogen explosion	0/20
	Italy	Ethylene explosion	3/22
	Columbia	Ammonia escape	30/22

Another criterion, although a secondary one, is the magnitude of the measures that must be taken to counteract the accident and to limit its consequences. In many disasters it is necessary to call up resources at a national and even an international level, as, for example, in Baton Rouge (Louisiana) in 1976 where, due to a release of chlorine gas, 10 000 people were evacuated, and no-one was seriously injured.

Finally, besides the human aspect, the impact on the environment can be so important that some chemical incidents must be considered as chemical disasters even when they do not affect humans. We all know the dramatic consequences of pollution of the sea by petroleum even if the accident occurs far from the coasts. The main elements of the definition therefore are:

- Extent of the contaminated area
- Size of the exposed population
- Amount of chemicals involved
- Toxicity of the chemicals
- Magnitude of the measures required (e.g. size of the population to be evacuated)
- Consequences on the environment

If we consider these criteria of major accidents, it is clearly difficult to define the various elements precisely, but we can say that for a highly toxic pollutant a risk will exist even if the contaminated area is small, and the exposed population and amount of chemicals are limited, as in a chemical plant. Conversely, if even moderately toxic pollutants are present in a large zone and/or reach a large population, it is statistically likely that there will be victims. Such a prognosis is therefore a matter of discernment and capability.

APPROACH TO A CLASSIFICATION OF CHEMICAL INCIDENTS

Origin

Chemical accidents may have natural origins such as volcanic phenomena, or industrial ones caused by breakage of pipes or containers, fires, explosions, spillages, and transportation accidents, the latter being now more frequent than the former. Also, chemical weapons have been used only recently, and are still used in different parts of the world.

Routes of contact and target organs

The routes of contamination may be:

- Inhalation of gases, fumes or volatile substances
- Ingestion of contaminated food and water
- Skin contact and cutaneous absorption

Inhalation of gases, fumes or volatile substances

Accidents due to inhalation are generally sudden (although the onset of the main symptomatology can be delayed), massive, and quite impossible to limit except by immediate evacuation of the contaminated area.

We all remember the use of chlorine during the First World War in Ypres (Belgium) and later, of yperite (mustard gas), and the Bhopal catastrophe, impressive by the number of victims. Such outbreaks are frequent, e.g. in Missisauga near Toronto in 1979, also due to chlorine; in Nebraska (USA) due to ammonia; many accidents in France caused by broken gas-pipes and also the natural catastrophe at Nyos Lake in Cameroon in 1986 (3) due to a massive release of carbon monoxide, suplhur oxide and hydrogen sulphide in a volcanic area which was responsible for the death of 1800 people and 3000 head of cattle.

The severity of such accidents is largely due to direct penetration of toxic gas into the pulmonary system where it can displace oxygen and lead to anoxia, although it does not itself have toxic properties (e.g. nitrogen, hydrogen). The gas may also be irritant, caustic, or corrosive for the respiratory tract, and also for the eyes and skin (e.g. chlorine, ammonia, phosgene, methyl isocyanate, yperite) or it can be resorbed and have a narcotic effect (methane) or a systemic effect that can be neurotoxic (such as disabling gases used in chemical warfare) or haemotoxic (cyanides, carbon monoxide). Many gases and vapours have mixed effects, such as phosphine, arsine and sulphur dioxide.

The site of such a catastrophe can sometimes be foreseen, for instance a dangerous plant that has been identified as such, but there are unforeseeable sites such as clandestine storage or a transportation accident.

A number of factors influence the severity of the event:

- The temperature and the meteorological conditions (i.e. wind, pressure, humidity)
- The behaviour of the exposed population:
  If people remain inside the buildings and are exposed to decreased oxygen pressure
  If they run outside the buildings
  If their respiratory rate is increased, for example in attempting to escape

In general, the effects of a massive inhalation of toxic substances appear very quickly, requiring immediate measures. The number of people affected is directly related to the density of population in the area, and can be very high. The toxic picture is in constant evolution in time and space, due to the easy and rapid spread of the gases which is impossible to stop. The only effective means of limiting its effect is to organize an efficient evacuation of the population; the wearing of masks and protective apparatus should be reserved for a limited number of people.

Besides the direct toxic effects of the chemicals, other factors have to be included in the picture, such as the consequences of fire and explosions like burns, blast, and various traumas.

Ingestion, food contamination and water pollution

If accidents due to inhalation are the most frequent and those requiring the most urgent measures, those due to ingestion and absorption of contaminated foods and water are not exceptional and some are responsible for a large number of victims. They can have an industrial, a natural, a criminal or a fraudulent origin. Often, the beginning is insidious. Poison Information Centres are the first to be aware that something abnormal is happening because of the calls they receive. Generally, the identification of the actual toxic agent is difficult and will require an epidemiological approach besides careful questioning of the victims and their relatives, and sample taking. The example of the 'Spanish oil' which occurred in 1982 shows how difficult it can be, as it is still not now completely clear.

In 1959, in Morocco, 10 000 people were victims of contamination of cooking oil by triarylphosphate and 10–15% retained definitive sequellae such as paralysis (4). The methylmercury outbreaks of Minamata (starting in 1953) and in Iraq (1971–72) (5) are other examples, as well as the recent contamination of wines by diethylene glycol and methanol in Austria and Italy. In the south of France also, smaller accidents regularly occur due to fraudulent production of pastis.

Often in such cases the contaminated area is larger than in outbreaks due to inhalation. The spread is slower and the diagnosis requires the contribution of many experts. Although panic does not develop in the same way it does exist, and here again, early and regular contacts with the media must be organized.

Skin contamination and transcutaneous penetration

The pattern of serious casualties due to skin contamination and still more to transcutaneous penetration is similar, but the diagnosis of systemic effects due to transcutaneous penetration is generally difficult. The enigma is even more difficult to solve and effective preventive measures are difficult to establish. As an example, there were two outbreaks caused by baby powder, the well known 'talc Morhange' in 1972 in France, where baby powder contaminated by 6.3% hexachlorophene was responsible for the death of 36 children and 204 victims, and contaminated baby powders in Ho-Chi-Minh City (Vietnam) in 1981, containing 1.7 to 6.5% warfarin which is easily resorbed by the skin, caused 741 victims, with 177 infants dying in less than nine weeks (6,7). In such cases collaboration of international experts and regular warnings in the local media contribute to the diagnosis and control of the outbreak. Chemical burns occur frequently in accidents due to liquids and to volatile agents. Their consequences can be limited by immediate measures and this necessity has to be foreseen when corrosive gases are spreading in a site.

In conclusion, hazardous chemical emergencies can be very different in their origins, their epidemiology and their approaches, although their final effects can be similar.

REFERENCES

(1) Tong T. A poison experience with environmental emergencies. *Vet Hum Tox* 1983; **25**(Suppl 1): 29–33.
(2) Raimondi R. Major hazards control. *Encyclopedia of occupational health and safety.* Geneva:ILO, 1983.
(3) Atchou G, *et al.* Les éruptions léthales de gaz carbonique dans les régions volcaniques du Cameroun. Aspects médicaux et causes possibles. *Médicine & Hygiène* 1987;**45**:2511–3.
(4) Albertini AV, Gross D, Zinn WM. *L'intoxication au phosphate de triaryle au Maroc en 1959.* Rapport médical édité à l'ordre de la Ligue des Sociétés de la Croix-Rouge, Genève. Stuttgart: Georg Thieme Verlag, 1967.
(5) Derban LKA. Outbreak of food poisoning due to alkyl-mercury fungicide. *Arch Environ Health* 1974; **28**: 49.
(6) Martin-Bouyer G, Khan NB, Linh PD, Tourneau J. An epidemic of a 'new' haemorrhagic disease in infants attributable to talcum powder contaminated with warfarin in Ho-Chi-Minh Ville (Vietnam). *Arch Tox* 1984; **Suppl 7**: 494–8.
(7) Fristedt B, Sterner N. Warfarin intoxication from percutaneous absorption. *Arch Environ Health* 1965; **11**(2): 205.

Further reading

Aldridge WN, Connors TA. Chemical accidents and toxicology. *Human Tox* 1985; **4**(5): 477–9.
Catastrophes toxiques. XXVe Congrès des Centres antipoisons, Paris, 21–23 sept. 1987. Collection Méd Lég. & Tox. Méd., n°137, Masson, Paris.
Gilad A, Silano V. Contingency planning for accidents and emergencies involving the release of potentially toxic chemicals. *Activities of the WHO Regional Office for Europe.* Presented at the Xth Intern. Congress of the EAPCC, Brighton UK, 3–6 August 1982.
Gerstner HB, Huff JE. Selected case histories and epidemiologic examples of human mercury poisoning. *Clin Tox* 1977; **11**(2): 131–50.
Gunn SW. La réponse internationale à des situations de catastrophe. *Médicine & Hygiène* 1986; **44**: 2240–2.
Weisman RS. A letter to the editor: chemical disasters. *Vet Hum Tox* 1985; **27**(5): 439.

Identification of toxic hazard

J. W. Bridges

Robens Institute of Industrial and Environmental Health and Safety, University of Surrey, Guildford, Surrey, UK

INTRODUCTION

In considering the identification of toxic substances in regard to a fire or rapid release of a chemical or chemicals there are two situations which should be addressed:

- Identification to prevent major incidents;
- Accessing information rapidly once an incident has occurred.

IDENTIFICATION TO PREVENT MAJOR INCIDENTS

The prediction of the toxicological hazard to a human or environmental species which may arise from a major incident must address:

1. The nature of the chemical(s) likely to be released
2. The level and duration of exposure to the chemical(s)

If dispersal is in the form of airborne material, the primary concern is likely to be with short-term exposure; however, if the chemical(s) is stable and gains access to water courses, agricultural land, etc., the effects of chronic exposure may also need appraisal. Adverse effects to man may occur directly or as a consequence of contamination of other organisms.

Nature of the chemical being dispersed

Although in many situations chemicals can be dispersed without undergoing significant degradation, this is by no means inevitable. Moreover, apparently stable non-toxic chemicals may at high temperature degrade to toxic moieties, e.g. polymeric products are widely used for building, packaging, etc., however on degradation they may release toxic species. It has been shown, for example, that when some polyurethane foams are burnt a number of highly toxic species such as hydrogen cyanide, carbon monoxide and bicyclic phosphorus esters are released.

Major chemical disasters—medical aspects of management, edited by Virginia Murray, 1990: Royal Society of Medicine Services International Congress and Symposium Series No. 155, published by Royal Society of Medicine Services Limited.

Another well known example is the formation of dioxins through the combustion of chlorinated phenols and biphenyls. Some products undergo changes if stored improperly. For example, malathion is classified by the World Health Organization, quite properly as 'Class III—Slightly Hazardous'. On storage malathion may, however, undergo conversion to the much more acutely toxic iso-malathion and this has had tragic consequences. A third concern is that in an incident a mixture of chemicals rather than a single entity is likely to be released. Not only must each significant component be identified but thought given to the toxicological consequences of multiple exposure.

Source of information on possible toxic effects to man

For most chemicals there is little or no information available on their direct toxicity to man. An estimation of likely human toxicity must therefore be made from data obtained in animal experiments. The primary considerations in selecting the appropriate collection of animal data for extrapolation purposes are the:

- Probable exposure period
- Expected route of exposure
- Identification of those likely to be involved in the incident. This should include consideration of potential exposure of at-risk groups, e.g. very young children, pregnant women, the elderly, etc.

Acute toxicity

The term 'acute' is generally used to mean exposure on one occasion of short duration only. Acute toxic effects may be lethal or non-lethal. To aid interpretation statistical inferences based on population effects in animals are commonly employed, particularly to define the lethal dose. The percentage of animals affected is expressed by a subscript hence LD_{50} is the lethal dose (usually expressed in milligram of chemical/kilogram animal body weight) to 50% of the animals. [NB: In acute toxicity tests involving whole atmosphere exposure, e.g. exposure by inhalation, the effect levels are often expressed in terms of EC (effective concentration) or LC (lethal concentration)] (1). The dose causing 50% of deaths rather than some other percentage figure is selected largely on historic grounds and because it can be determined with the greatest accuracy. Many variables may be an influence on the actual LD_{50} value obtained. Two-three-fold differences in LD_{50} often occur between animals of different ages, sex and between strains of animals of the same species (2). Much larger interspecies differences are not unusual. Since the Seveso Directive is based on an incident in which 2,3,7,8-tetrachlorodibenzo-p-dioxin (TCDD) was released with other chemicals into the atmosphere it is appropriate to cite this as an example. Ingested TCDD is about 100 times less acutely toxic to mice than to guineapigs, and the Syrian hamster is about 600 times less susceptible than the guineapig. Differences of this magnitude between three rodent species make extrapolation from rodent to man highly problematical. For reasons of economy and convenience the majority of toxicology investigations are carried out in rodents, and with a lot of chemicals there is no other information on which to establish a toxicity rating. Other variables include timing of observation, housing conditions, diet, etc. As a consequence, repeat LD_{50} tests under apparently very similar conditions often produce variations of more than 40%. Thus the LD_{50} is best viewed as an approximate indication of lethal potency and must never be regarded as an absolute figure.

Table 1 *Some international classifications of acute toxicity*[a]

(a)	(b)	(c)	(d)	(e)	(f)
Extremely toxic >1	Very toxic <15	Designated Poison <15	Category I <50	Group I <5	Extremely hazardous <5
Highly toxic >1 to 50	Toxic >25 to 200	Poisonous substance	Category II >5 to 500	Group II >5 to 50	Highly hazardous >5 to 50
Moderately toxic >50 to 500	Harmful >200 to 2000	Deleterious substance <300	Category III >500 to 5000	Group III solids: >50 to 500	Moderately hazardous >50 to 500
Slightly toxic			Category IV >5000	Liquids: >50 to 2000	Slightly hazardous >500
Practically non-toxic >5000 to 15 000					
Relatively harmless >15 000					

[a]Note: Data have been attenuated. Figures shown are for acute oral LD_{50} values in rats expressed in mg/kg^{-1}. Other requirements not included in this Table.
Key: (a) Hodge & Sterner Classification; (b) EEC Annex VI; (c) Poisons—Deleterious Substances Control Law (Japan); (d) Federal Insecticide, Fungicide and Rodenticide Act (USA); (e) Transport of Dangerous Goods (United Nations); (f) Classification of Pesticides (WHO).

LD_{50} values are often used by government agencies, in isolation from any other data, as the means of ranking chemicals for their toxicological hazard (see Table 1). This approach is encapsulated in the Seveso Directive of the European Economic Community (EEC). There are a number of serious criticisms of this simplistic way of identifying and comparing toxic hazards from major incidents, namely:

1. The dose which just causes lethality by the route relevant to the exposure situation is in principle a more valid index for assessing hazard than the oral dose which will kill 50% of a population. Unfortunately there is no fixed relationship between an LD_{50} value and say an LD_1 value, e.g. the $LD_{50} : LD_1$ ratio has been shown to vary by up to 70-fold for a number of pesticides. (Dr K N Woodward, unpublished data). [NB: This problem could be overcome by calculating from the LD_{50} value a worst case situation, where LD_1 data is not available or by using minimum lethal dose data] (3)
2. For major incidents, exposure by inhalation or through the skin rather than by the oral route is most likely, and therefore acute toxicity findings for these routes of exposure are normally more relevant than results based on oral administration. (Again, a 'worst case' calculation could be employed to extrapolate data from the oral route to the dermal and inhalation exposure situations where such information is unobtainable)
3. Chemicals with a high LD_{50} (i.e. a low lethality) may none the less have highly undesirable acute effects at lower doses which may even be irreversible. For example, chemicals causing narcosis or severe irritancy could lead to individuals suffering accidents in a major incident. The importance of mutagenic potential must also be considered though the effects which may arise are more likely to be expressed in the long term rather than immediately.

4. LD_{50} gives little or no indication of delayed toxicity due to acute exposure, nor of likely toxicity arising from chronic exposure, e.g. via contaminated food, drinking water, etc. (4)
5. In order to assess risk, dispersal characteristics, stability, etc., must be taken into account (see below)

For some chemicals, inhalation hazard to man has been evaluated and the findings embodied in the Health and Safety Executive, the National Institute for Occupational Safety and Health and other guidelines in the form of short term exposure limits or ceiling values. Although these recommended limits are intended to be related to normal adult working environments, they may none the less be a useful guide for judging potential toxic hazard from the sudden release of such chemicals into the atmosphere. However, they should not be used to rank chemicals according to hazard. It should be noted that at present there is no agreed method of assessing potential acute hazard from exposure to a mixture of chemicals despite the fact that this is likely to be the most common situation in a major incident.

Other toxicology considerations

Many chemicals causing cancer are not particularly acutely toxic. Nor does acute lethality data as it is normally derived give any indication of hazard to the unborn child. If sustained exposure to a chemical occurs then consideration of data on its chronic toxicity, reproductive and allergic effects may be necessary. From an administrative viewpoint these data are much more difficult to evaluate and rank than acute lethality data because the sites and forms of toxicity may vary very considerably, species differences tend to be greater and reproducibility of findings poorer (5). A decision tree approach or an expert computer system for utilizing such data is probably most appropriate for administration by non-technical experts concerned with identifying hazard. An example of a very simple decision tree incorporating both acute and possible chronic effects is given in Fig. 1.

Assessing inherent toxicity to environmental species

In considering the environmental impact to species other than man the primary concern is normally the potential effects on populations rather than individuals. Lethality and mutational effects are of particular relevance. Unfortunately, the amount and quality of information on likely effects on environmental species is very limited (6), although the situation is improving as increasingly companies are being asked to provide acute toxicity data on a few 'representative' aquatic and terrestrial species (7). There are major difficulties in extrapolating such information to other species; however, it is possible to use a crude decision tree scheme for rating chemicals according to their likely impact on environmental species (see Fig. 2).

Exposure conditions

Ease of dispersal

This will be influenced by the form of the dispersing event itself, but also by factors such as the volatility of the chemical of interest, its reactivity with other molecules, etc. Thus a highly toxic but very low volatility chemical may in practice constitute

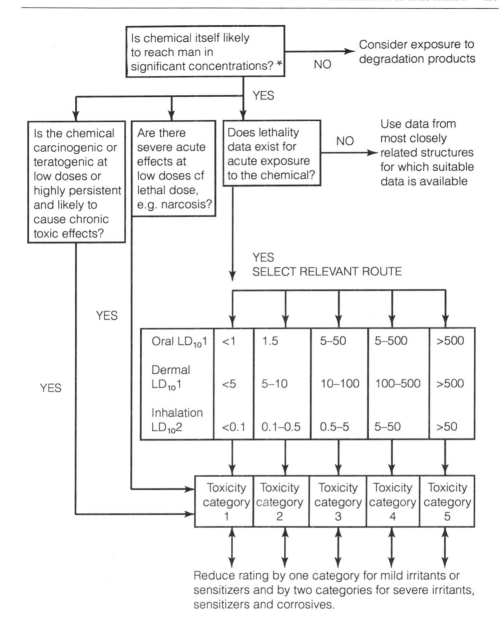

Figure 1 *A simple decision tree scheme for rating chemicals according to their toxic hazard to man from major incidents. NB: Toxicity category 1=highest hazard group toxicity. Category 5 represents chemical with no significant hazard. 1. mg/kg body weight; mg/litre of air for four hours; *requires information on probable dispersal conditions.*

a rather minor hazard in a major incident in comparison to a less toxic agent with high volatility. However, it should be remembered that toxicity by dermal exposure may be a hazard with low volatility chemicals, particularly those which are lipophilic. Dispersion through water courses, e.g. drains, may also occur causing a rapid spread of chemical. It is also important that the emergency services

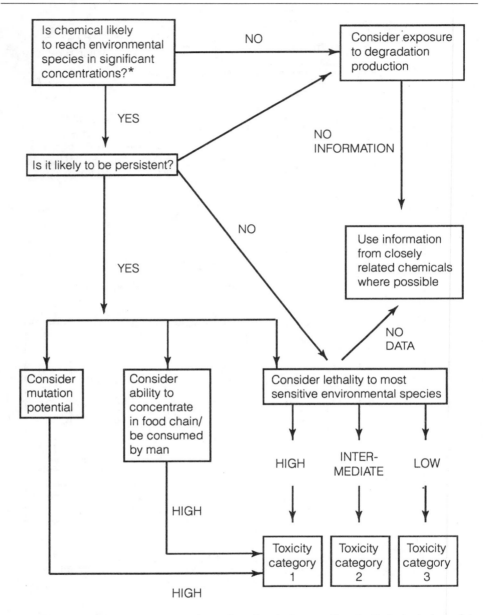

Figure 2 *A simplified decision tree for rating chemicals according to their toxic hazard to environmental species as the result of a major incident.*
*requires information on probable dispersal conditions.

are aware of the potential hazards of using various procedures, e.g. extensive use of water may put out a fire but lead to increased dispersal of a toxic chemical.

Persistence

The toxic action of a chemical may be terminated by extensive dilution (e.g. in air) or chemical (abiotic) or biological (biotic) degradation. Some chemicals are resistant to both abiotic and biotic attack, e.g. polychlorinated biphenyls, and may remain in the environment for long periods of time. Such substances may be accumulated in organisms living in the locality and hence constitute a potential chronic toxic hazard both to the organisms themselves and to those who feed off them including man.

Site specific factors

In addition to intrinsic considerations such as those above, for a reliable assessment of the toxic hazard from a potential major incident, site specific factors ought to be borne in mind. These should include:

1. Identification of the most likely dispersal mechanisms and the quantity of material which may be released
2. Release location, i.e. on land, sea, inland water, in the air, and the topography, prevailing winds, temperature, etc.
3. Population distribution of human and other species

Accessing information rapidly following incident

A priority following an incident is to obtain rapid reliable information on the possible toxic hazards. This information may be crucial to:

- Devising appropriate treatment for exposure victims
- Identifying the evacuation needs both in terms of the nature of such an evacuation and its likely duration
- Limitation of the incident's spread including avoidance of procedures which may unintentionally lead to exacerbation of an incident
- Allay public concern

In an incident there are three main potential sources of information: inventories, chemical analysis and characterization of effects on people and/or environmental species.

Inventories

Typically inventories will change with time, be they related to a store, a plant manufacturing or processing chemicals, or a transport unit (road, rail, sea or air). The quality of the information may also be highly variable. Ideally each inventory ought to identify in a readily accessible form all the chemicals present, the amounts involved and the hazards from each (see above) in a format which is quickly understood by non-technical experts. It ought too to indicate the hazard from combustion products. Non-relevant information should be excluded. A system of spot checks is needed to ensure that inventory information is correct. There is a considerable need to validate the information available in those data sheets presently available and to provide it in a common format suitable for computerization.

Chemical analysis

Because inventories are seldom complete and in an incident may not be accessible, the second line of defence is chemical analysis. To be of value such analysis needs to be rapid and reliable. Unfortunately, such methodology is suitable for relatively few chemicals and may not be available at an incident, particularly a transport accident, for some time. Analytical methods where available are often particularly valuable as a cross check on inventory information. Manufacturers should be very strongly encouraged to provide appropriate analytical methods for chemicals of particular concern.

Effects on people and/or environmental species

Occasionally the early effects on people and/or environmental species prove a valuable indication of the nature of the chemical(s) being released. However, this is true for only a very limited number of chemicals. For most the early effects are not at all characteristic.

FUTURE NEEDS

In addition to the development of more sensible means of ranking chemicals according to the hazard they present in a major emergency there is a clear need for:

1. An effective procedure for proper logging of incidents including the definition of the effects in man and other species and the measures taken to ameliorate these. This is essential if we are to learn from incidents both in terms of prevention and more effective response to emergencies involving the release of toxic chemicals. A detailed report on near misses is also vital if we are to develop the most effective emergency services.
2. A national/international data bank/advisory centre to provide prompt reliable information on analytical procedures, treatment and. incident limitation strategies. Such a centre could also provide an information resource on training methods and conduct research and disseminate findings of incident analysis. An up-to-date list of readily available experts should be held by such a centre. The centre would take responsibility for coordinating a suitable support team once an incident occurred. Such a team might help both in investigative work and in providing information and advice.
3. Realistic training exercises on incidents involving toxic chemicals in various pertinent situations.
4. Regular assessment of the preparedness of all the emergency services. This should include evaluation of the attitudes of staff at all levels who work with hazardous chemicals since the best way to prevent major incidents is to have effective safety management and high safety consciousness for all involved.

ACKNOWLEDGMENT

The author is indebted to Dr K N Woodward for his assistance in drawing up the decision tree in Fig. 1.

REFERENCES

(1) Brown VK. *Acute toxicity theory and practice*. Chichester: John Wiley, 1980.
(2) Calabrese EJ. *Principles of animal extrapolation*. Chichester: John Wiley, 1983.

(3) BTS Report. A new approach to the classification of substances and preparations on the basis of their acute toxicity. *Hum Toxicol* 1984; **3**: 85–92.

(4) Bridges JW, Hubbard SA. Principles, practice and problems in toxicology. In: Gardner AW, Wright J, eds. *Occupational Medicine* 1982; **2**: 257–82.

(5) Bridges JW. The assessment of toxic hazards. In: The assessment and control of major hazards. *I Chem E Symposium Series No. 93*, 413–28.

(6) Butler GC, ed. *Principles of ecotoxicology*. SCOPE 12. Chichester: John Wiley, 1978.

(7) Schmidt-Bleek F, Haberland W, Klein AW, Caroli S. Steps towards environmental hazard assessment of new chemicals. *Chemosphere* 1982; **11**: 383–415.

Risk assessment of major chemical disasters and the role of the poisons centre

Theodore G. Tong

Arizona Poison Information Centre, The University of Arizona, Tuscon, Arizona, USA

INTRODUCTION

Spills, leaks, fires and other accidents during the manufacture, transport, use and storage of hazardous chemicals and toxic substances are occurring throughout communities in the United States at an alarming frequency. Actions during a hazardous chemical or toxic substance release are frequently conducted in a confused and inefficient fashion when on-scene responders, in the absence of any coordinated pre-incidental operational plan for response, raise questions on what to do and where to obtain help. Response on these occasions typically involves numerous authorities and jurisdictions representing law enforcement, fire, safety, public health, and emergency medical responders.

Lack of coordination of warning and notification procedures are further complicated on these occasions by insufficient access to the knowledge and skills needed to identify the materials released and to determine the health problems they may cause.

In many communities where these incidents pose considerable risk, poisons centres have become an important participant in the network of agencies, services and individuals with designated responsibilities and tasks for managing and giving assistance during these emergencies.

RISK ASSESSMENT

As the chemicals frequently involved in major disasters are mixtures, the symptoms and complaints experienced by individuals who are, or who have already been exposed are very often non-specific in character. Chemical agents usually have multiple organ system effects and depending on the route, duration, amount and concentration of the exposure, the onset and duration of symptoms will vary widely. In any risk assessment process involving toxic substances there is no substitute for scrupulous collection of details particularly on the physical condition of anyone exposed and the circumstances that surround the incident.

Ocular and dermal injury can occur following contact or exposure to materials such as oxidants, corrosives, and vesicants. Chemicals absorbed can produce

Major chemical disasters—medical aspects of management, edited by Virginia Murray, 1990: Royal Society of Medicine Services International Congress and Symposium Series No. 155, published by Royal Society of Medicine Services Limited.

Table 1   *Examples of special problems in hazardous materials incidents*

Irritant gases:
  Chlorine
  Ammonia
  Oxides of nitrogen and sulphur
  Acids
  Phosgene
  Aldehydes
  Isocyanates

Simple asphyxiants:
  Nitrogen
  Methane
  Carbon dioxide

Chemical asphyxiants:
  Carbon monoxide
  Nitrites
  Cyanides
  Hydrogen sulphide

Toxic hazards:
  Heavy metals, zinc, nickel, lead, mercury, arsenic, chromium
  Pesticides: organophosphates, carbamates

Others:
  Paraquat
  Polychlorinated biphenyls

significant systemic toxicity. Some chemicals can cause both cutaneous damage and systemic toxicity following exposure or contact with them. The majority of toxic injury encountered during hazardous chemical and toxic material incidents is through inhalation (Table 1). Specific antidotes are indicated for serious poisoning with chemical asphyxiants (i.e. carbon monoxide, cyanide, the methaemoglobin formers), organophosphate, and carbamate pesticides (Table 2).

However, risk assessement will frequently show that in the overwhelming majority of cases, casualties from chemical incident exposures will only require administration of symptomatic and supportive care.

Table 2   *Examples of emergency pharmacotherapy in hazardous materials exposures*

Oxygen
Atropine
Pralidoxime
Cyanide antidote kit
Methylene blue
Chelating agents:
  BAL
  d-penicillamine
  Calcium disodium EDTA
  DMSA
  DMPS
Calcium gluconate

The role of poisons centres in risk assessment

The notion that poisons centres have an important responsibility for providing a variety of response activities, such as risk assessment during hazardous chemical or toxic substances release incidents, has been given much recent attention (1,2,3).

As the resource for information on the pathophysiological effects of chemicals and toxic substances, a poisons centre's immediate aim in risk assessment is to determine:

1. Identity materials released or at risk of being released
2. Real or estimated quantities involved
3. Specific nature of the release or type of accident
4. Reactions observed between released materials and the environment or any known casualties or injured

Estimations are then established for the probability of short-term and long-term toxicity that might be experienced from contact, or exposure to the hazard or hazards. Where the hazardous materials incident is complex and 'major' in scope, special consultants and expertise are called upon to provide additional support and assistance. Thus, the ability of poisons centres to competently and thoroughly assess the health threats of chemical and toxic substance release incidents is a necessity.

Poisons centres have become designated in some local and regional emergency response plans as the focal point for alerting treatment facilities and public safety agencies of possible dangers and appropriate courses of action to take during exposure to hazardous and toxic materials; most centres will not recommend specific testing, containment, decontamination or disposal procedures but will refer such inquiries to the appropriate local, regional, or state agencies responsible for these activities and services. Usually, consultation with poisons centres medical staff is a policy and procedure followed whenever advice on specific antidote pharmacotherapy is being considered. Appropriate precautions to take to avoid contamination are emphasized whenever the poisons centre has determined that a health hazard may exist.

In addition, poisons centres in the USA have a vital role to play in minimizing public confusion and fear by offering readily accessible details on expected health hazards and making appropriate referrals to experts on containment, clean-up, and disposal of hazardous materials.

Poisons centre risk assessment requirements

Centres engaged in hazardous materials response efforts are expected to have rapid access to computerized information on hazardous materials with listings of their physical and chemical properties and details on their safe handling, containment and decontamination.

Poisons centres aiming to assist in toxic emergency response must:

1. Have full-time specialists trained and proficient in the retrieval, analysis and communication of medical, toxicological, and chemical information
2. Be accessible for information and assistance on a 24 hour-a-day seven-days-a-week basis to public safety and medical personnel; they must be similarly available to the public during incidents
3. Have resources organized in such a manner to permit rapid access to technical and clinical information dealing with hazardous materials

4. Have procedures and capabilities for recording keeping and review
5. Be located in a medical facility with ready access to consultants from various medical, laboratory, industrial, and occupational health related clinical and scientific specialties
6. Have interest and capability to provide training to medical and other health specialists on matters related to toxicology and hazardous substances

During an incident, the information a Centre should be able to provide includes physical and chemical property data, reactivity and toxicity information, and advice on medical management. In addition, the centre through its consultants, should aim to provide the medical personnel with access to a range of expertise including environmental and industrial toxicologists, occupational health specialists, hazardous wastes and materials specialists. The evaluation of the toxic exposure will include identifying instances where antidotes may be of value (Table 3).

Table 3 *The poisons centre's role in hazardous materials emergencies*

1. Participate in a coordinated, community-specific response plan with clearly designated responsibilities and defined procedures when a hazardous materials emergency occurs
2. Assist incident responders in identifying and assessing the threat to health and environment
3. Facilitate the linkage between toxicological expertise and information resources with incident responders and the emergency management system; the goal for such ties is to arrive at appropriate decisions dealing with health and environmental risks
4. Assist in the mobilization of medical resources to provide rescue and emergency care of those injured or ill from exposure to toxic release
5. Provide appropriate medical management information to medical personnel treating victims
6. Be a mechanism by which health effects from exposures can be accurately followed up and documented post-incident
7. Be the designated toxicological focal point for dissemination of accurate, clear, consistent, and appropriate information to the public during toxic incidents
8. Offer educational programmes and opportunities to medical and public safety personnel on control, management, and response to hazardous chemical incidents
9. Evaluate toxicological information and data on hazardous materials and become an accessible repository of this information and data
10. Become involved in a surveillance role to help identify and remove undetected environmental toxic hazards from the community

INSTANCES OF POISONS CENTRE INVOLVEMENT IN CHEMICAL INCIDENTS

During several recent widely publicized hazardous chemical accidents, poisons centres have found themselves the centre of enquiry from on-scene incident responders, the media and a confused, anxious, and sometimes angry public for information on possible acute health effects, decontamination procedures and recommendations for treatment. The experience of centres that have been involved in these circumstances are quite consistent and similar with regard to the type of information assistance and expertise referral requested, regardless of the chemicals or materials released. A review of some major incidents shows that poisons centres are an excellent resource for coordination of emergency medical personnel dealing with poisoned patients, incoming to emergency treatment facilities with potential medical problems.

Several case histories are given here to demonstrate the considerable contribution poisons centres can make to accurate risk assessment and advice on immediate action to minimize adverse consequences of these threats (3,4,5). The centres played an important role by correctly determining the seriousness of the toxic exposure.

21 November 1979: 3.30 pm, San Francisco, California

A fire was reported to have started, probably ignited by an electric heater at a location in an area of mostly manufacturing and warehousing facilities adjacent to downtown San Francisco. The blaze had grown to become a four-alarm incident within minutes, fueled by leaking chemicals illegally stored in the structure. As responding firefighters fought the unusually heavy, thick, acrid, and greenish-brown coloured smoke, the nearby on-ramps to the San Francisco Bay Bridge were closed, snarling dense rush-hour traffic on this late afternoon trying to leave the city before the Thanksgiving Day holiday.

A number of firefighters were overcome by smoke and exhaustion. In one instance, a 48-year-old firefighter required transport from the scene to the San Francisco General Hospital for evaluation. On arrival at the Emergency Department, he was in acute respiratory distress, cyanotic and lethargic. No evidence of myocardial involvement could be found on examination. He failed to improve following administration of 40% oxygen. Blood drawn for arterial blood gas analysis was an unusual chocolate-brown colour.

The San Francisco Bay Area Poison Control Center (SFBAPCC) specialists, situated in the Emergency Department, were consulted by physicians who were confronted with this dilemma. Methaemoglobinaemia, caused by inhalation of a toxic by-product of combustion, was suggested by the poisons centre as the likely aetiology. Accordingly, the subsequent administration of methylene blue produced dramatic and rapid improvement and an uneventful recovery of this firefighter.

Early recognition and successful resolution of this life-threatening toxic problem, helped dramatically to focus attention of the city's fire and public health departments on the importance of a poisons control centre as a resource during emergencies that involve toxic and hazardous materials.

13 January 1980: 6.55 am, San Francisco, California

San Francisco firefighters, responding to multiple alarms, rushed to the scene of a blaze in an area close to the city's downtown. Upon arrival, it was apparent to the incident command that chemicals stored in the building were involved. The SFBAPCC was called at 7.10 am by fire and public health department officials urgently requesting the assistance of a poison information specialist at the scene to identify the toxic hazards and to assess the threat to health from this fire. The Center responded immediately by dispatching the director to the scene.

The large two storey building was the office and warehouse of the same firm involved in the November 1979 fire. Under the guise of being a pharmaceutical manufacturer, this firm was a leading producer of isobutyl nitrite, a chemical commercially promoted and sold as a perfume or room deodorizer known as 'Rush'. Vapours of 'Rush' and other butyl nitrite compounds are alleged to enhance sexual performance when inhaled and are purchased solely for this purpose.

This fire, which eventually completely destroyed the building took scores of firefighters nearly six hours to control; it was not until two days afterwards that workers from surrounding office complexes were able to re-enter the area without experiencing respiratory and eye irritation. There were no serious injuries encountered during this episode.

Prompted by the growing number of similar incidents, the San Francisco Fire Department (SFFD), in late January 1980, convened an *an hoc* advisory committee to assist and give guidance in the formulation of a city-wide contingency plan to respond to the problems of hazardous materials emergencies. This group, composed of designated representatives of the SFFD, SFBAPCC, city departments of public health, water, public works, the mayor's office of emergency services, a number of other experienced individuals in occupational medicine, nursing, public health, industrial safety, and emergency planning, met regularly for several months to study the issues. Findings were made and specific recommendations presented to the SFFD by this advisory committee. These specific action suggestions were then extensively examined and studied by the department with participation by agencies from city, region, and state, and hazardous materials management consultants. Nearly a year later, a notification and alert plan was developed, adopted, and implemented by the fire department. The advisory committee was also asked to continue serving the department as a consultant on matters related to the planning and conduct of emergency response to hazardous materials incidents.

Major findings by the *ad hoc* Advisory Group to the San Francisco Fire Department, 1980

1. The poisons centre should be a central communications point in any hazardous material emergency response plan
2. The centre should develop standard protocols for emergency response, covering antidotes, first aid, notification of emergency medical personnel, and treatment facilities
3. A hazardous materials incident response team should be assembled, comprised of individuals who can be called for technical assistance on toxicology information and can give experienced on-scene help
4. Any responder at the scene must be trained and experienced in areas of toxicology, industrial hygiene, and basic combustion chemistry; have appropriate reference materials; be aware of the department's plan of operation for hazardous emergencies; be familiar with the use and limits of personal protective equipment; and have expertise in the use of essential on-scene measurement techniques
5. An emergency hazardous materials response plan should be developed for the city, with notification procedures and contingency options clearly outlined
6. A procedure should be developed for medical follow up of exposed firefighters through the poisons centre's toxicological/medical consultants
7. Minimum standards for training and personal protective clothing requirements should be established for fire department personnel who have responsibilities in hazardous materials response

3 April 1983, 4:15 am, Denver, Colorado

Just after 4:15 am on 3 April 1983, a spill of 20 000 gallons of nitric acid occurred in the central Denver railyards. The acid spread over a 300×300 foot area and an acid cloud began to rise over the city. The rapid spread of fumes ultimately led to an evacuation of 3000 residents.

The Rocky Mountain Poison and Drug Center was one of the initial agencies involved in the management of the spill. Specialists and consultants from the Center outlined the potential toxic effects of nitric acid fume inhalation and supplied medical treatment information to workers involved in the clean-up of the spill, hospitals and health workers, the media and the public throughout the entire incident, which took nearly three days to secure.

The increased need for information from the poisons centre resulted in a 200% increase in the centre's average daily call volume with a total of 648 calls received on 3 April 1983.

14 August 1985 approximately 3:00 pm, New York City

The New York City Poison Control Center was advised by police that a metalworking plant in the Borough of Queens was burning out of control. It was known that the plant had on site 74 drums of cyanide each containing 55 gallons (exact chemical composition unknown).

A public advisory was immediately issued from the centre about the hazards of the situation along with instructions about use of protective equipment and on-site first aid. The New York Hazardous Material Emergency Unit, several mobile emergency room vehicles, the department of environmental service, police, fire, and emergency medical services units were all participating as incident responders.

During the first hours of the incident, the poison information specialists contacted all of the emergency departments throughout the area that would potentially receive casualties from the incident in order to assure that medical personnel were familiar with the use of the Lilly Cyanide Antidote Kit. In addition, they were reminded of the possibility that any individual brought from the fire site might not be poisoned with cyanide, but that other toxic by-products of combustion, such as carbon monoxide, might be involved.

The poison control centre quickly became aware that the hospitals likely to receive patients from the scene had very limited supplies of the antidote kits. The centre became the lead agency to coordinate the acquisition of the antidote. A telephone call from the centre to Eli Lilly and Company in Indianapolis, Indiana, resulted in an immediate air shipment of 60 cyanide antidote kits into the disaster area within two hours.

SUMMARY

In summary, the role of many poisons centres has expanded beyond the traditional scope of prevention and treatment of accidental childhood ingestions and acute drug overdoses. Forced by circumstances and necessity, many centres have become useful resources of information and referral assistance during chemical release accidents. In the process of risk assessments, poison control centres must be prepared to act quickly and correctly on these occasions. Poison control centres have found that the most productive experiences of risk assessment have occurred when special efforts were taken during the planning process to improve communications and to establish resources for accurate and complete information prior to a chemical or toxic substance release and not during such an incident.

REFERENCES

(1) Tong TG, Becker CE, Foliart D, *et al.* A model poison control system. *West J Med* 1982; **137**: 346–50.
(2) Perrin EV, Micik S. Poison control centers and the toxic environment. *Emerg Med* 1982; **14**(17):95–8.
(3) Tong TG, Joe G, Morse LH, *et al.* A poison center experience with environmental emergencies. *Vet Hum Toxicol* 1983; **25**(suppl 1): 29–33.
(4) Spiller SK, Wruk KM, Montanio CD, *et al.* Poison center disaster management: a strategic plan. *Vet Hum Toxicol* 1985; **27**: 301.
(5) Weisman RS, Goldfrank L, Bellini R. Chemical disasters (Letter). *Vet Hum Toxicol* 1985; **27**: 439.

SESSION V

MEDICAL ASPECTS OF MANAGEMENT
OF MAJOR CHEMICAL DISASTERS

Management of respiratory effects

Denis Edwards

Intensive Care Unit, University Hospital, South Manchester, UK

INTRODUCTION

The effects of various corrosive chemicals when inhaled on the lung are all broadly similar (1) and these are comparable to the effects of smoke inhalation (2). This is because smoke produced in domestic fires nearly always contains a variety of noxious agents and it is they, rather than the carboniferous products of combustion, which produce the characteristic clinical problems.

The respiratory effects seen are divided into three phases (3): early, intermediate and late (Table 1). These will be considered separately.

EARLY RESPIRATORY EFFECTS—THE FIRST SIX HOURS

The most immediate life-threatening problem is hypoxia caused by gases displacing oxygen from the atmosphere (4,5). As with fires, this effect is more pronounced in enclosed spaces. The hypoxia can lead to coma and the victim is unable to effect self-rescue. After rescue any victim must be assumed to be hypoxic and should be treated with supplemental inspired oxygen, preferably at a high flow rate (10–15 litres/min). If there is any doubt about the ability of the victim to maintain the airway or the adequacy of ventilation then endotracheal intubation and mechanical ventilation needs to be undertaken—at the scene if necessary.

There is a spectrum of injury which ranges from an irritating cough or sensation of sore throat to immediate or early death. The factors governing the type and severity of response include the type of chemical involved, the dose inhaled or absorbed, the duration of exposure, the presence or absence of other injuries such as thermal cutaneous burns and individual susceptibility such as atopy or pre-existing pulmonary or cardiac disease.

Cerebral hypoxia leads to coma and the victim is unable to effect self-rescue. This leads to further inhalation of toxic gases and exposure to hypoxic environment and in fires more severe cutaneous burns.

The signs of respiratory distress include those of hypoxia which are a change in the level of consciousness, heart rate or blood pressure, vasoconstriction with pallor of the skin and sometimes accompanied by sweating, and in extreme cases

Major chemical disasters—medical aspects of management, edited by Virginia Murray, 1990: Royal Society of Medicine Services International Congress and Symposium Series No. 155, published by Royal Society of Medicine Services Limited.

Table 1 *Respiratory effects of chemical inhalation*

Early:	
6 hours	Hypoxia
	Bronchospasm
	Pulmonary oedema
	Systemic toxic effects
Intermediate:	
<48 hours	Bronchospasm
	Laryngeal oedema
	Pulmonary oedema
	Bronchiolar oedema/sloughing
Late:	
>48 hours	ARDS
	Secondary infection
	Fibrosis

central cyanosis. There may be signs of respiratory distress which are related to increased activity of the respiratory muscles or evidence of fatigue particularly in the diaphragm. These are:

- Tachypnoea (>40 breaths per minute)
- Falling respiratory rate
- Use of accessory muscles
- Intercostal indrawing or recession
- An irregular respiratory rate or pattern
- Paradoxical respiration

In paradoxical respiration, the contractions of the diaphragm and intercostal muscles are dysco-ordinated as a result of diaphragmatic fatigue. The chest and abdomen move in opposite directions during the respiratory cycle. It is a sign of impending apnoea and imminent death.

Endotracheal intubation and mechanical ventilation may be technically difficult and the most senior/skilled operator available should carry it out. Anaesthetic drugs may be required. For this, and other reasons, one ought to construct rescue or disaster plans that include the transport of senior intensive care personnel, i.e. consultants, to the scene at the earliest time.

Available equipment should include a portable mechanical ventilator and a monitor/defibrillator. Some inhaled gases can be absorbed systemically and it is at this point that specific antidotes need to be applied (these are beyond the scope of this presentation but are discussed elsewhere).

Even in the absence of signs of hypoxaemia or respiratory distress patients can be significantly or severely hypoxic and at the earliest possible moment arterial blood should be withdrawn for measurement of blood gases. The decision to ventilate is based on a combined assessment of the clinical state and the blood gases. In some cases the patient may be in extreme distress with reasonable gases, but should be ventilated. In other cases the patient should be ventilated even if clinically well, if the PaO_2 is <8kP$_a$ on supplemental inspired oxygen. To wait for a rising $PaCO_2$ is to court disaster as the rises are not linear but exponential and are associated with rapid falls in PaO_2, especially in the patient with pneuchymal lung damage. A common mistake in the early phases of pulmonary injury is to administer bronchodilators prior to correction of hypoxia. By abolishing the homeostatic reflex of hypoxic pulmonary vasoconstriction these can lead to worsening hypoxaemia.

Table 2 *Sequence of action after chemical inhalation*

The victim is rescued
↓
Oxygenated/ventilated
↓
Other first aid measures,
e.g. I.V. fluids
↓
Transfer to specialized centre

If victims of toxic gas inhalation are deemed to require ventilation and therefore endotracheal intubation, the technique of intubation is crucial. Once again it cannot be overemphasized that an experienced operator is required. The fully conscious patient may require intravenous anaesthesia and muscle relaxants (suxamethonium). The moribund patient can be intubated with neither of these. Failure to intubate rapidly after administration of relaxants or sedatives or delay in intubation in moribund hypoxic patients can lead to disaster.

Corrosive agents may cause swelling and oedema of the upper airway very quickly after the incident. This is one of the reasons why intubation may be difficult and why it should be performed as soon as possible. Some agents such as NO_2 or SO_2 can cause immediate bronchospasm. Although bronchodilators including steroids are usually given it is difficult to know how effective they really are (6). Certainly they should not be given without prior administration of high concentrations of oxygen as the beta$_2$-agonists in particular can worsen hypoxia in a patient breathing air.

The bronchospasm can be delayed for six to 24 h and victims need to be observed during this period no matter how well they seem to be.

INTERMEDIATE RESPIRATORY EFFECTS—SIX TO 48 HOURS

The major hazard during this period is that chemical irritation of the bronchial mucosa causes progressive oedema. The most irritant agents cause lysis of the mucosa which sloughs away. At this point the patient will suffocate rapidly if breathing spontaneously.

Hopefully the significance of the respiratory injury will have been appreciated and the patient will be intubated and mechanically ventilated. This may require the generation of high peak inflation pressures and there is the constant danger of borotrauma including intrinsic positive end expiratory pressure (PEEPi), this can lower blood pressure by lowering cardiac output, which leads to a reduction in tissue oxygen consumption (VO_2).

$$VO_2 = \text{cardiac output} \times (\text{arterial} - \text{mixed venous oxygen content})$$

$$\text{mean arterial pressure} = \text{cardiac output} \times \text{systemic vascular resistance}$$

It is important to maintain ventricular filling pressures at optimal levels but even with this inotropic support may be needed. Dobutamine is the agent of choice for this. For this level of support full invasive monitoring is mandatory. The most striking, dramatic and potentially dangerous complication of this phase is that the endotracheal tube may be blocked by plugs of mucosa and mucus debris.

This is often complete and unresponsive to suction. The tube may have to be changed—a difficult and dangerous manoeuvre under the circumstances. In extreme cases the whole of the bronchial tree may lose its mucosa over a matter of hours. This is associated with significant loss of fluid, albumen, electrolytes and blood and transfusion therapy has to be adjusted accordingly.

LATE RESPIRATORY EFFECTS—MORE THAN 48 HOURS— RECOVERY OR DEATH

There are two major complications that may arise at this stage. They are pulmonary infection and the Adult Respiratory Distress Syndrome.

Infection is common because of the denuded bronchial epithelium. A variety of organisms may be implicated including staphylococci, Gram-negative rods and anaerobes in addition to the usual respiratory pathogens which are pneumococci and haemophilus. Antibiotic therapy at this stage may have to be with combinations of agents or one of the newer more powerful broad spectrum agents. The combination of a 'naked' bronchial tree and an endotracheal tube by-passing the usual upper airway defences against infection can be a recipe for disaster from the infection point of view. Meticulous care needs to be given to such procedures as bronchial suction and physiotherapy.

Respiratory infections frequently lead to bacteraemia with all its attendant sequelae including sepsis syndrome and septic shock. A detailed discussion of these conditions is beyond the scope of this presentation, but suffice it to say that the sepsis syndrome is frequently associated with generalized multisystem organ failure which will need further artificial support and that septic shock in its full blown form still has a mortality of 90% in most centres.

Having hopefully survived all the above mentioned problems the patient now faces the largest obstacle to his recovery—the Adult Respiratory Distress Syndrome (ARDS). This has a characteristic pathophysiology which includes increased pulmonary venous admixture, increased physiological dead space, increased pulmonary capillary permeability and reduced compliance. ARDS was first described as a complication of major trauma and was described as a common cause of death in the Vietnam war.

Indeed it was such a frequent occurrence after some battles, and one in particular, that it became known for a time as 'Da Nang Lung'. Its causes today are divided into direct and indirect. The inhalation of toxic gases would be one of the direct causes. However, it can complicate the systemic effects of some chemicals particularly if they cause hypotension. Also the combination of a direct insult to the lung such as smoke or chemical inhalation and an indirect one such as caustic or thermal burns to the skin can cause a particularly fulminant form of the syndrome which may manifest itself during the early phase described (7,8).

Virtually by definition, patients with ARDS will require mechanical ventilation. Despite this the majority will require high fractional inspired concentration of oxygen (FIO_2). Because of the high levels of alveolar dead space large tidal volumes will be needed which in the presence of reduced pulmonary compliance will lead to high peak inflation pressures. The patient is again at risk from barotrauma. The ventilator should be adjusted so that peak inflation pressures do not exceed 60 centimetres of H_2O. This may require adjustment and sometimes reversal of the inspiratory to expiratory time ratio. A longer inspiratory time will allow the least compliant areas of the lung to be ventilated. In order to reduce the need for high levels of FIO_2 and the degree of pulmonary venous admixture external positive end expiratory pressure ventilation (PEEPi) is often used. There have been doubts expressed about the efficacy of PEEPi in view of the continued poor outcome from ARDS—the mortality being in excess of 70% in the majority of published series. Almost certainly the explanation lies in the fact that PEEPi lowers cardiac output in the majority of cases. This often occurs without a fall in blood pressure as there is a compensatory increase in systemic vascular resistance (see formula above). This is unfortunate as it leads to a reduction in the total amount of oxygen delivered to the tissues—the oxygen delivery (DO_2).

$$DO_2 = cardiac\ output \times arterial\ oxygen\ content$$

Unless cardiac output is being measured this effect remains undetected and arterial oxygen tension may even increase. In many patients, therefore, the use of PEEPi may worsen outcome lowering DO_2 and producing tissue hypoxia. This problem is worsened by the fact that in ARDS—whether of direct or indirect aetiology, the tissues depend on very high levels of DO_2.

SUMMARY AND CONCLUSIONS

The management of respiratory complications of disasters involving chemicals can vary from a few minutes of oxygen therapy by mask, with immediate improvement, or several weeks of mechanical ventilation followed by death from multisystem organ failure. Apart from specific antidotes available in only a minority of cases management is based on the principles of A,B,C—Airway, Breathing, Circulation (7,8). Procrastination about intubation and ventilation can be disastrous. The decision to ventilate depends on a rapid assessment of clinical signs and arterial blood gases. The attendance of a skilled intubator, by definition an anaesthetist in the majority of instances is mandatory.

To obtain full recovery skilled and experienced management is required from or even before the time of rescue. The first step is to convert the 'victim' to a 'patient' that is to deliver him alive to the intensive care unit. Thereafter in the severest cases a long series of complications may occur which require multiple and sophisticated therapeutic interventions. The true test of any disaster response is not how many victims are rescued alive at the scene, but how many of those survive to reach hospital, and how many leave hospital alive. Preventable deaths, even those in hospital, should be recorded and investigated so that the response can be modified in the future.

REFERENCES

(1) Moylan JA, Chan C-K. Inhalation injury—an increasing problem. *Ann Surg* 1978; **188**(1): 34–7.
(2) Brown J. Management of injury due to smoke inhalation. *J Roy Soc Med* 1982; Vol 75(Suppl 1): 44–51.
(3) Trunkey DD. Inhalation injury: symposium on burns. *Surg Clinics N Am* 1978; **58**(6): 1132–40.
(4) Clark CJ, Campbell D, Reid WH. Blood carboxyhaemaglobin and cyanide levels in fire survivors. *Lancet* 1981; i: 1332–5.
(5) Jackson DL, Menges H. Accidental carbon monoxide poisoning. *JAMA* 1980; **243**(8): 772–4.

(6) Beeley MJ, Crow J, Jones GJ, Minty B, Lynch RD, Pryce DP. Mortality and lung histopathology after inhalation lung injury. *Am Rev Respir Dis* 1986; **133**: 191–6.
(7) Achauer BM, Allyn PA, Furnas DW, Bartlett RH. Pulmonary complications of burns: the major threat to the burn patient. *Ann Surg* 1973; **127**(3): 311–19.
(8) Navar PO, Saffle JR, Warden GD. Effect of inhalation injury on fluid resuscitation requirements after thermal injury. *Am J Surg* 1985; **150**: 716–20.
(9) Crapo RO. Smoke-inhalation injuries. *JAMA* 1981; **246**(15): 1694–6.

Management of chemical burns of the eye

John Beare

Western Ophthalmic Hospital, London, UK

SUMMARY AND INTRODUCTION

Chemical burns of the eye can result in permanent blindness if the urgency of the situation is not recognized (1). Copious and immediate irrigation with water or saline remains the most important aspect of management (2). Prevention is undoubtedly better than cure and the use of correctly fitting and appropriate safety spectacles or goggles *must* be enforced where noxious chemicals are handled (3).

The toxicity of certain chemicals to the eye has been known for centuries. The red eyes of sewer workers caused by hydrogen sulphide gas were noted by Ramazzini, firing his interest in occupational diseases and culminating in his classic treatise on the subject in 1700 (4,5). Changing industrial practices have meant that some substances which were formerly common causes of serious ocular injury such as sulphur dioxide from refrigerators (6) are now less common. Industry is still responsible for the majority of chemical hazards, but the rising incidence of non-accidental chemical injuries is of increasing importance, assuming almost epidemic proportions in London at present (7-9).

Serious injury is fortunately uncommon considering the large number of chemical incidents involving the eye (10), although some chemicals are more likely to cause significant damage, in particular strong acids and alkalis. It is important to distinguish between ocular injury due to *systemic* absorption of chemicals or drugs and that due to *external contact* of chemicals with the eye. Several excellent reference works deal comprehensively with the former subject of ocular toxicity from systemic absorption of drugs and chemicals (1,2,11-13) which will not be dealt with further in this paper.

Modern disasters

The huge chemical disaster in Bhopal in 1984 resulted from a massive leak of over 40 tons of methylisocyanate (MIC). Over 2500 people died mainly as a result of the pulmonary effects of the vapour, to which more than 200 000 may have been exposed. Eye injuries were common, resulting mainly in superficial punctate erosions of the corneal epithelium, although total corneal epithelial loss was seen in those worst affected. Many patients were temporarily completely incapacitated, but there were no cases of deeper corneal injury or vascularization in the cases

Major chemical disasters—medical aspects of management, edited by Virginia Murray, 1990: Royal Society of Medicine Services International Congress and Symposium Series No. 155, published by Royal Society of Medicine Services Limited.

examined, and the superficial injuries rapidly healed (14–17). Persistent eye watering has been reported in some patients (18).

Protective mechanisms

The defensive mechanisms of the eye can be rapidly overwhelmed by noxious chemicals. Increased tearing will tend to dilute the chemical, but strong alkalis in particular rapidly penetrate the normal cornea (11,19,20). Bells phenomenon (a reflex upward turning of the eye when the lids are closed) tends to protect the upper cornea, although in serious contact injuries the whole cornea and limbus may be damaged. Severe blepharospasm caused by the pain of acute chemical injuries may make adequate irrigation of the eye extremely difficult.

Determinants of severity of injury

The major determinants of the severity of injury are the nature of the chemical, its concentration and pH, the quantity involved, the period of contact with the eye (i.e. the speed with which irrigation is begun), and its physical state (whether gas, vapour, liquid, or solid). Even mildly basic or acidic chemicals can cause substantial injury if the period of contact is prolonged (21,22).

The causes of chemical eye burns can be divided into *accidental* (e.g. industrial, agricultural, and household incidents) and *non-accidental*. The more serious injuries tend to be from acids, alkalis, and corrosives.

ACCIDENTAL CAUSES

A huge number of different substances are accidentally splashed into the eyes both at home and at work every day. Fortunately the vast majority of these substances cause only superficial injury to the eye and probably only a very small percentage of these cases ever attend hospital, making a full recovery without treatment.

Household products

Accidents commonly occur at home where a number of agents have the potential for causing serious eye injury, e.g. household ammonia, and drain cleaners containing sodium hydroxide. Other noxious substances are freely available through hardware stores for use as cleaning agents, e.g. spirit of salts (30% hydrochloric acid solution).

Occupational exposure

Potentially very dangerous chemicals of an enormous variety may be handled. If a chemical is hot, a thermal burn may be superimposed on the effects of the chemical burn. Liquids under pressure may similarly cause severe associated mechanical injury to the eye.

Alkalis

Strong alkalis have been shown to penetrate the normal rabbit cornea within 15 seconds of instillation (19), although the actual rate of penetration depends to some extent on the cation, being most rapid in the case of ammonia which causes the most severe injuries (21,22). When the pH is greater than 11.0, devastating injuries are common.

Household ammonia (commonly sold as 7–9.5% solution in water in the UK) is widely available and can cause serious injury. It is commonly used as a weapon in cases of assault. Ammonia is used on a huge scale in industry in various manufacturing processes, in fertilizers, etc., and is thus a frequent and serious potential hazard.

Sodium hydroxide (NaOH,lye), e.g. in drain cleaners, caustic potash (KOH), and calcium hydroxide as lime or in mortar and cement are all common causes of serious eye injury.

Acids

The penetration of acids tends to be limited to some extent by the formation of insoluble complexes with surface proteins, although strong acids (pH < 2.5) may produce very severe injuries similar to strong alkalis, with permanent corneal and intraocular damage (23). Exploding car batteries (which contain sulphuric acid) account for a number of these injuries where serious mechanical injury to the eye from flying debris may be combined with chemical injury (24).

Corrosives

Compounds of arsenic, phosphorus, sulphur, chlorine, aniline dyes, creosote, fertilizers and pesticides may all cause serious eye injuries with permanent corneal scarring.

Detergents, organic solvents

Alcohols, aldehydes, ketones, esters and ethers tend to produce milder injuries. These agents all cause superficial damage to the corneal epithelium which rapidly heals, rarely causing any permanent damage. Cyanoacrylate glues may seal the eyelids together for several days and cause superficial corneal injury.

NON-ACCIDENTAL CAUSES

Assault

An increasing problem in major cities is the use of chemical sprays in 'mugging' (25). There has been a recent marked rise in the incidence of this type of assault in London (7,8). At the Western Ophthalmic Hospital in Central London we saw one such case due to mugging in 1984, three in 1985, 16 in 1986, 37 in 1987 and 40 cases in 1988. Of these patients, 15% suffered very serious injuries with effective permanent blindness in the affected eye (9). Quite apart from the toll in terms of human misery, this does represent a very substantial economic burden to the National Health Service, each patient costing an average of at least £500 to treat. Ammonia was the likely agent in the most severe cases, although a study is in progress with The National Poisons Unit, Guy's Hospital, London in an attempt to identify precisely which chemicals are being used in personal assault with chemicals (26).

Vesicant war gases

Serious eye problems were common in those soldiers who survived nitrogen mustard gas attacks in the First World War. Severe corneal burns with total corneal epithelial loss resulted, with later onset of gross corneal oedema, corneal ulceration and vascularization (1). The symptoms of poor vision, watering and pain often persisted for many years after the acute event and were often bilateral. Similar injuries have been seen recently in relation to the Iran/Iraq conflict.

Lacrimators (tear gas)

Lacrimators such as CS gas or Mace are commonly used for riot control or personal protection ('antirape'). They cause extreme eye irritation and tearing even at very low concentrations due to stimulation of corneal nerve endings. No tissue damage usually occurs, but serious eye injury with permanent corneal scarring has occurred when the chemical was discharged very close to the eye, where mechanical injury may have contributed (2).

GRADING OF SEVERITY OF INJURY AND SYMPTOMS

Roper-Hall describes four grades of chemical eye injury from mild to very severe (27–29), paying particular attention to the presence and degree of limbal vessel ischaemia, and the degree of corneal opacification at presentation, both of which correlate with the long-term visual prognosis. (See Colour Figs 1–6)

Chemical conjunctivitis and superficial keratitis

The mildest injuries cause irritation and watering, with slight redness of the eye, although with no demonstrable damage on staining with fluorescein at slit lamp examination.

The intensely irritating red eyes which occurred in the aftermath of the bombing of major cities in Germany in the Second World War were a result of chemical irritants, while photochemical smog in large cities (2) and swimming pool conjunctivitis are other examples of very mild chemical injury. Occupational exposure to soap, fertilizers, hydrogen sulphide, pitch, explosives, pesticides and to satinwood or boxwood may all cause incapacitating conjunctivitis and superficial keratitis unless suitable protective eyewear is worn (1).

Superficial corneal oedema

Organic solvent vapours characteristically cause fine epithelial oedema leading to blurred vision and irritation which may be delayed until several hours after exposure. Staining of the cornea with fluorescein would show no obvious abnormality although epithelial oedema would be visible on the slit lamp. The symptoms resolve without treatment.

Corneal epithelial loss

Minimal to total loss of the corneal epithelium may occur. If there is extensive corneal epithelial loss, the eye will be very painful and the profuse watering and blepharospasm will make it difficult for the patient to see, quite apart from the

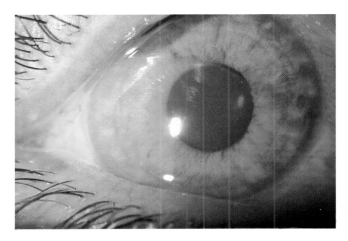

Figure 1 *Partial corneal epithelial loss in a mild chemical burn. Excellent prognosis.*

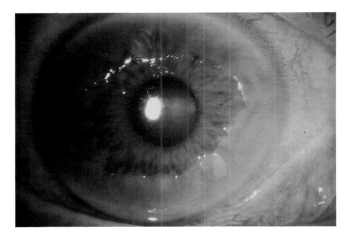

Figure 2 *Concentrated nitric acid burn showing opacification of surface epithelium and epithelial loss. Good prognosis.*

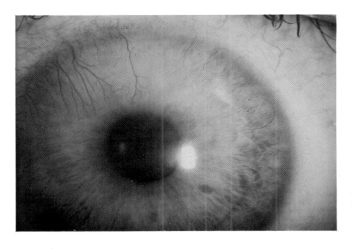

Figure 3 *12 months after moderate severity ammonia burn showing progressive vascularisation of upper cornea. Visual acuity 6/18.*

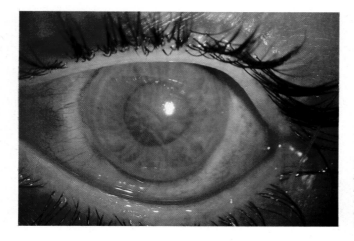

Figure 4 *Severe acute ammonia burn with limbal ischaemia, marked corneal oedema, dilated pupil and early cataract (one day after assault with ammonia spray).*

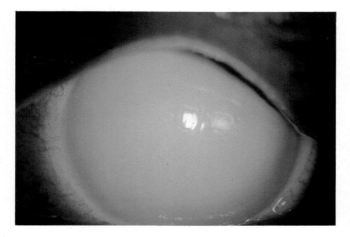

Figure 5 *Same eye as Fig 4 on Day 2 showing total corneal epithelial loss (stained with flourescein).*

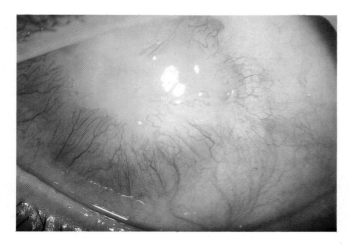

Figure 6 *Same eye as in Fig 4 and 5, 14 months after injury showing gross corneal vascularisation, and vision of perception of light only.*

difficulties of examination and treatment. Where there is no limbal ischaemia (closure of episcleral vessels at the junction of cornea and sclera) after the acute injury, the prognosis for normal vision is excellent, even if fluorescein staining shows total corneal epithelial loss. In contrast, where there is severe limbal ischaemia involving over 180 degrees of the corneal circumference the long-term visual prognosis is often dismal, due to very extensive later corneal vascularization and scarring, often with associated intraocular damage (see Figs 1–6).

Deeper corneal and intraocular damage

Deeper penetration of the cornea will lead to destruction of corneal stromal cells (keratocytes), nerves and blood vessels (20), while intraocular damage may cause both acute and chronic rise in intraocular pressure, cataract, uveitis and even retinal damage (30). Extensive destruction of the conjunctiva may result in formation of a symblepharon, with obliteration of the conjunctival fornices. Also, loss of mucus producing conjunctival goblet cells with additional damage to the lacrimal gland ductules and accessory lacrimal glands may result in tear film instability and symptoms of a dry uncomfortable eye. Stenosis or occlusion of the lacrimal canaliculi may produce a watering eye.

In severe chemical burns (Grades III and IV) there is marked pain, and loss of vision. The absence of pain in such injuries is usually a sinister sign and as in severe thermal burns of the skin may imply destruction of nerves in the cornea.

In severe burns it may not be possible to see the iris through the grossly oedematous cornea, and this always indicates a catastrophic injury (28). In these eyes a hypopyon or hyphaema (a horizontal level of liquid white cells or blood in the anterior chamber, respectively) is commonly seen after a few days, often with a rapidly maturing cataract. Deep involvement of both cornea and sclera may be accompanied by signs of anterior segment ischaemia, and there may be accompanying scleral necrosis.

Pfister comments that the best result that can be obtained in an eye after a severe alkali burn is a totally vascularized and scarred cornea that has not undergone ulceration, and in which glaucoma has not developed (23).

EMERGENCY MANAGEMENT

At site of injury

Regardless of the nature of the chemical, immediate copious irrigation is of the utmost importance. No time should be wasted in either trying to discover the nature of the chemical or to look for specific irrigants or 'antidotes'. If no other means is available, the entire face should be submerged in a container or basin of tap water and the eyes opened and closed continuously. Sterility should be temporarily ignored. It is more essential for the chemical to be diluted and washed away as quickly as possible (31) since any delay in washing out the eye increases the likelihood of severe damage. The provision of emergency eye wash stations (32) at work is crucial where noxious chemicals are in use, and employees should be frequently reminded both of their position and correct use by the use of wall charts and regular instruction, using videotapes and other teaching aids.

An intravenous infusion set attached to a bag of normal saline is a very convenient and effective means of irrigating the eye, and is appropriate for occupational health services, emergency services and also hospitals, all the required equipment being readily available (see Fig. 7).

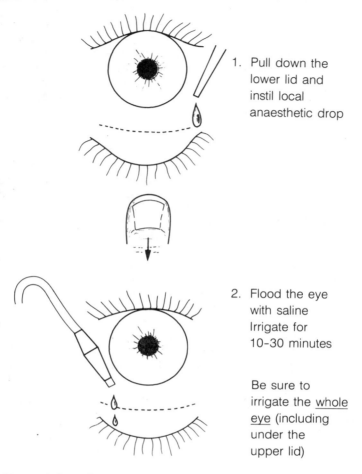

1. Pull down the
   lower lid and
   instil local
   anaesthetic drop

2. Flood the eye
   with saline
   Irrigate for
   10–30 minutes

   Be sure to
   irrigate the whole
   eye (including
   under the
   upper lid)

Figure 7 *How to irrigate the eye.*

Irrigation should be continued for at least 10 minutes, or 30 minutes or longer in the case of strong acids or alkalis, until the conjunctival sac is neutral on pH testing with universal indicator paper (33) or using an indicator such as 0.1% bromophenol blue in the irrigating fluid (28).

Irrigation

Various *special irrigating solutions* have been suggested for the management of eye injuries due to particular chemicals. Examples include 0.05 M sodium edetate for lime burns, normal saline for silver nitrate burns, calcium gluconate solution for hydrofluoric acid, 30% polyethylene glycol-400 for phenol burns, dimercaprol for lewisite burns, 2% sodium thiosulphate solution for mercury fulminate burns and 3% copper sulphate solution for white phosphorus burns (11). Where these chemicals are in use at work it would seem appropriate to have a supply of the specific irrigant available in the occupational health department, assuming of course that the chemical involved in the injury is known. However, any delay in washing out the eye is unacceptable, and in general tap water, normal saline, Hartmanns solution (28) or a universal buffer solution are the best choice of

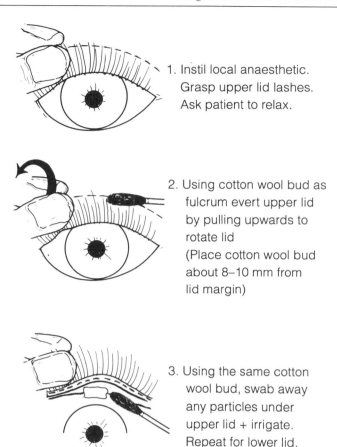

1. Instil local anaesthetic.
   Grasp upper lid lashes.
   Ask patient to relax.

2. Using cotton wool bud as
   fulcrum evert upper lid
   by pulling upwards to
   rotate lid
   (Place cotton wool bud
   about 8–10 mm from
   lid margin)

3. Using the same cotton
   wool bud, swab away
   any particles under
   upper lid + irrigate.
   Repeat for lower lid.

Figure 8 *How to evert an eyelid*

irrigants. Neutralizing solutions, e.g. citric and boric acids to neutralize alkali, and sodium bicarbonate for acid burns (8), whilst theoretically advantageous are probably no more effective than neutral solutions.

Method of irrigation (emergency and hospital)

Pain and blepharospasm may make irrigation very difficult. Warming the irrigating fluid and the use of local anaesthetic drops, e.g. benoxinate, amethocaine or lignocaine, may make irrigation more comfortable for the patient. It is most important to evert the lids to ensure that any residual coagulum of chemical is removed, and it is ideal if this can be done at the site of injury. The technique of eversion of an upper lid is easy once learned (see Fig. 8), but may present problems in a frightened patient in severe pain who cannot open his eyes. This search for and removal of residual particulate chemical is particularly important in lime burns, where 0.02 M EDTA solution may be very useful in removing adherent chemical. A lid speculum may assist irrigation in hospital, but if adequate irrigation is not possible after instilling local anaesthetic drops it is worth considering a short general anaesthetic particularly in children. Any untoward delay is to be avoided. Some authors have suggested a facial nerve block to relieve blepharospasm (21). Double eversion of the upper lid in hospital over a Desmarres retractor may enable better visualization and cleaning of the upper conjunctival fornix.

Some authors have used a commercially available irrigating contact lens (21) or an intravenous cannula inserted through the lid to provide continuous irrigation for several hours as an inpatient.

EMERGENCY TREATMENT IN HOSPITAL

Examination

All but the most trivial injuries should be seen by an ophthalmologist. This is to ensure both that irrigation has been adequate and also that any residual chemical has been removed from the conjunctival fornices. Irrigation should be repeated even if already performed at the site of injury. After irrigation, the visual acuity should be checked in both eyes separately with glasses if worn. On superficial examination the eye may appear *deceptively normal*, and the slit lamp gives a much more accurate view of any damage. Fluorescein staining is required to reveal the full extent of the corneal and conjunctival epithelial loss. In severe injuries the cornea will appear cloudy due to oedema, extensive closure of limbal blood vessels may cause a blanched appearance, and the pupil may be semidilated due to iris damage. Intraocular pressure should always be checked although this may be technically difficult in a very watery painful eye, and there is often marked associated lid swelling due to lid skin burns.

Acute medical care

Eye injuries are of extreme importance although obviously attention must simultaneously be given to any associated injuries, particularly if potentially life threatening, e.g. laryngeal or pulmonary oedema from inhalation of chemicals.

After irrigation the major concerns in the acute stage are to prevent optic nerve damage from raised ocular pressure, and to protect the cornea from ulceration, perforation and infection (21). Acute rise in intraocular pressure (34,35) should be treated with topical beta-blockers, e.g. timolol, often in addition to oral carbonic anhydrase inhibitors, e.g. Diamox.

In the presence of corneal epithelial damage it is sensible to prescribe a topical broad spectrum antibiotic such as gentamicin or chloramphenicol until the epithelium is healed, since infective keratitis is not uncommon. Delayed epithelial healing is common after severe alkali burns, and some authors have used 'bandage' soft contact lenses to speed this process. Mydriatic drops such as cyclopentolate, homatropine or atropine may be useful in relieving pain, although atropine may cause blurred vision for up to two weeks as was noticed by many of the Bhopal victims, and a shorter acting mydriatric may be a better choice, particularly in elderly patients where there is a small risk of angle closure glaucoma from mydriasis.

The use of steroid drops in acute chemical burns is an area of controversy (33). There is fairly widespread agreement that topical steroids should be used during the acute stage. Some authors suggest reducing the dosage or stopping steroids after the first week since they may enhance corneal stromal melting and ulceration, although this is disputed by others. Collagenases produced by invading white blood cells may lead to corneal ulceration or even perforation in severe chemical burns. Topical ascorbate (Vitamin C) or 10% citric acid drops, and collagenase inhibitors such as 10–20% acetylcysteine may be useful in preventing corneal ulceration and perforation in alkali burns (36,37).

Attempts at the prevention of symblepharon formation by the use of doughnut shaped conformers or daily glass rodding to break down adhesions are often unsuccessful.

Emergency surgery

A number of different surgical procedures have been suggested as a means of limiting eye damage in the acute stage of severe chemical burns. These include anterior chamber paracentesis (washout), conjunctival peritomy, and 'auto-hemotherapy' (subconjunctival injection of the patients own blood). There have been no controlled trials of these operations in human subjects, but they each have some support from animal studies and various authors have claimed success with individual patients. Conjunctival or mucous membrane grafting in the acute stage after injury again has its advocates. Some surgeons have even performed lamellar or penetrating keratoplasty (corneal graft) shortly after injury, although the results tend to be poor.

Long-term care

Symptoms of a dry uncomfortable eye are common after severe chemical burns and tear film substitutes, e.g. hypromellose drops, may be useful. Chronic glaucoma is common due to damage to the aqueous drainage apparatus, while other eyes become hypotonic due to ciliary body damage. Scarring of the lacrimal ductules contributes to the dryness of the eye, while the often heavily scarred and vascularized cornea has an irregular surface which tends to wet poorly and is subject to recurrent corneal epithelial breakdown. All these features, combined with a high incidence of secondary glaucoma, makes patients with severe chemical burns poor candidates for corneal grafting. Casey (38) states that 'grafting the alkali burned cornea is a most frustrating experience' and also that it is difficult to estimate the incidence of rejection since the grafts often fail before rejection becomes the dominant feature. The long term results after repeated grafting in chemical burn cases are only approximately 30% successful (39).

Corneal grafting is not usually attempted until at least 12–18 months after the acute injury. If grafting fails, a keratoprosthesis may be the last hope for the retention of some vision in these very severely injured eyes, but this operation does have a high complication and failure rate (40). Plastic surgical procedures are frequently required in order to correct cicatricial lid deformities, trichiasis (ingrowing lashes) and symblepharon.

PREVENTION

Prevention is undoubtedly better than cure.

Where noxious chemicals are in use, frequent, thorough and appropriate education of the workforce and occupational health services about the risks posed by the chemicals that they handle are essential. Unpleasant photographs of badly injured eyes may be of some help in emphasizing the point of this instruction.

Management should ensure that all employees are equipped with correctly fitting, comfortable and tough eye protection which is appropriate for the job, and there should possibly be penalties for those staff who repeatedly refuse to wear the eye protection supplied.

Correct irrigation may prevent serious damage to the eye.

PATHOPHYSIOLOGY

A great deal of research has been carried out in the hope of improving the often dismal visual results in severe chemical burns, usually working on experimental alkali burns in rabbits (11,36,41–43). There have been many useful developments in treatment as a direct result of this important research, although the management of the effects of severe chemical burns on the eye continues to present an enormous challenge.

REFERENCES

(1) Duke-Elder, Sir William. *A system of ophthalmology, Part 2: Injuries*, Vol XIV, Chap XII Chemical injuries. London: Henry Kimpton, 1972: 1011–207.
(2) Potts AM. Toxicology of the eye. In *Casarett and Doull's Toxicology*, 3rd ed (eds). New York: Macmillan, 1986: Chap 17, p. 478.
(3) Read HP. 3d, ANSI eye protection rules shifts from design to performance, *Occup Health Saf* 1988; **57**(2): 32–4,82.
(4) Ramazzini B. *De morbis artificum diatriba, Mutinae* (1700).
(5) Lebensohn JE. *An anthology of ophthalmic classics*. Baltimore: Williams & Wilkins, 1969, pp. 399–402.
(6) Grant WM. Ocular injury due to sulphur dioxide. *Arch Ophthalmol* 1947; **38**: 755–61, 762–74.
(7) Morgan SJ. Chemical burns of the eye: causes and management. *Br J Ophthalmol* 1987; **71**: 854–7.
(8) Beare J, Wilson R, Marsh RJ. Ammonia burns of the eye: An old weapon in new hands *Br Med J* 1988; **296**; 590.
(9) Beare J. Eye injuries from assault with chemicals: A review of 64 cases (unpublished data), 1989.
(10) McGarvie MJ, Murray VSG. *Incidents involving chemical contamination of the eye*. London: National Poisons Information Service, 1985.
(11) Grant WM. *Toxicology of the eye: drugs, chemicals, plants and venoms*. 2nd ed. Springfield: Thomas, 1986.
(12) Gilmartin B. The Marton Lecture. Ocular manifestations of systemic medication. *Ophthalmic Physiol Opt* 1987; **7**(4): 449–59.
(13) Fraunfelder FT. *Drug induced ocular side effects and drug interactions*, 2nd ed. Philadelphia: Lea & Febiger, 1982.
(14) Andersson N, Kerr Muir M, Mehra V. Bhopal eye. *Lancet* 1984; **ii**: 1981.
(15) Andersson N, Kerr Muir M, Salmon AG. Bhopal disaster: Eye follow-up and analytical chemistry. *Lancet* 1985; **i**: 761–2.
(16) Salmon AG, Kerr Muir M, Andersson N. Acute toxicity of methylisocyanate. A preliminary study of the dose response for eye and other effects. *Br J Ind Med* 1985; **423**: 795–8.
(17) Andersson N, Kerr Muir M, Mehra V, Salmon AG. Exposure and response to methylisocyanate: results of a community based survey in Bhopal, *Br J Ind Med* 1988; **45**(7): 469–75.
(18) Andersson N. Persistent eye watering among Bhopal survivors (letter). *Lancet* 1986; **ii**(8516): 1152.
(19) Siegrist A, Konzentriert Alkali und Saure Wirkung auf das Augen. *Z Augenheilkd* 1920; **43**: 477–81.
(20) McCulley JP. Chemical Injuries. In: Smolin G, Thoft RA, eds. *The cornea: scientific foundations and clinical practice*. Boston/Toronto: Little Brown & Co, 1983: Chap 14, 422–35.
(21) Nelson JD, Kopietz LA. Chemical injuries to the eyes: Emergency, intermediate, and long term care. *Postgrad Med* 1987; **81**(4): 62–75.
(22) Pereleux A. Chemical burns of the eye. *Bull Soc Belge Ophtalmol* 1986; **217**: 35–43.

(23) Pfister RR. Chemical injuries of the eye. *Ophthalmology* 1983; **90**: 1246–53.

(24) Moore AT, Cheng H, Boase DL. Eye injuries from car battery explosions, *Br J Ophthalmol*, 1982; **66**: 141–4.

(25) Klein R, Lobes LA. Ocular alkali burns in a large urban area, *Ann Ophthalmol* 1976; 8(10): 1185–9.

(26) Beare J, Murray VSG. Attempted identification of chemical agents in eye injury by analysis of tear samples (unpublished data) 1989.

(27) Roper Hall MJ. Thermal and chemical burns. *Trans Ophthalmol Soc UK* 1965; **85**: 631–46.

(28) Eagling EM, Roper-Hall MJ. *Eye injuries an illustrated guide*. London: Butterworths, 1986.

(29) Hughes WF. Alkali burns of the eye II. Clinical and pathological course. *Arch Ophthalmol* 1946; **36**: 189–214.

(30) Smith RE, Conway B. Alkali retinopathy. *Arch Ophthalmol* 1976; **94**(1): 81–4.

(31) Scheie HG, Albert DM. *Textbook of ophthalmology*. Philadelphia: WB Saunders, 1977.

(32) Cox WR. Eye wash stations provide first aid cover for chemical contamination, *Occup Health Saf* 1986; **55**(9): 59–60.

(33) Wright P. The chemically injured eye. *Trans Ophthalmol Soc UK* 1982; **102**: 85–7.

(34) Paterson CA, Pfister RR. Intraocular pressure changes after alkali burns. *Arch Ophthalmol* 1974; **91**: 211–8.

(35) Chiang TS, Moorman LR, Thomas RP. Ocular hypertensive response following acid and alkali burns in rabbits. *Invest Ophthalmol* 1971; **10**: 270.

(36) Pfister RR, Paterson CA, Hayes SA. Topical ascorbate decreases the incidence of corneal ulceration in alkali burned corneas. *Invest Ophthalmol Vis Sci* 1978; **17**: 1019–24.

(37) Pfister RR, Paterson CA. Ascorbic acid in the treatment of alkali burns of the eye. *Ophthalmology* 1980; **87**: 1050–7.

(38) Casey TA, Mayer DJ. *Corneal grafting, principles and practice*. Philadelphia: WB Saunders, 1984: Chap 20, 241–52.

(39) Brown SI, Bloomfield SE, Pearce DB. A follow-up report on transplantation of the alkali burned cornea. *Am J Ophthalmol* 1974; **77**: 538.

(40) Fyodorov SN, Moroz ZI, Zuev VK. *Keratoprosthesis*. Edinburgh, London, Melbourne, New York: Churchill Livingstone, 1987.

(41) Pfister RR, Koski J. Alkali burns of the eye: pathophysiology and treatment. *South Med J* 1982; **75**: 417–22.

(42) Levinson RA, Paterson CA, Pfister RR. Ascorbic acid prevents corneal ulceration and perforation following experimental alkali burns. *Invest Ophthalmol Vis Sci* 1976; **15**: 986.

(43) Paterson CA, Pfister RR, Levinson RA. Aqueous humor pH changes after experimental alkali burns. *Am J Ophthalmol* 1975; **79**: 414–9.

Management of skin contamination

John S. C. English

Department of Occupational Dermatoses, St John's Hospital for Diseases of the Skin, London, UK

INTRODUCTION

In the aftermath of a major chemical disaster appropriate and swift action may save lives and at the very least reduce morbidity. Fortunately such disasters are rare, but when they do occur many people may be affected, for example the Bhopal and Seveso incidents.

Because the chemical industry deals with many hazardous chemicals and processes they are usually aware of potential problems. There are 62 000 chemicals currently used in the industry, of which 5% are somewhat hazardous and 1% very hazardous. In fact, the relative risk for fatalities occurring in workers involved in the chemical industry is the lowest compared to other industries (1) (Table 1).

HOW DO CHEMICALS AFFECT THE SKIN?

The skin is a fairly resilient organ and people's susceptibility to chronic irritant exposure varies. However, there is not such a wide variation in response to acute chemical damage. Chemicals can damage the skin by a severe change in the pH, defatting the skin, a hygroscopic action and coagulative necrosis. During chemical contamination thermal burns may occur if the chemical is hot.

Many chemicals are capable not only of causing burns but of being absorbed, and causing toxic effects leading to acute yellow atrophy of the liver or renal failure. Burns from acids and alkalis may cause acidosis or alkalosis, both requiring treatment. Of 95 chemical burns recorded at the Birmingham Accident Hospital (2), 39 were caused by acids, 19 by alkalis and 28 by other inorganic agents. A few of the more important causes of chemical burns are discussed:

Alkalis have hydroxyl ions which are caustic and the high pH will burn the skin. They are soluble in water and therefore skin contamination should be treated immediately with copious irrigation.

Acids have hydrogen ions and a low pH, the skin is damaged more by alkalis than acids. Copious irrigation with water is the immediate treatment. A buffer solution containing potassium dihydrogen phosphate 70 g, disodium hydrogen phosphate 180 g and water 850 ml has been recommended for both acid and alkali skin contamination but tap water is more readily available.

Major chemical disasters—medical aspects of management, edited by Virginia Murray, 1990: Royal Society of Medicine Services International Congress and Symposium Series No. 155, published by Royal Society of Medicine Services Limited.

Table 1 *The relative risk for fatalities per working life of 1000 people (= 100 million hours).*

	Relative risk
Chemical industry	3.5
Steel	8
Coal mining	40
Construction	67
Flying personnel	250
Professional boxers	7000

Phenol is rapidly absorbed through intact skin causing damage to the CNS and kidneys. Local necrosis is proportional to concentration and small amounts of water or alcohol may increase the absorption. Deluge washing with large amounts of water or swabbing with polyethylene glycol should be employed.

Chromic acid produces ulceration and necrosis, it may be absorbed and cause renal failure. Deeper burns may require excision and grafting. Superinfection with *Streptococcus pyogenes* may be a missed cause of delayed healing (2).

Hydrofluoric acid causes severe necrosis and lesions may be more extensive than they appear to be. The burns are very painful. Immediate treatment should include copious washing with water or a saturated solution of sodium bicarbonate, then a paste of 15–10% magnesium sulphate and glycerin rubbed in and 10% calcium gluconate is injected intralesionally, to reach the deeper areas of necrosis. If hydrofluoric acid gets under the nails necrosis of the finger tips may occur, the nails should be cut back.

Phosphorus ignites on exposure to air. Burns should be kept moist until all particles are removed. Small residual particles can be detected by phosphorescence in a dark room (2) or by small quantities of copper sulphate solution applied to the contaminated area, which will reveal particles by forming black copper phosphide. Severe metabolic changes may occur and patients who have suffered phosphorus burns should be carefully monitored.

IMMEDIATE MANAGEMENT

The primary—and essential—treatment of all chemical burns is removal of all contaminated clothes and copious washing (except for metallic potassium and sodium, which ignite in water). Specific antidotes are available for only a few chemicals. The patients should then be transferred to hospital.

Hospital treatment

When patients are admitted to hospital the Accident and Emergency Department need to know what chemical or chemicals are involved. In the UK and many other countries it is customary for all major burns to be treated by plastic or orthopaedic surgeons working in Regional Burns Units. Therefore the patients may have to be transferred.

It is essential to make an immediate assessment of the severity and extent of the burn. Superficial burns cause erythema, partial-thickness burns blisters and eschars and full-thickness burns cause an eschar which sloughs. After copious and prolonged flooding (hopefully done before arrival at hospital) subsequent treatment depends on the nature of the burn. All burns are subject to infection with *Clostridium tetani* and prophylaxis for those not already protected is advocated. The burned area should be covered by sterile gauze or antibiotic impregnated paraffin gauze to enable transfer to a burns unit.

SURVIVAL

The mortality from burns depends upon the percentage of skin involved. Young adults can be expected to survive burns where 18–22% of skin is involved, whereas the elderly may not survive a 10% burn. The depth of necrosis depends on the concentration, duration of contact and time before treatment is instituted.

SUMMARY

Prevention and education is paramount. Contaminated clothing should be removed and the contaminated skin immediately irrigated with copious quantities of water. The patient should then be transferred to an appropriate hospital for further assessment and treatment.

REFERENCES

(1) Theiss AM. Accident risk. In: Harrington JM, ed. *Recent advances in occupational health* No 2. Edinburgh: Churchill Livingston, 1984: 17.
(2) Cason JS. *Treatment of burns*. London: Chapman & Hall, 1981: 188–205.

Medical management of chemical disasters involving food or water

Glyn N. Volans

National Poisons Unit, Guy's Hospital, London, UK

INTRODUCTION

Incidents concerning the ingestion of contaminated food or water can take on truly disaster proportions but they will differ in their presentation from industrial and transport accidents. Instead of the dramatic event with full response from the emergency services, a slower evolution is likely with the first presentations being to General Practitioners, Accident and Emergency Departments, Environmental Health Officers, Occupational Health Services and even Outpatient Departments. Many, or even most, of the cases will have mild symptoms which give little cause for concern, or they may be symptom free apart from the anxiety produced in response to announcements about the incident.

The medical management of such incidents will, however, follow a similar pattern to other forms of chemical disasters. Triage may be essential to select those patients needing treatment or further observation and an informed toxicological assessment of the risks of the incident is necessary at an early stage. In practice such information does not always exist and the existing information resources need to be further developed to fulfil this role.

The outcome of each incident needs to be adequately documented and assessed and the importance of standardized record keeping and sample collection is evident. Treatment will mostly be symptomatic and supportive and will usually be well within the resources and the experience of a British receiving-hospital. Specific treatment with antidotes will occasionally be needed, for example atropine/pralidoxime for treatment of organophosphate poisoning. However, supplies of antidotes are not always immediately available and for a major incident they could be inadequate. The problems of production and supply of antidotes are currently being addressed internationally in a programme organized by the International Programme on Chemical Safety (WHO/ILO/UNEP, Geneva) (1), and we might hope to see better arrangements for dealing with such incidents in the future.

I shall review briefly some of the existing experiences of major incidents involving chemical contamination of food and water and suggest actions that need to be taken and areas for further discussion.

Major chemical disasters—medical aspects of management, edited by Virginia Murray, 1990: Royal Society of Medicine Services International Congress and Symposium Series No. 155, published by Royal Society of Medicine Services Limited.

CHEMICAL DISASTERS FROM FOOD CONTAMINATION

I have failed to identify any recent comprehensive review of chemical contamination of food and no single database gives access to all the relevant reference sources.

However, in the case of pesticide contamination of food Ferrar and Cabral (2) examined all the recorded incidents since 1900 that they could find. They listed 37 well documented epidemics and classified them into the four different types shown in Table 1.

Table 1 *Pesticide contamination in food (2)*

Causes of 37 well documented epidemics recorded since 1900

1   Food prepared using intermediates contaminated with pesticides
2   Food prepared from raw materials treated with pesticides
3   Accidental addition of pesticides to food
4   Food contaminated by pesticide misuse

Epidemics from food prepared with intermediates contaminated with pesticides during storage and transport (Type 1) include organophosphate contamination incidents such as the one most recently reported in Mexico which affected 559 people who were poisoned by parathion, 16 of whom died. Previously, in India, the same chemical poisoned 360 people causing 102 deaths.

Incidents involving food prepared from raw materials treated with pesticides (Type 2) can be equally serious and include those related to seeds dressed with mercury as a fungicide, such as the outbreaks in Turkey (estimated at 3–5000 cases, of which 11% died) and Iraq (estimated 6500 cases and 459 deaths).

These incidents all occurred in developing countries, but the developed countries have not escaped cases of accidental addition of pesticides to food (Type 3) and food contaminated by pesticide misuse (Type 4). Type 3 includes the addition of sodium fluoride to meals in a hospital in the USA in 1943; 263 people were affected and 57 died. A Type 4 incident was reported in the USA as recently as 1985 when over 1100 cases of aldicarb poisoning were recorded after consumption of contaminated water melons.

Other recent epidemics of chemical food poisoning include the Spanish Toxic Oil Syndrome with all its unsolved problems (3), and the fraudulent contamination of alcoholic drinks with methanol in Italy and Egypt. These latter episodes are of particular interest for the way in which they presented as chemical emergencies to Poisons Information Centres. In Milan, Bozza-Marrubini and her colleagues (personal communication) made a clinical diagnosis of methanol intoxication and subsequently worked with their local laboratory to develop assays for methanol and its metabolites both to access toxicity and to help trace the suspect wines. In Egypt the contaminated products were liqueurs and again management was based on clinical findings (Fahim, personal communication). Subsequently samples from that outbreak were assayed in our laboratory in London as a part of an ongoing international collaboration.

Deliberate chemical contamination of food

A disturbing trend in recent years has been the use of deliberate contamination of food for possible criminal or terrorist gains. The problem seems likely to increase as demonstrated by a recent paper which identified 18 publications circulating in the USA with the express aim of instructing the reader on how to plan for deliberate contamination of food and how to profit from this (4).

We have reviewed the National Poisons Information Service (NPIS) records and identified both the chemicals used in previous incidents, and the types of food allegedly contaminated. Table 2 demonstrates the wide range of substances and the type of products that have been contaminated.

Table 2 *Substances used in deliberate contamination of food (source NPIS Records)*

Cyanide, cannabis, caustic soda, diethylene glycol, glass, insecticides, metallic mercury, paraquat, rat poison and thallium

Foods contaminated or allegedly contaminated:

Wine, fruit juices, fruit, confectionery, turkey, coleslaw and butter

Fortunately not all these incidents involved serious risk and in some cases contamination was not proven. Nevertheless, there appears to have been at least three more incidents in the UK this year so far, and there is an urgent need to develop both information and analytical resources to respond to future incidents. With this in mind the NPIS and Reading Scientific Services Limited, a Food Research Unit at Reading University, are discussing the ways in which existing data sources and analytical expertise can be coordinated to improve the response to future incidents.

CHEMICAL CONTAMINATION OF DRINKING WATER

The need for collaboration of information services in response to possible contamination of water supplies was recognized some years ago and a joint approach to such incidents was agreed by the NPIS and the Water Research Centre (WRC), Marlow, Buckinghamshire (5).

A major stimulus to the collaboration was an incident in 1984 when the River Dee was polluted by a major chemical spill of which the main component was phenol (6). There were four major intakes for potable water from below this site, serving a population in excess of one million consumers. For a number of reasons there was a delay in recognition of the chemical spill, and by the time that it was reported the water had not only reached the consumers, it had also been treated with chlorine so that the toxicological risk assessment had to consider chlorophenols as well as phenol. From the known toxic effects of these compounds, acute gastro-intestinal disturbance and headache could be predicted, but the water would have an unpleasant taste and consumption could be expected to be reduced. From calculations on the amount of chemical released and the volume of the water supply the concentrations of phenols and chlorophenols reaching the consumer could be estimated. These were thought to be largely below the levels where the water would be considered unsafe, as was later confirmed by analysis of water samples from a number of sites on the supply system. Nevertheless, there were many consumer complaints to the Water Authority and an epidemiological study demonstrated a clear difference in gastro-intestinal symptoms between exposed and unexposed groups (7). The public alarm caused by the incident may well have led to some psychogenic symptoms but I think that most people would accept that minor toxicological effects were demonstrated. Since that time the relevant Water Authority has introduced an improved monitoring and response system for water pollution by chemicals, including the use of high performance liquid chromatography and water tasters (8). It is encouraging to report that with this scheme there has been a decrease in the frequency with which that authority has had to close down parts of its water supply.

When the Water Research Centre and the NPIS reviewed previous incidents and existing information, it was concluded that each had a role to play in the alerting system for any major incident because, in general, each has developed information resources to serve different enquirers and each has acquired different expertise. By agreeing to act in collaboration these resources can be used to best effect, and can ensure that decisions on water supply and risk to patients can be coordinated as appropriate (5).

The Lowermoor incident

The informal agreement between the WRC and the NPIS has ensured a rapid and successful exchange of information in a number of instances when chemical contamination of water was suspected. However, the recent incident at Lowermoor, North Cornwall (6 July 1988) involved many other parties, and demonstrates the need for a more comprehensive plan for response to water contamination.

On the date in question 20 tonnes of concentrated aluminium sulphate was accidentally discharged into the water treatment works above the town of Camelford. This resulted in contamination of the water supply to up to 20 000 people (10 000 residents and estimated 10 000 tourists). The cause of the incident is described in detail in the excellent report by Dr John Lawrence (9) and I will not go into detail here. Suffice it to say that in the early hours after the contamination the staff of the Water Authority did not know exactly what had happened and that some of the actions taken were subsequently found to be inappropriate. When information became available it was correctly predicted that the aluminium sulphate would lower the water pH and not only increase the water aluminium concentration but also release copper, lead and zinc from plumbing. It was noted that the strongly acid water would have a bad taste and a brown sludge and that people would be unlikely to drink it. By the time that the water was palatable it was predicted that it would be safe and the Water Authority issued reassuring statements. In practice people did drink the water and many reported symptoms, notably nausea, vomiting, diarrhoea, sore eyes, mouth ulcers and itching skin rashes. Some felt generally unwell and described worsening of existing conditions including arthritis and skin rashes. Analytical results confirmed water aluminium concentrations of 10–50 mg/l for 1 to 3 days. This is 50–250 times the EEC limit, but it must be noted that the limit is set for aesthetic reasons (taste and appearance) and not because of proven toxic effects.

Higher aluminium concentrations were reported in the supply system and some tap water, but levels over 100 mg/l render the water undrinkable, and some were samples taken from hot water systems which in any case, are not advised for drinking. The highest recorded levels of lead, zinc, and sulphate represented no risks and most samples were within accepted EEC limits. Raised copper concentrations in water were recorded up to three times the EEC limit for cold water taps, and these could have contributed to the gastro-intestinal symptoms, headache and rash. However, the elevation of copper concentrations was short lived, as shown also by the reports of transient blue staining of hair, nails and laundry.

Overall, the analytical results supported the toxicological view that prolonged toxic effects would not be expected. Unfortunately, however, the understandable concerns of the population were not heeded to their satisfaction, and people felt that they were being denied information and access to experts in toxicology. In consequence the media have highlighted these concerns, and by January 1989, the Parliamentary Under Secretary of State for Health established an Advisory Group to investigate the Lowermoor incident under Chairmanship of Professor Dame Barbara Clayton. Their report will be awaited with interest, not only for its comments on the toxicological evaluation of the incident, but also for its views on the response to such incidents in future.*

Table 3 *Application of analytical toxicology in chemical disasters*

Analytical resources

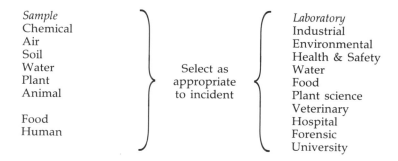

Sample		Laboratory
Chemical		Industrial
Air		Environmental
Soil	Select as	Health & Safety
Water	appropriate	Water
Plant	to incident	Food
Animal		Plant science
		Veterinary
Food		Hospital
Human		Forensic
		University

Considerations in sample collection in chemical disasters
1 Agree a general policy between all involved parties
2 Choose an agency to start/coordinate process
3 Determine appropriate samples (collection technique, size, container, preservatives)
4 Ensure samples are adequately labelled (material, place, subject, date, time, preservative)
5 Decide whether repeat samples are needed
6 Arrange appropriate storage/transport
7 Decide the time scale for analysis (urgent, routine, research?)
8 Arrange forum to report/discuss results to avoid waste of time

Assessment of analytical toxicological data
1 *Analytical interpretation*:
    Use method with adequate selectivity, sensitivity and reliability ('quality control')
    Compare result to those reported previously in various groups after various doses ('feasibility control')
2 *Clinical interpretation*:
    Discuss analytical findings in light of other data (time course of episode, clinical chemistry, pharmacology of suspect agent, etc.)
    If necessary, extrapolate from analytical results with similar compounds/groups of compounds
3 *A dialogue* between an experienced analyst and clinican is vital!

This report was published in July 1989, and confirms the lack of evidence for long-term toxic effects. It also proposes that for incidents such as this, there should be advanced planning to ensure sound management including the provision of medical and scientific information to the public and the media (10).

ANALYTICAL CONSIDERATIONS IN MAJOR CHEMICAL DISASTERS

Although the role of chemical analyses in incidents of chemical contamination of food and water is addressed here, the same considerations can be applied, with little change, to other types of major chemical disasters.

The WHO report on the Spanish Toxic Oil Syndrome (3) states in its conclusions that:

1. Owing to the emergency nature of the situation in 1981, proper organization of the collection of case-related oils and proper coordination of chemical and toxicological studies were not carried out.
2. Available evidence from chemical analyses and animal experiments is difficult to evaluate owing to the fact that different oils were examined in different laboratories, and uncertainty prevails as to whether or not truly case-related oil samples were examined.

The problems of sample collection after that incident are easily understood when allowance is made for the stresses and the urgency which faced clinicians, administrators and investigators alike. The same problems will almost certainly be repeated in future incidents unless we plan for sample collection as part of our response to future incidents. A suggested scheme for this is given in Table 3 which details not only the analytical resources required and sample collection considerations, but also key factors in assessment of the chemical and toxicological significance of the results.

CONCLUSIONS

In conclusion, planning is needed for response to chemical incidents involving food and water and it must be recognized that such incidents differ from other major chemical incidents. The following actions could be considered in particular:

1. Collection of data on past experiences
2. Establishment of a network of relevant information and expertise
3. Planning for early toxicological assessment of the risks and comparison with preliminary findings
4. Planning for appropriate sample collection and identification, and a network of laboratories able to analyse such samples
5. Arrangements to ensure that interpretation of analytical results involve dialogue between analysts, clinicians and other experts
6. Experience gained from future incidents should be well documented and accessible for use as an information resource and training tool.

Finally, it should be recognized that in incidents concerning contamination of food and water, the media have a major role to play and it is the responsibility of those handling the incident to ensure that the media are adequately informed, and that every effort is made to avoid inappropriate alarm whilst attempting to prevent toxic effects.

REFERENCES

(1) International Programme on Chemical Safety. Joint IPCS/CEC Project on Evaluation of antidotes used in treatment of poisoning. Report of the Preparatory Phase. ICS/87.30. International Programme on Chemical Safety. 1988.

(2) Ferrer A, Cabral JRP. Epidemics due to pesticide contamination in food. In: *World conference on chemical accidents*. Edinburgh: CEP Consultants Ltd. 1987: 385–7.

(3) Grandjean P, Tarkowski S. *Spanish toxic oil syndrome*. Copenhagen: World Health Organisation Regional Office for Europe, 1984.

(4) Dietz PE. Dangerous information: product tampering and poisoning advice in revenge and murder manuals. *J Foren Sci* 1988; **33**: 1206–17.

(5) Fawell JK, Volans GN. Toxicology information service responses to chemical incidents involving drinking water. In *World conference on chemical accidents*. Edinburgh: CEP Consultants Ltd, 1987: 200–2.

(6) Jones F, Fawell JK. Lessons learnt from the River Dee pollution incident, January 1984—Public Health. In *World conference on chemical accidents*. Edinburgh: CEP Consultants Ltd, 1987: 223–6.

(7) Jarvis SN, Straube RC, Williams ALJ, Bartlett CLR. Illness associated with contamination of drinking water supplies with phenol. *BMJ* 1985; **290**: 1800–2.

(8) Jones AN, Westwood TA. Lessons learnt from the River Dee pollution incident, January 1984—pollution control. In *World conference on chemical accidents*. Edinburgh: CEP Consultants Ltd, 1987: 296–9.

(9) Lawrence J. *Report of an inquiry into an incident at Lowermoor Water Treatment Works of South West Water Authority on 6 July 1988*. Brixham: CIC Brixham Laboratory, 1988.

(10) Clayton B. Advisory Group, Water Pollution at Lowermoor, North Cornwall. *Report of the Lowermoor Incident Advisory Group*—Chairman: Professor Dame Barbara Clayton. pp. 22 Cornwall and Scilly District Health Authority, Truro—July 1989.

SESSION VI

FOLLOW UP OF MAJOR CHEMICAL DISASTERS

Chairman: Dr D. Taylor

Disaster epidemiology: lessons from Bhopal

Neil Andersson

Department of Epidemiology and Tropical Medicine, Centre for Tropical Disease Research (CIET),
Faculty of Medicine, Universidad Autonoma de Guerrero, Acapulco, Mexico

INTRODUCTION

Before the first week of December 1984, few epidemiologists had ever heard of
methyl isocyanate (MIC) and, in the first days after the catastrophe, there was
little information about the substance available to relief workers on the scene.
Rumours about cyanide and phosgene circulated freely, and the people who had
the best knowledge about what had happened, the management of the Union
Carbide factory that produced carbamate pesticides on the northern outskirts of
Bhopal, were under house arrest. The arrival of a WHO adviser from Geneva
on the third day brought with it some relief, armed as he was with biochemistry
information to the effect that MIC disappears on contact with water, and that
there could not possibly be any MIC left.

But this temporary comfort had more to do with worries of relief workers who
had walked around the exposed communities not knowing whether they might
themselves suffer ill effects. In reality, the information was of very little use in
evaluating the situation. There was no need for the scanty toxicological data about
LD_{50}s. A single glance at the dead people and animals surpassed most of the
toxicological data available. But how they died, who had been exposed, how large
a dose they received, what were the non-fatal consequences of this exposure,
were questions without answers from available reference material. Most future
industrial disasters will produce a similar scenario. Some of the practical difficulties
and achievements of disaster epidemiology in Bhopal are discussed below.

POLITICS AND EXPOSURE CATEGORIES

Just as the occurrence of industrial disasters highlights the political or commercial
pressures, so do such events concentrate the frustrations and difficulties
experienced in establishing exposure categories in everyday 'cold' epidemiology.
Since industrial disasters, almost by definition, involve the breakdown of
managerial and state control, the new assertions of this control in the immediate
wake of the disaster are frequently exaggerated and distorted in a way that
produces additional and sometimes insurmountable difficulties for the disaster

*Major chemical disasters—medical aspects of management, edited by Virginia Murray, 1990: Royal Society of
Medicine Services International Congress and Symposium Series No. 155, published by Royal Society of Medicine
Services Limited.*

epidemiologist. If either of the two fundamental epidemiological parameters (exposure and effect) is distorted in any way, it reduces the value of the endeavour, even before trying to take account of effect modifying factors, confounders, or missing data. The Seveso disaster provides an example (1–3).

At noon on 10 July 1976, a runaway chemical reaction at the plant synthesizing trichlorophenol (TCP) released a cloud of toxic chemicals over nearby residential areas. The cloud was later admitted to involve not only TCP but highly toxic dioxin (TCDD) and, contrary to the public perception of the disaster, the location of the factory turned out not to be in Seveso, but in neighbouring Meda. The exposure also affected neighbouring Cesano Maderno and Desio. If the difficulty in establishing exactly what had been released and where it was released was not enough, the rigid classification of exposure in Seveso followed lines of expedience rather than entirely scientific criteria. The exposure zones were classified A, B and R, based originally on soil samples of TCDD (averaging 580.4, 3 and $0.9\mu g/m^2$ for Zones A, B and R, respectively) (3). Reliable as the individual soil measurements might have been, the problem came in drawing a line between zones for purposes of epidemiological enquiry. At one level it was necessary to be pragmatic in efforts to deal with the continued risk of TCDD, with its long half-life, by defining a geographic area to be sealed off and later to be buried under one metre of soil and (in places) concrete. But such practical lines should not have had anything to do with an epidemiological measurement process. In Seveso, the exposure categories for the immediate interventions were used also as categories of exposure for a wide range of epidemiological studies (1–3). Under these circumstances, despite the substantial epidemiological skills available to the project, it is not surprising that it produced relatively unconvincing findings.

As in Seveso, there has been a temptation in Bhopal to delineate formally between who was not exposed and who was exposed, and their level of exposure. While it is relatively easy to demonstrate that communities 20 kilometres away were not exposed, the outer limits of real exposure and the gradient of exposure outward to that point is not so easy to establish. Because of its long half-life, it will probably be possible to measure dioxin levels in Seveso many years after the release; MIC, on the other hand, has a half-life of only two minutes (4). This effectively rules out environmental measurements to establish exposure categories. With all its imperfections, we have used proximity to a high death cluster, as measured in the two weeks immediately after the disaster, as a rough indicator of probable exposure to MIC (5,6). Until it is possible to develop a reliable marker of previous exposure, epidemiological studies should not accept geographic boundaries between levels of presumed exposure. There is simply not enough evidence to know what happened and who, once exposed, went where. In the first hours after the release of MIC, many people panicked and ran away from the Union Carbide factory, into the chemical cloud. Factors such as this individual behaviour are very important determinants of individual exposure. Political 'space' is necessary for further accumulation and systematization of evidence of the individual exposure and effects. When it becomes necessary to establish exposure zones, the need to be pragmatic should not override—as may be the case with exposure zones in Seveso—the need to be scientific.

MULTIPLE EPIDEMIOLOGICAL METHODOLOGIES

No single epidemiological technique, on its own, would have been adequate for the tasks in Bhopal. To characterize the nature and extent of eye damage in order to plan appropriate relief strategies, we used a combination of existing and modified methodologies:

1. rapid appraisal procedures were used to gain initial insight into exposure categories and the range of health consequences of exposure
2. this provided the basis for 'cluster cohorts', which could be added to, in an epidemiologically interpretable manner, to increase the coverage of the scheme as more time and resources became available
3. inexpensive questionnaire formats derived from locally available materials were developed that could be put into service in a matter of hours and also serve for longitudinal follow up; and
4. clinical data from ongoing out-patient consultations were collected in a form that could be used for case-referent epidemiological monitoring

Rapid appraisal procedures

Outside the realm of formal epidemiology, procedures of rapid appraisal have become quite well systematized in the evaluation of development projects (7,8). In Bhopal, these techniques were useful in gaining first hand initial impressions of exposure categories and the range of effects suffered by the patients, as well as the extent of the population dislocations and the medical response. Beginning before daybreak on the third day after the disaster, the team of Indian and British ophthalmologists and an epidemiologist traversed the entire exposure area, changing modes of transport (car, tricab and foot) to gain access to all types of household in the exposure area. We also visited several unexposed Bhopali communities of similar socio-economic status, to obtain an impression of background conditions. Thus, in a matter of six hours, hundreds of very brief interviews—each limited to three questions that were repeated for people encountered throughout the exposure and non-exposure areas—provided preliminary data on perception of exposure, deaths and movement of people. Visits by our team to hospitals and clinics were oriented mostly towards evaluation of the range of effects on the eye, particularly addressing the initial fear that tens of thousands of people had been blinded by the gas. The same procedure could apply for many other health consequences.

Cluster cohorts

Once some idea of broad exposure zones existed, eight exposed and two-non-exposed clusters of households were designated for rapid surveys and clinical examinations. Although it was possible to obtain a reasonably recent aerial map of the city, there was no up to date formal sampling frame which indicated population density and other factors necessary for a probabilistic sample; there was also no time to wait for development of a sampling frame. The use of cluster surveys based on a purposive sample is not a new methodology and is highly suited to disaster epidemiology. But the time and resource constraints of a disaster situation can accentuate problems of small numbers and missing data, which can affect any epidemiological endeavour, so that they take on an importance not really contemplated in non-disaster contexts. To a large extent, methodological considerations were influenced by the specific mandate to determine the consequences for human sight. It was necessary to examine sufficient people to get a clear idea of the effects and to determine appropriate treatment of exposure victims in order to avoid long-term consequences. These examinations, while covering a reasonably sized sample in a short time, had to be sufficiently reproducible and detailed to permit later monitoring of eye consequences. Finding a balance between these considerations led to the sample that we have now followed for nearly five years. Even with this very restricted size, in the first year of follow up it was possible to contact only 50%. In the two year follow up regular contact was developed with some 85% of the original sample, With intensive investment over the next year, it was possible to increase this to 93% (6). By the five year follow up, the figure should be close to 98%. Resources did not permit much more than full ophthalmological examination of the selected sample; much less would it have been possible to examine fully all 250 000 survivors or to follow them over time.

Other community-based epidemiology studies initiated after the mass exodus on the 12th day post-disaster (for the 'restart' of the plant to dispense with the remaining toxic chemicals), were in an even worse position than this small cluster survey. Many of the worst affected families did not return to their homes. The dwellings of some of these were taken up by other families and exposure histories became very confused as more and more was heard about possible compensation. This may well have the same effect as the manipulation of exposure categories in Seveso, underestimating the true effect of the exposure. In our clusters, even with the follow up initiated before the mass exodus, there is a danger of bias due to more intensive follow up among the exposed than unexposed people; unexposed people may have found annual household visits and detailed eye examinations quite surprising. To a large extent, it has been possible to avoid this detracting from validity of the enquiry, by dividing our exposed clusters into those with heavy and light exposure. This division was done without the examining ophthalmologists' knowledge, based on death rates measured in the clusters during the first survey in December 1984. It was thus possible to consider gradients between high and low exposure (6).

Appropriate questionnaire design

There is no model questionnaire that can be applied in the disaster situation. There are, however, a number of classical errors that, committed in the disaster situation, may be more expensive than in 'cold' epidemiology. Blunderbuss questionnaires enquiring superficially about a wide range of perceptions and possible effects, insensitive questions that do not take adequate account of social norms, imprecise questions that do not elicit a clear (and quick) answer, leading questions and questions that beg recall bias are all common errors that must be avoided. The disaster situation calls for special discipline in limiting questions to the minimum required for planning the medical response, eschewing considerations such as 'it would be interesting to know . . .'. An approach is required that respects human suffering, and reciprocates information supplied with immediate medical attention. The team concerned with eye consequences of MIC exposure in Bhopal developed a very limited number of questions while actually providing relief work in an affected community. Each question, as it arose, was tested on the nearby households. The final questionnaire inquired about age, sex, duration of exposure, action taken, treatment received, initial effects (open question), eye effects, deaths in the household, and was accompanied by a respiratory and detailed eye examination, following a standard protocol (5). A subsequent cycle recorded smoking habits, occupation and education, since these factors tend not to change much over time.

In order to get the initial documentation of effects carried out alongside relief efforts, there was no time for printing questionnaires. The actual instrument for collection of data was a hard covered exercise book for each cluster, with the pages cut in half from top to bottom, providing a half page for every person, that could line up next to the questions and examination protocol written on the hard cover. These books were purchased at a local stationery store and, within two hours of finalizing the questionnaire, they were ready for field use. Subsequent modifications of the questionnaire based on initial experience were simply written into each of the ten books. They also provided a permanent record for follow up of the clusters. This experience from Bhopal demonstrates the feasibility of rapid initiation of fieldwork. The initially limited size of the community-based service could later be supplemented, multiplying the cluster cohort framework as resources permitted.

Expansion of the cluster cohorts

The principal objective throughout this epidemiological exercise has been to develop appropriate eye care for the victims. In the course of developing community eye services for the exposed population in Bhopal, initial priority was given to medical care of people with eye problems while monitoring their progress in the eight exposure and two non-exposure clusters. In the months that followed, the clinical care was expanded from the outpatient base at the Bhopal Eye Hospital though a Community Service Programme to provide basic eye care for an increasing proportion of the exposed population. This programme involved the addition of further cluster cohort modules, each of them (like the original 10 clusters), made up of eight exposure and two non-exposure clusters. Eye care services may be modified from time to time on the basis of changes in eye conditions among affected people. In each cluster of approximately 50 houses, a house-to-house survey determines age and sex structure of the population, and inquires about deaths in the past year and about any current eye problems. These cases are referred to a mobile eye clinic in the cluster for ophthalmological examination. In each cluster, whether exposed or not, an eye health promoter is recruited and trained in recognition of the main eye problems affecting these communities, and in maintenance of a monthly register of births and deaths. This has permitted systematic expansion of the original cluster cohort scheme, providing clinical care while monitoring the emergence of any new eye problems at community level, in an epidemiologically interpretable manner. By the time of the fifth year follow up, it is hoped, these eye care services will be extended to most of the 200 000 exposed and to approximately 60 000 unexposed people, along with a measurement and analytical capability that will permit better planning for appropriate medical care. Community-based epidemiological procedures in the disaster situation must accompany and be based upon medical management of the consequences.

Case-referent monitoring

People that present voluntarily for medical attention after a disaster provide another valuable source of epidemiological data. One of the first products of the epidemiological evaluation of eye consequences was the establishment of the Bhopal Eye Hospital, within two months of the disaster. The out-patient data at this hospital have been collected in such a manner as to permit periodic evaluation of the emergence of an excess of conditions that might be associated with MIC exposure, using as comparison certain conditions not likely to be related to MIC exposure. This inexpensive use of routine data emerging from clinical care has been called 'case-referent monitoring'. Like other study designs, our case-referent studies on chronic eye effects among the survivors have problems regarding adequate exposure history. Since the enquiry takes place after both exposure and the appearance of the disease, in the context of discussion about compensation it is very difficult to obtain reliable exposure data. In this situation, we elected a disease reference series (for example, refractive errors as a reference group for chronic eye irration) which we did not expect to be selected in terms of MIC exposure (6,9).

The eye as a 'sentinel organ'

It is almost always difficult, at the outset of post-disaster epidemiological follow up, to determine what to follow over time; this was a particular problem in Bhopal, when there was very little idea about the nature of MIC or its effects. In our case, the specific mandate was to establish the extent and nature of eye consequences of MIC exposure in Bhopal, in order to plan and provide appropriate medical responses. A later interest was to establish what other epidemiological value the data from this clinical service might have. As it turns out, many of the pathologies associated with chemical poisoning can be reflected in the eye. The moist surface of the eye may respond similarly to the alveolar surface from the point of view of acute burns from hydrophilic exothermic reactions, as happens with MIC. Examination of the eye also provides an opportunity to examine directly both arteries and veins; furthermore, the afferent pupillary reflex and colour vision provide an indicator of motor and sensory neurotoxicity. Eye infections, particularly bacterial infections, may provide a clue to general state of immunity and the risk of infections in other organs. Watering and irritation may signal altered responsiveness. Phlyctenular keratoconjunctivitis provides a clue to underlying disease, such as tuberculosis.

GAINS FROM A MULTIDISCIPLINARY APPROACH

With all its limitations and practical difficulties, the early epidemiology fieldwork of several relief teams and Indian scientific agencies in Bhopal provided working estimates of the numbers of deaths and the main physical problems among the survivors (10–12). There was no idea in the first few weeks about the likelihood of late deaths, late eye or lung consequences, or whether the substance or substances released were teratogenic, mutagenic, carcinogenic or neurotoxic. There is no single scientific method that will distinguish these effects. What is required is a synthesis of methods; in Bhopal, this included an epidemiological perspective during initial clinical observation and relief work, later formal epidemiological studies by Indian investigators, analytical chemistry and toxicology.

The release of MIC resulted in the death of around 2000 people, most of them, it is thought by clinicians who were in Bhopal soon after the event, from acute pulmonary oedema resulting from the burns occurring during the highly exothermic reaction of MIC with water content of lung secretions and tissues (5,11,12). One of the short-term findings of our rapid appraisal was that no case of blindness could be attributed to the exposure (10), yet longer term follow up of the exposed population indicated that this did not mean they were free of eye or other consequences. A large case-control study confirmed that increased risk of persistent irritant eye symptoms was related to duration of exposure to the gas (9,13). Similar long term ocular effects were found by other clinicians (14). Three years follow up revealed an excess of eye irritation, eyelid infections, cataract and a decrease in visual acuity among the exposed people. None of these findings could be accounted for by chance (95% confidence), social class or age (6). Among human survivors from Bhopal, chronic effects on the lungs have been found by epidemiological follow up up to two years after the event (15). Our three years follow up demonstrated that breathlessness was twice as common a complaint in the heavily exposed clusters than in those with lower exposure, a finding that could not be explained by different age or smoking patterns (6). Detailed clinical studies of Bhopal survivors suggest long-term immunological effects, including the potential of MIC to produce hypersensitivity reactions (16,17) and the reduction of phagocytic ability of mononuclear peripheral blood cells (18). The studies of Varma (19), the Indian Council for Medical Research (20) and Kanhere (21), even with their deficiencies, provide adequate evidence for developmental and reproductive effects, according to criteria of the 1989 United States Environmental Protection Agency Guidelines for Development Toxicity Risk Assessment. Studies of neuromuscular problems in survivors, particularly muscle weakness (14,22), indicate that this might also be a problem area.

In comparison with the large number of animal studies on the acute effects of MIC (23–29), relatively few toxicological studies have contemplated long-term consequences of exposure. But the accumulating evidence is not encouraging. ECG abnormalities (particularly premature ventricular and atrial contraction, small t-waves and multiple p-waves) were found in rats four months after a single exposure to MIC (30). Chronic respiratory damage (30–32) and chronic eye inflammation (28,31) are also well documented. Altered local immunity was postulated as a possible explanation for these findings (33). Formal immunological studies indicate persistent bone marrow suppression, suppression of the lymphoproliferative responses of splenic leucocytes to B and T cell mitogens and decreased thymus/body weight ratios (27,29,34–36). Our toxicological studies of the chronic effects of acute exposure to MIC in Lister Hooded rats, apart from dose-related and progressive infiltrates of lymphocytes in the lung, liver, spleen, kidneys and glands surrounding the eye, also produced dramatic 'rheumatoid' syncitializing of the pulmonary epithelium at 5 and 15 ppm (37). When incubated at low temperatures MIC is also mutagenic in Salmonella (38) and increased fetal deaths, reduced placental weights, and fetal body weights, were observed in mice exposed to MIC during gestation (20,39). Several carcinogenicity animal studies are underway, although none has yet been reported. We found several cases of pulmonary pre-malignancy in Lister Hooded rats exposed to 15 ppm of MIC in a dynamic atmosphere (37).

These results demonstrate the value of multidisciplinary research in the disaster situation; the implications, incomplete as they are, are serious when it is considered that some 200 000–300 000 people are involved. There remains an enormous amount of toxicological research to be done on MIC and its degradation products, with special attention to immunological consequences of exposure. In order to exclude the occurrence of these consequences among the human survivors, it will be necessary formally to study infections and allergies, and deaths from these conditions in Bhopal.

THE ROLE OF EPIDEMIOLOGY IN DISASTER ANTICIPATION

There has been no shortage of calls for governments, industry, international organizations and trades unions to take action in anticipation of disasters. The

Trade Union Report on Bhopal (40), for example, calls upon governments to set safety standards for locating plants and for the use of chemicals, to establish monitoring systems and contingency plans, to arrange safe transport of hazardous materials, to institute a legal framework for provision of information about hazards to workers and the public, and to institute more active inspection processes by trained people who have the resources to do their job. It called on trade union organizations to play a more active role in systematizing and disseminating information on hazards, to seek adoption of control programmes through national processes, to promote the establishment of local health and safety committees and to institute training procedures. The recommendations, undeniably logical and correct as they are, do not take full account of the different interests within the governments nor the difference in interests at times between governments and ordinary people. The need for foreign exchange, and various processes of direct and indirect payoffs militate strongly against adoption of these measures.

Chemical manufacturers and importers have been called upon frequently to institute safer operating procedures, including design, training and storage. They have been called upon to provide better information about their processes and to generate contingency plans for major accidents, in all countries where they operate. Yet these calls have not been met with serious action. Most businesses operate in terms of short-term interests, and risks of disaster are probably weighed up as a sort of business risk, with similar implications perhaps to the crashing of a currency or the emergence of a strong competitor. Among the lessons to be drawn from Bhopal and Seveso is that these business interests do not have a strong perspective of disaster anticipation. It should not be difficult for governments to insist periodically that companies handling dangerous industrial processes be required to respond to a series of 'what if' scenarios.

International organizations like ILO and WHO have been called upon to provide comprehensive guidelines for the use of hazardous chemicals and to distribute hazard information. Yet the number of possible chemical processes is so large that it would be difficult to disseminate information on all of these to the local level. Important as it undoubtedly is, the vast bank of information on chemical hazards is unlikely to reach the local level where it can best contribute to the anticipation of industrial disasters. An important potential role of international agencies is to support research into the toxic properties of chemicals along more useful lines. The experience from Bhopal emphasizes that estimates of LD50s or LC50s provide little useful information as determining factors in disaster anticipation or response (41). Knowledge of other acute and chronic consequences is also important, and there is a desperate need to develop models of sublethal toxicity testing. It is not so important where this type of information is generated; what matters is its clarity and whether it is available when it is really needed. In Bhopal it was not available when needed.

It is necessary to go beyond rhetorical demands that big business changes its character, or that governments do what they have been unable or unwilling to do for years. Setting aside the unfeasible notion of training workers in every factory in every developing country in the nature of thousands of chemical processes, a priority on training introduces the concept of systematic pressure generated by improved local capabilities to measure hazards and to produce results in a usable form. In Bhopal, it was possible to initiate this training in the aftermath of the 1984 disaster. But it is relatively easy to become involved after a disaster, and then to invest an enormous amount in rapid response, medical care including the construction of hospitals and the purchase of expensive and otherwise unaffordable instruments and equipment. Epidemiology also has a role to play in anticipation, now, of the next Bhopal.

An ever widening range of man-made and technological disasters can be expected in the future. Awareness is growing among governments of the value of local epidemiological capabilities in the disaster situation, as in day-to-day planning. The development of cluster survey methodology in Bhopal has fuelled risk monitoring options in other developing countries. Since the Bhopal catastrophe, repeated surveys of nearly 100 000 families in some 500 'sentinel site' communities in Mexico, Nicaragua, Honduras, Guatemala, El Salvador and Panama have generated information on background frequencies of exposures and diseases. The same process has been proposed for monitoring local level exposures to the hazards of small industry, informal employment and individual use of pesticides. The project is made up of a series of quite inexpensive study cycles (3–6 each year) to determine background frequencies of disease and to measure the impact of educational and other intervention programmes focused on specific health risks. Perhaps the greatest gain of the initiative is the reproduction of epidemiological capabilities in these countries and an increasing awareness of their ability to measure impact.

To be more relevant to the reduction of man-made disasters, such as Seveso and Bhopal, this surveying process would have to be complemented by a 'risk mapping' of all hazardous industrial processes. The ensuing data base would provide not only background frequencies of disease for later comparisons, but a framework from which potential hazards of industrial processes could be measured systematically and without the sometimes excessive disturbance that characterizes 'one off' studies. The main thrust of this sort of approach lies not only in the immediate information produced, but in the training element (41). In each of the countries using the sentinel site methodology, epidemiologists are being trained with a combination of fieldwork and university-based theoretical exercises. Local training in epidemiology—including rapid response epidemiology, set studies and community participatory methods—is the cornerstone for any realistic disaster anticipation strategy.

CONCLUSION: A GROWTH INDUSTRY

Earthquakes, floods, droughts and war all come and go. But industrial disasters can be guaranteed to be on the increase. The economic recession affects rich and poor countries quite differently, with a product that can only be described as 'disastrogenic' in the poorer countries. In rich countries, the increased labour organization, production costs and competition, particularly in the face of a reduced potential market, forces producers to look at poorer countries. These countries, in turn, are usually characterized by weak labour organization and limited state intervention to protect worker and community health. As contrasts between rich and poor countries intensify, technological disasters become more likely.

Various elements make up the disastrogenic cycle. The potentially dangerous plant is located in a heavily populated area; there has been insufficient attention to safety in the process design; there are dangerous and irresponsible operating procedures; there is inadequate maintenance and hygiene monitoring; faulty equipment; there are cutbacks in manning; there is inadequate training of a workforce not familiar with the work processes; there is a certain unresponsiveness to safety complaints on the part of management and government; the workers, the community living nearby and even junior management lack information about the nature of substances they are handling; epidemiological capabilities are in short supply and there is a lack of disaster planning. Different components of training could have some influence in this: training of medical and industrial hygiene staff at postgraduate level in specialist occupational and environmental health institutes; the development of distance learning modules, whereby teachers and specialists visit developing countries to train local government and academics; and the collaboration with labour organizations in developing countries. All these attempt to reduce the pressure that maintains the 'disastrogenic' cycle, that can theoretically be broken at any of a number of points: state intervention, the international companies becoming more responsible, better support from bilateral and multilateral agencies or stronger union organization. The feasibility and influence of each of these attempts will vary from place to place. But there is also another target group for disaster anticipation that is seldom considered systematically: the community.

People who live near chemical plants or other hazardous processes, it can be reasonably argued, benefit from available jobs and, quite often, infrastructure such as roads, electricity, water, health services or education that may otherwise not have been available. They are also the ones, as in the case of Seveso and Bhopal, who pay the price in the case of disaster. Disaster anticipation means training to develop a base that can exert pressure for change, a base from where developments can be monitored and improvements negotiated for on scientific grounds. If governments, international and bilateral agencies, universities and research institutes, or the companies themselves, are looking for a practical base for disaster anticipation, a locus for consolidation of the various elements outlined above, then the communities living around the production plants and likely to be affected by any disaster should be involved. Increasing community participation is proposed here, consistent with the Alma Ata interpretation of Primary Health Care (41), as a direction to guide development and not as a formula to be applied mechanically. As a starting point, ways should be sought to stimulate discussion about the benefits and potential costs; an opportunity for this might be the announcement of availability of jobs. Community consultation in the location of plants can serve as kindling for informed dialogue with those who, in the event of the disaster, will pay the price. School children can provide a useful means of transmitting knowledge on environmental concerns to their families, including development of the habit of asking 'what if' questions in the monitoring of those factories. Church groups and other community organizations can provide a focus for dialogue about these environmental issues. If informed and rational pressure can be generated across this wide base, and reinforced by official policy, disaster anticipation may become a reality.

SUMMARY

Official encouragement of rapid initiation of epidemiological enquiries is crucial in the immediate aftermath of disasters, man-made or natural. As part of an attempt to develop appropriate eye care strategies following the disaster, traditional epidemiological techniques were adapted in Bhopal, including rapid appraisal procedures, development of new questionnaire formats, the evolution of epidemiological monitoring based on clinical records, cluster survey methodology and testing of a clinical approach that assists broader inferences about the effects of the exposure.

Multidisciplinary research, including clinical epidemiology, analytical chemistry, toxicology and histopathology, have together cast some light on the probable long-term effects of MIC exposure. In the aftermath of the Bhopal disaster, it has been possible to train local scientists and relief workers in epidemiological techniques, and these people now provide the long-term follow up to monitor late consequences of the exposure. Epidemiology also has an important role in anticipation of further disasters, attempting to break the 'disastrogenic cycle' (inappropriate situation, inappropriate design, inadequate training and supervision, manpower cutbacks, poor information and no disaster preplanning). Priorities include developing capabilities of epidemiological measurement. There is a need for more relevant toxicological information than merely LD50s, which are not very useful in the disaster situation. People who live near chemical plants or other hazardous processes pay the price in the case of disaster. They should be involved earlier in the process of developing a coherent strategy of disaster anticipation.

ACKNOWLEDGMENTS

Clinical eye care and ophthalmic relief work after the disaster was supported by the Royal Commonwealth Society for the Blind (RCSB). The RCSB also supports the Bhopal Eye Hospital, under the able direction of Dr Manohar Ajwani, and its Community Eye Programme supervized by Mr Mohan Tiwari. The lessons expressed in this paper are the author's interpretation, in large measure, of their tireless work to serve their gas-affected countrymen. They should not be held responsible, however, for any errors and they do not necessarily agree with the opinions expressed. I am sincerely grateful for their confidence and friendship. I am also grateful to Dr Anne Cockcroft for her support in the course of this work and for helpful comments on various drafts of this text.

REFERENCES

(1) Bisanti L, Bonetti F, Caramaschi G, *et al.* Experiences from the accident of Seveso. *Acta Morph Acad Sci Hung* 1980; **28**: 139–57.
(2) Bertazzi PA. Epidemiology in the investigation of health effects of man-made disasters. In: Hogstedt C, Reuterwall C, eds. *Progress in occupational epidemiology.* Amsterdam: Elsevier Science Publishers BV, 1988: 3–14.
(3) Bruzzi P. In: Coulston F, Pocchiari F, eds. *Accidental exposure to dioxins. Human health effects.* New York: Academic Press, 1983: 5–28.
(4) Brown WE, Green AH, Cedel TE, Cairns J. Biochemistry of protein-isocyanate interactions: a comparison of the effects of aryl vs. alkyl isocyanates. *Environ Health Perspec* 1987; **72**: 5–11.
(5) Andersson N, Kerr Muir M, Mehra V, Salmon AG. Exposure and response to methyl isocyanate: results of a community based survey in Bhopal. *Br J Indust Med* 1988; **45**: 469–75.
(6) Andersson N, Ajwani M, Mahashabde S, *et al.* Long term effects of MIC; three year followup of Bhopal survivors. Submitted for publication.
(7) Wood GD. The social and scientific context of Rapid Rural Appraisal. *IDS Bull* 1981; **12**(4): 3–7.
(8) United Nations. *Systematic monitoring and evaluation of integrated programmes: A source book.* New York: UN, 1978.

(9) Andersson N, Kerr Muir M, Ajwani MK, Mahashabde S, Salmon A, Vaidyanathan K. Persistent eye watering among Bhopal survivors. *Lancet* 1986; **ii**: 1152.

(10) Andersson N, Kerr Muir M, Mehra V. Bhopal eye. *Lancet* 1984; **ii**: 1481.

(11) Kamat SR, Mahashur AA, Tiwari AKB, *et al.* Early observations on pulmonary changes and clinical morbidity due to the isocyanate gas leak at Bhopal. *J Postgrad Med* 1985; **31**: 63–72.

(12) Dave JM. The Bhopal methyl isocyanate incident: an overview. In Scheifer HB, ed. *Highly toxic chemicals: detection and protection methods. Proceedings of an international symposium*. September 1985, Saskatoon, Canada. Canada: University of Saskatchewan, Toxicology Research Centre, 1–37.

(13) Andersson N, Kerr Muir M, Salmon A, *et al.* Bhopal disaster: eye followup and analytical chemistry. *Lancet* 1985; **i**: 761–2.

(14) Misra NP, Pathak R, Gaur KJBS, *et al.* Clinical profile of gas leak victims in acute phase after Bhopal episode. *Indian J Med Res* 1987; **86**(suppl): 11–19.

(15) Kamat SR, Patel MH, Pradhan PV, *et al. Sequential respiratory, psychologic and immunologic studies in relation to MIC exposed subjects at Bhopal: interim report of analysis after two years follow up*. Bombay, India: Seth GS Medical College, Department of Respiratory Medicine, 1989.

(16) Karol MH, Taskar S, Gangal S, *et al.* The antibody response to methyl isocyanate: experimental and clinical findings. *Environ Health Perspect* 1987; **72**: 169–175.

(17) Karol MH, Kamat SR. The antibody response to methyl isocyanate: experimental and clinical findings. *Bull Eur Physiopathol Respir* 1988; **23**: 591–7.

(18) Saxena AK, Singh KP, Dutta KK, *et al.* Inhalation toxicity studies in rats. Part V: Immunologic response of rats two weeks after exposure; phagocytic response, endotoxin susceptibility, local lung immunity, mitogen and DTH response. *Indian J Exp Biol* 1988; **26**(3): 195–200.

(19) Varma DR, Ferguson JS, Alarie Y. Reproductive toxicity of MIC in mice. *J Toxicol Environ Health* 1987; **21**: 265–75.

(20) ICMR. *Health effects of the Bhopal gas tragedy*. New Delhi, India: Indian Council of Medical Research, 1986.

(21) Kanhere S, Darbari BS, Shrivastava AK. Morphological study of placentae of expectant mothers exposed to gas leak at Bhopal. *Indian J Med Res* 1987; **86**(suppl): 77–82.

(22) Bharucha EP, Bharucha NE. Neurological manifestations among those exposed to toxic gas at Bhopal. *Indian J Med Res* 1987; **86**(suppl): 59–62.

(23) Alarie Y, Ferguson JS, Stock MF, *et al.* Sensory and pulmonary irritation of methyl isocyanate in mice and pulmonary irritation and possible cyanidelike effect of methyl isocyanate in guinea pigs. *Environ Health Perspect* 1987; **72**: 159–67.

(24) Maginniss LA, Szewczak JM, Troup CM. Biological effects of short-term high-concentration exposure to methyl isocyanate. *Environ Health Perspect* 1987; **72**: 35–8.

(25) Nemery B, Sparrow S, Dinsdale D. Methyl isocyanate: thiosulphate does not protect. *Lancet* 1985; **ii**: 1245–6.

(26) Bucher JR, Gupta BN, Adkins B, et al. Toxicity of inhaled methyl isocyanate in F344/N rats and B6C3F1 mice. Acute exposure and recovery studies. *Environ Health Perspect* 1987; **72**: 53–61.

(27) Bucher JR, Gupta BN, Thompson M, *et al.* The toxicity of inhaled MIC in F344/N rats and B6C3F1 mice: repeated exposure and recovery studies. *Environ Health Perspect* 1987; **72**: 133–8.

(28) Salmon AG, Kerr Muir M, Andersson N. Acute toxicity of methyl isocyanate: a preliminary study of the dose response for eye and other effects. *Br J Ind Med* 1985; **42**: 795–8.

(29) Kolb WP, Savary JR, Troup CM, Dodd DE, Tamerius JD. Biological effects of short-term high-concentration exposure to methyl isocyanate. *Environ Health Perspect* 1987; **72**: 189–95.

(30) Tepper JS, Weister MJ, Costa DL, *et al.* Cardiopulmonary effects in awake rats four and six months after exposure to MIC. *Environ Health Perspect* 1987; **72**: 95–103.

(31) Gassert T, Mackenzie C, Kerr Muir M, Andersson N, Salmon AG. Long term pathology of lung, eye and other organs following acute exposure of rats to methyl isocyanate. *Lancet* 1986; **ii**: 1403.

(32) Mitsumori K, Boorman GA, Gupta BN, Bucher JR. Four day repeated inhalation and recovery study of MIC in F344 rats and B6C3F1 mice. *Fundam Appl Toxicol* 1987; **9**: 480–95.

(33) Salmon AG, Kerr Muir M, Andersson N. Comparison of toxicology and epidemiology of methyl isocyanate at Bhopal (Abstract). *Human Toxicol* 1987; **6**: 410.

(34) Luster MI, Tucker AN, Germolec DR, *et al*. Immunotoxicity studies in mice exposed to MIC. *Toxicol Appl Pharmacol* 1986; **86**: 140–4.

(35) Tucker AN, Bucher JR, Germolec DR, *et al*. Immunological studies on mice exposed subacutely to MIC. *Environ Health Perspect* 1987; **72**: 139–41.

(36) Hong HL, Bucher JR, Canipe J, Boorman GA. Myelotoxicity induced in female B6C3F1 mice by inhalation of MIC. *Environ Health Perspect* 1987; **72**: 143–8.

(37) Mackenzie CD, Andersson N, Cameron K, *et al*. Long term effects of MIC in Lister Hooded Rats: possible implications for Bhopal survivors (in press).

(38) Shelby MD, Allen JW, Caspary WJ, *et al*. Results of *in vitro* and *in vivo* genetic toxicity tests on MIC. *Environ Health Perspect* 1987; **72**: 183–7.

(39) Schwetz BA, Adkins B, Harris M, Moorman M, Sloane R. Methyl isocyanate: reproductive and development toxicology studies in Swiss mice. *Environ Health Perspect* 1987; **72**: 149–52.

(40) ICFTU-ICEF. *The Trade Union Report on Bhopal*. Geneva, 1985, p 15–16.

(41) WHO/UNICEF. *Primary health care*. Geneva, New York: World Health Organization, 1978.

(42) Andersson N, Martinez E, Cerrato F, Morales E, Ledogar R. The use of community-based data in health planning in Mexico and Central America. *Health Policy Planning* 1989; **4**(3): 197–206.

Psychological impact

James Thompson

Department of Psychiatry, Middlesex Hospital, London, UK

INTRODUCTION

Although I have been involved in many disasters and have seen many depictions, I never fail to *feel* something about what has happened there. This is one of the features about disasters which often makes people reluctant to carry out research into them. The immediate aftermath of a disaster is a very emotional time for everyone who is there. Often the last thought is of epidemiology; the normal humanitarian instinct is to try to help as quickly as possible.

This chapter on psychological impact may be the last in the book, but I would argue that in terms of chronic effects, and of demands on health care, the number of patients with psychological problems may be twice as many as the immediate casualty list. From some of the data we have on chemical and 'contamination' disasters, it might well be that the psychological impact rate is about one order of magnitude higher. What does this mean, and what is meant by 'psychological impact'?

It is usual, when one considers a disaster, to think of expanding rings of people who have been affected. After the King's Cross fire, with which I have been most closely associated, there were 31 dead, about seven people severely injured, and a total casualty rate including those suffering from smoke inhalation, etc., not above 60. Yet we know from follow-up that there are some 120 people who are handicapped in a psychological sense, because of their experiences of the disaster.

The immediate ring consists of those who are directly involved in the disaster. The secondary ring comprises the distressed relatives of the people who have been injured and killed, and the tertiary ring consists of those brought in to help clear up the catastrophe. There are doubtless further rings which ripple out, but they are of less consequence in terms of their impact on health care. However, there is now the problem that depictions of disasters are so vivid that many people suffer psychological effects simply because they witness reports in the media which bring back memories of previous problems.

REACTION TO DISASTERS

What happens to people in disasters? Traditionally there are five stages of human reaction to disaster—threat, warning, impact, recoil and post-impact.

Major chemical disasters—medical aspects of management, edited by Virginia Murray, 1990: Royal Society of Medicine Services International Congress and Symposium Series No. 155, published by Royal Society of Medicine Services Limited.

Threat

The question of risk perception is very interesting, and it is worth looking at the wide range of disasters to which people feel that they may be vulnerable, and at perceptions in the public mind.

If people are asked to estimate the likelihood of their experiencing various events, some things are overestimated, whereas others are underestimated. There is a bias in terms of judged frequency of death for dramatic events which are likely to be reported by the media. Disasters are what I call 'large parcel events'—large numbers of people dying together become newsworthy, whereas large numbers of deaths distributed over time and space are not seen as disastrous.

People's estimates are in rough concordance with actual death rates, but when they are asked to estimate the likelihood of those causes of death they use a restricted band of estimates.

Psychologists assert that most people can only count up to seven in psychological terms, unless they are trained in specific judgments. This is relevant because perception of risk is one of the determinants of human behaviour, and one of the problems in the context of confusion over health risks is that we have not yet found a way of describing risks in a manner which most people can understand. One proposal for overcoming this problem is to have risk levels which refer to the orders of magnitude of death rates. It is obviously hard to understand a range of different causes of death, and a simplification of this sort might assist us in communicating information about the relative risk levels of different types of hazards.

The problem with risk perception and threat is that people vary considerably in how they judge whether they believe themselves to be at risk. In terms of the psychology of accidents, one of the most common causes is an underestimate on the part of the operators of the real risks of their actions within the system, as happened at Chernobyl.

Warning

The state of warning is when people are given news that something is happening, for instance, an accident at a chemical works, and that it is necessary to monitor the situation or perhaps necessary to evacuate the area.

A common belief, reinforced by 'disaster movies' is that when notice is given of a chemical plant disaster people will panic, jump into their cars and clear the area. This is a misconception held both by the public and by the authorities. In fact, when warnings are given there is usually little response in the early stages. It is very hard to get people to change their well established patterns of behaviour. At the Summerlands fire people queued up to pay their bills, whilst the plastic was burning round them; at Kings Cross many people continued to catch trains, although it was obvious from the smoke that a fire was in progress. When tidal waves are announced there is even a proportion of people who will go to the shore to witness the wave rather than take cover. Careful epidemiological studies of floods in American flood plain areas show that in the early stages of giving advice, many people carry on with their normal activities. When statements were made on the television that flood water was about to hit houses, 22% of people continued with normal activities, 60% evacuated, and the remaining 18% watched television or listened to the radio to try and decide what to do.

There is therefore a resistance to taking action as a consequence of warnings, and it can be shown that before almost every disaster adequate warnings were given.

Such warnings are so contrary to normal perceptions that the reaction has been called 'negative panic'. The notion of panic is misunderstood. The situations in which people make frantic and irrational attempts to escape are relatively few, and tend to be restricted to people in confined spaces who are struggling to get out in a limited time.

In general people do not panic, they react sluggishly to warnings and they tend to follow their normal behavioural pattern.

Impact

The impact itself depends very much on what sort of disaster occurs; this influences the eventual conditioned responses and stimulus features seen later in our patients. In the recent catastrophe of the *Herald of Free Enterprise* at Zeebrugge, the change from normality to direct life threat was probably in the order of 50 seconds. That was a very swift event. There are even quicker ones—in the Clapham train crash normality switched to abnormality in no more than ten seconds. However, in some of the poisoning disasters, such as Seveso, there may not be an immediate impact; the impact comes not from observing one's life as threatened, but getting information through other people. One of the most crucial things which is apparent when there are 'insidious contamination threats' is a damage of the trust relationships between people and authority figures. However, when the impact is palpable there is generally an activation of the flight/fight system. We find a massive disorienting anxiety response, and people report the situation retrospectively as unreal; they appear to be monitoring and reacting to everything around them, and becoming extremely vigilant in this state. However, people's recall of those events, though very vivid, can sometimes be confused and their timing of events can be wrong. There is sometimes confusion about what happened immediately post-impact, and the sequence of events.

Recoil

Recoil is when the immediate danger is over, and people are showing reaction to it. Again, the recoil depends on whether there is a perceptible 'all clear' signal. If there is such a signal, for instance being allowed off the plane by terrorists, or when an earth quake stops, there is an immediate phenomenon of recoil, which is really massive anxiety relief. People become euphoric. They are so happy to be alive that everything seems to be all right. They sometimes minimize their injuries because of the absolute relief of being out of the traumatic situation. I believe that this reaction gives the people who are viewing these disasters a somewhat distorted impression of what is happening to the individual.

Post-impact

After the recoil people are generally very anxious to re-establish social links; they need company. Our social animal needs become extremely dominant and it makes people coming out of disaster situations particularly vulnerable to rumour and to social conformities.

The whole question of how we should react, what is the truth in the situation, and what we should do now can be potentially a very unstable situation, and it is usual after massive earth quakes to find people in loosely coherent groups, very prone to rumour, and not functioning very successfully.

There is a reasonable amount of post disaster work which people carry out quite spontaneously. Depending on the nature of the disaster, there are varying amounts of focused and effective public intervention. The difficulty with chemical disasters is that one does not have a statable 'all clear' signal. The case of Three Mile Island is an interesting example, because the stresses involved were largely psychological. What happened at Three Mile Island however, is relevant to the whole question of chemical disasters. A situation existed in which people had to judge whether or not they were at risk; they needed to know whom to believe, and that was also the situation in the aftermath of Bhopal and Seveso. The researchers in the Three Mile Island follow up found that the most pervasive feeling was that people did not know what to believe; they felt that they were facing something new, which no one knew anything about, and that sort of feeling is profoundly damaging both to people and to the management of communities. The epidemiology in Three Mile Island showed a reliable, though not a major increase in psychological distress in the population, which was evident 18 months later; a reliable, though not a large increase in the amount of health consultations, and an increase in a variety of disorders which can be categorized under 'anxiety'.

In the King's Cross disaster there were some similarities in that most of the people brought in as injured were not burned, they had inhaled smoke and had witnessed a frightening event. They were treated and then released. In our study of this event we have tried to include everyone who was involved, even peripherally, in that experience. In doing so, we had what is in my experience a unique situation, in that the Chairman of the enquiry, Desmond Fennel, allowed us to write to everyone who had made a witness statement, to ask how they were and if they would complete a questionnaire about what symptoms they had, how they were feeling, and whether they were still thinking about the disaster. We are still in the midst of the study, but what we have found so far I can report briefly.

First, however, it should be noted that it is very difficult to contact all the victims. Attempts to follow them up are still done in an extremely haphazard way, partly because some people have difficulty in understanding that there is such a thing as psychological impact. They assume that the impact will be shown by someone who is crying, tearing their hair, shivering and generally demonstrating emotion. But average disaster victims are not like that; they will say that they are all right, and often it is family and friends who suggest that they are not.

We found that the main symptoms reported by victims, and confirmed later at interview, were all related to anxiety. The most common complaint of a disaster victim is that they are feeling edgy, they are alert, they are hypervigilant, and are looking out for further problems. In terms of their mental life, they have intrusive memories of the event, and try and take steps to avoid any reminders of the incident, something which takes up energy, diminishes their concentration and lessens their ability to carry out normal activities.

The second most common feature is that people show 'social dysfunction'. They complain that they cannot carry out their work the way they used to, that they cannot even carry out their normal spare time activities in the same way, and that they are underfunctioning. The next most frequent complaint is of a wide range of psychosomatic conditions.

It is therefore difficult to make assertions about the effects of chemicals or other potentially damaging agents. One of the effects of having been a disaster victim seems to be a generalized fatigue and higher sensitivity to all one's bodily pains. Even that statement, however, is a value judgment. It may be that people do have more headaches and aches and pains because of some vulnerability and mediated effects.

The final category, depression, is somewhat surprisingly not the most dominant feature of disaster victims. However, it is likely that someone who has gone through a disaster will use the psychosomatic complaint quadrant as a means of gaining admission to medical care.

What other emotional effects do people suffer? We found that the most common emotion is anger. Anger is usually a coping response, an attempt to do something, but the form this took was more of a seething resentment; resentment that they were being 'picked on', that this had happened to them, that they had an injury for which life itself had not compensated them. There are other victims who survive terrible injuries and make excellent recoveries in psychological terms, yet who still admit to being edgy and sensitive about some issues, who will never enter a room without checking where the exit signs are, etc.

TREATMENT OF DISASTER VICTIMS

What should one provide in the way of intervention and treatment? In a major chemical disaster the initial first 72 hours will contain the immediate actions which are necessary and essential to deal with the injured, but in terms of real impacts on health care there will be about ten times more people suffering emotional effects.

The first task of someone trying to participate in disasters from the psychological point of view is to establish proper functional relationships with the key people there. We do not have disaster plans in a functional sense, at least as far as follow up is concerned. It is a haphazard collection of social work initiative, social services departments, occasional psychology and psychiatry departments, area voluntary groups, and disaster relief funds. I believe strongly that we need to have steering groups in place before disasters happen, so that all the issues of professional territoriality are dealt with as quickly as possible.

The essence of such a group is to listen, to search through various networks for any means of acquiring lists of the people involved. In the case, for example, of the King's Cross Fire this is an extremely difficult task. Many people may have experienced the fire and yet not been traced.

I would suggest that the next thing is to accept that any form of psychological intervention, however unskilled, is probably beneficial. In the early stages of supporting people in disasters, anyone who is willing to discuss the issue or who is brave enough to listen while unpleasant, dangerous, difficult things are said by the victim, should do so. That is what I regard as a humanitarian minimum. I am aware that some people may take the wrong approach, but the overwhelming effects of being able to discuss the issue are worth while.

This is emphasized by some of the correlations we found with distress on the general health questionnaire in the King's Cross study. People who felt angry about the fire had a higher distress score. Those who spoke about the fire to other people had lower distress scores. Another strong correlation with distress was the fear that the person had of being unable to escape and that their life was at risk.

Although there is some dispute as to what is the major reason for psychological distress after a disaster, I believe that the major explanatory variable is the nature of the event itself, the reason being that our correlations with distress are higher for measures of inability to escape and fears of another fire, than they are with neuroticism or compensation. There are associations with compensation and neurotic personality prior to the event, and distress later, but they are, in our experience, not as strong as those which can be triggered simply by asking 'did you think you were going to die?'. The one item which shows a negative direction is whether they have talked about the fire since the event, not necessarily with professionals but in general terms. We believe that any form of talking in the early stages is probably helpful. There is also evidence from other sources that the act of writing down painful personal experiences has a slight lifting effect; even talking about it reduces perceived stress, and in a follow up study it actually reduced the amount of consultation with Health Centres in the subsequent year.

I would suggest the need for a standard debriefing and standard questionnaires, and then propose two levels of treatment. The first is whatever can be given as a humanitarian minimum immediately, and then a screening procedure to identify those most severely affected, using the General Health Questionnaire as the basis. That can be followed with an offer of treatment. Our study of the King's Cross victims seems to show that immediate help does have an effect, because the badly burned victims who were given psychological help immediately now have lower distress scores than totally uninjured people who were not given any treatment in the early stages.

There is obviously a need for more follow up studies, preferably controlled studies, of such interventions after major disasters, and we are now conducting those.

Conclusions and recommendations

Many agencies and professional groups may be involved in the medical management of a major chemical disaster. There is a need to recognize the role of each agency and group in order to promote integration of their activities and the most effective medical management of a chemical disaster.

The recommendation was made to create a working group under the aegis of the Royal Society of Medicine, which should consider ways of achieving:

1. **The development of links between national agencies and professional groups, the development of definitions of the roles and responsibilities of each**, and the publication of this information. Examples of relevant agencies and professional body groups are listed alphabetically:
   - Academic and non-academic institutions in the field of toxicology, occupational health, epidemiology and public health.
   - Emergency Services: fire, ambulance and police.
   - Government: such as the Health and Safety Executive, the Department of Health and Local Authorities.
   - Health professionals and professional bodies.
   - Industry, including individual companies, industrial associations, for example the Chemical Industries Association, and industry based occupational health services.
   - Medical services: such as Accident and Emergency Departments, Intensive Therapy Units and laboratory services.
   - Poisons information services.
   - Support services: such as British Red Cross, the St Johns Ambulance Brigade, the Royal National Lifeboat Institution and the Women's Royal Voluntary Service.
2. **The need to promote and form new links with international organizations** based in Europe, partly in the light of the preparations needed for the 1992 Unified European Market, and worldwide, such as the International Programme on Chemical Safety (WHO/ILO/UNEP).

   The benefit of such links would include the development of common standards, the participation in joint projects with a reduction in duplicated work, the establishment of, or the support to, an International Toxic Alert Scheme, and information exchange on chemical disasters. Some links between centres with toxicological and medical expertise have already been developed, but these need to be promoted and expanded.

Major chemical disasters—medical aspects of management, edited by Virginia Murray, 1990: Royal Society of Medicine Services International Congress and Symposium Series No. 155, published by Royal Society of Medicine Services Limited.

3. **The feasibility of a centre or centres** with the following objectives:
   - To record and co-ordinate the different roles of agencies and professional groups that might be involved in the management of a major chemical disaster.
   - To facilitate access to databases, information and advisory services available on an emergency and non-emergency basis.
   - To provide information and advice to outside agencies, professional groups, public and media on resources available for assessment of health and environmental impact of a chemical disaster.
   - To provide medical support for contingency chemical disaster planning at all levels and in all areas of the country.
   - To define training needs of agencies and professional groups that might be involved in the medical management of a major chemical disaster and to develop the teaching resources needed for the different training programmes.
   - To devise appropriate systems to involve the toxicological and medical centres of expertise in chemical disaster management and the evaluation of the medical management of individual disasters.
   - To advise on ways of developing surveillance schemes to evaluate and follow up exposed human populations and, possibly, toxicological effects on the environment.

Dr Derek Taylor
Dr Virginia Murray
Dr Robin Philipp
Dr Michel Gilbert